ở cth lot
ßa

db - 1995

Cousin Joe

COUSIN JOE

Blues from New Orleans

Pleasant "Cousin Joe" Joseph
AND Harriet J. Ottenheimer

The University of Chicago Press   Chicago and London

Born in 1907 in Wallace, Louisiana, just outside of New Orleans, COUSIN JOE became a professional entertainer during the 1920s, starting with impromptu street performances and progressing to gigs at the Famous Door and other local clubs, to recording and performing in New York City, and finally to world tours. In 1972 his album *Bad Luck Blues* was named "Blues Album of the Year" in France.

HARRIET J. OTTENHEIMER is professor of anthropology in the Department of Sociology, Anthropology, and Social Work at Kansas State University.

Throughout this book, some names have been changed or omitted, and the description of some episodes has been altered.

The University of Chicago Press, Chicago 60637
The University of Chicago Press, Ltd., London

96 95 94 93 92 91 90 89 88 87   54321

Library of Congress Cataloging-in-Publication Data
Cousin Joe, 1907–
    Cousin Joe: blues from New Orleans.

    Bibliography: p.
    Discography: p.
    1. Cousin Joe, 1907–   . 2. Blues musicians—
United States—Biography.   I. Ottenheimer, Harriet,
1941–   . II. Title.
ML420.C72A3   1987   785.42'092'4 [B]   87-5561
ISBN 0-226-41198-2

To Rahsaan, Mignonne, and Jarrell Cato

Belle and William Joseph

Contents

Illustrations

Acknowledgments

There are two principal phases that we have been through with this book: an early one, in the 1960s, when most of the narrative was taped and transcribed, and a later one, mostly in the 1980s, when most of the writing and editing was done, and additional narratives were taped (and transcribed) to supplement the original material. The work was done in two locations: New Orleans, Louisiana, and Manhattan, Kansas. In the early years when both of us were in New Orleans, we were able to work together on an almost daily basis. In the later years, after Harriet moved to Kansas, we made heavy use of the mail and telephone systems and visited one another as often as we could (but not as often as we would have liked to). Joe made one trip to Kansas in 1980 and Harriet made four trips to New Orleans—two in 1980, one in 1981, and one in 1985. Needless to say, many people helped and encouraged us through the years.

In New Orleans, special mention must be made of Danny Barker, then curator of the New Orleans Jazz Museum and long-time friend of Cousin Joe's, who introduced us to one another in 1966. At Tulane University, Dick Allen, Munro Edmonson, Jack Fischer, Arden King, and Norma McLeod were early supporters of our work together. Clay Watson and Alan Jaffe were also involved in the early years of the project. Some of the early work was funded by the National Institute of Mental Health. In the 1980s, Don Marquis, curator of the New Orleans Jazz Museum, provided encouragement as well as rare photographs from the museum collection, and Ethelyn Orso provided lodging, encouragement, and invaluable friendship. The Department of Anthropology at Tulane University extended the courtesy of an Adjunct position for Harriet in 1980, and Curtis Jerde, head of the William Ransom Hogan Jazz Archives at Tulane, provided access to the archives' holdings. Also at Tulane, Frederick Starr provided encouragement for the project.

In Kansas, the members of the Department of Sociology, Anthropology, and Social Work at Kansas State University provided various forms of encouragement through the years, especially Wayne Rohrer, who read and commented on the entire manuscript and helped with some of the historical details, and Lonnie Athens and Isidore Walliman, who made useful suggestions concerning publication. Eugene Friedmann and Marvin Kaiser, heads of department, provided support and encouragement as well. In the Department of Psychology, Leon Rappoport also provided encouragement and suggestions. Karen Henderson, Christie Campbell, and Beth Hermann all shared in the work of typing, printing-out, copying, and mailing of the various drafts. Phil Royster and Antonia Pigno read large portions of the manuscript and provided critical comments (it was Phil who first encouraged us to consider using standard spelling and grammar).

Several groups on the Kansas State University campus combined efforts to sponsor Cousin Joe's visit to Kansas in 1980 including the departments of Sociology, Anthropology, and Social Work, History, and Music, the Minorities Research and Resource Center, and the Black Student Union. A small Summer Research Grant from the K.S.U. Graduate School's Bureau of General Research helped to support Harriet's visit to New Orleans in 1980. An additional small grant from the K.S.U. Graduate School provided salaries for students to help with the job of transcribing tapes. Vic Amburgey, Peggy Stevenson, Hal Rager, and Gerald Goff performed this difficult task admirably. Assistance with expenses during the 1981 visit to New Orleans was provided by the Department of Sociology, Anthropology, and Social Work. Most of the photographs at K.S.U. and some of those from New Orleans were taken by Holly Miller. One was taken by Martin Ottenheimer. Also in New Orleans, Joe Guillotte arranged for Warren Gravois to make copies of the photographs in the New Orleans Jazz Museum collection. In Kansas, Robert Deus helped with Havana street names, and Bill Kellstrom helped to identify the name of the drug used for syphilis in the 1930s. Many people helped with the discography. In Kansas, Bill Harshbarger and Afan Ottenheimer lent critical ears to the task of identifying instruments and musicians on commercial recordings from the 1940s. Suzanne Steel, at the University of Mississippi Blues Archive, John Storm Roberts, at Original Records, and John Berthelot, at Great Southern Records, all sent materials. In England, John Broven, Ann and Derek Stirland, Alan Farey, Alyn Shipton, and Dave Penny helped with details. In New Orleans, in Kansas, and in New York, Maurice Martinez read the entire manuscript, corrected critical details, and provided invaluable support and encouragement.

At various times our families have had to contend with the attention that this project took from them. Joe's son, Michael, in the early years, and Harriet's sons, Afan and Davi, in the later years, have all suffered more or less graciously through their parents' absences. Special thanks must be offered to our spouses: Joe's wife, Irene, and Harriet's husband, Martin. These two fine people have somehow managed to find it in their hearts to continue to encourage us, for all of the twenty years that it took us to complete this project. We suspect they are even more pleased than we that the book really did have an end.

1

Country Boy

I'm just a country boy,
Tryin to get along in this big ol town . . .

MY DADDY was a mean man! So mean, boy he used to jump on my mother just for nothing. Just for meanness. He would beat my mother for breakfast, dinner, and supper. Almost three times a day. If he'd say something to my mother and she'd answer him back, he'd knock her down. My mother used to keep black eyes all the time. She was a good woman, but my daddy was a mean man.

He got that meanness from his father. My grandfather was mean, too. My grandfather used to whip my grandmother with one of those eight-plait whips they used to whip horses with. Yeah! He'd use that when he was driving the mules. Six and eight mules, hauling that sugar cane. My grandfather could hit that first mule on his left ear with that whip. Never miss. Pyap! And he used to whip my grandmother with that.

I must have been about two years old when my grandmother ran away from my grandfather and about ten when my mother ran away from my father.

My grandmother left my grandfather in the middle of the night. Twelve o'clock at night. It was in St. John Parish. Right up there about thirty-nine miles from New Orleans, but on the other side of the river. Wallace, Louisiana. My grandmother made my grandfather believe she was going to the john. They used to have those outhouses in the country, you know. Had a little house, nine feet high, and a cracker sack for a door. Had that nailed up on there. A sack! They didn't have any lumber to make the door.

So my grandmother went on out to the john and my step-grandpa was on the other side of the fence, waiting for her. Like Romeo was waiting for Juliet. My grandmother had given my step-grandpa just a dress and a slip and things for her to wear when she came out, because she only had her gown on when she came out. So he had this wrapped up in a paper sack and was all ready. Had *his* clothes on. And they went somewhere and waited till train time.

They caught the ferry. They had a fellow, named one of those Cajun names. Bebin. He had an outboard motor and he used to charge people so much to cross the river in his boat. My step-grandfather'd paid him and made arrangements for him to take them across the river so they could catch the train on *this* side of the river. Caught the train, came down to New Orleans.

And my grandfather still waiting for my grandma to come out of the john! Till the day he died, he waited. That's from the beginning. I'm coming from the beginning.

My grandma and my step-grandpa found a house in New Orleans—on Annette Street—and my step-grandpa stayed with my grandmother till she died. I think she was about sixty-eight when she died. He lived to be about ninety and used to go fishing every day. Used to *walk* to Lake Ponchartrain with his fishing pole and a basket. He liked to fish.

Now, when they came down to New Orleans, then my father and my mother brought *me* there, too. They say I was two years old when they brought me. I was raised in New Orleans. That's why I don't know much about the country. I usually tell people I'm from New Orleans, but I'm originally from where I was born, and I was born in a little town of very few people, called Willow Grove, on a plantation, in Wallace, Louisiana. It was December 20, 1907. You know, when I tell people I'm from the country, they don't believe me. Even in New York, people tell me, "You don't speak like nobody from down there."

I say, "That's where I'm from! Gumboland! Yeah!"

Well, after we came to New Orleans, I can remember I was living on Lowerline and Zimpel in a two-room-and-a-kitchen house. My father and my mother, their bedroom was the first room. The second was our room—my sister and I.

My mother and father had six children: three boys and three girls. Now, my oldest sister, she died before I was born. In fact, two of my sisters I didn't know at all. And my two brothers, they died when they were babies, you might say; two or three years old, or four, maybe.

My daddy had a horse and a wagon and he had a job delivering groceries for a grocery store. He was making nine dollars a week. He used to have a credit book and if we wanted anything at the grocery store we'd get it and the grocery man would put it on the book and would take it out of my father's salary, whatever it was, at the end of the week. My daddy used to raise hell with me because I used to go buy candy and I'd get a whipping for *that*.

We were raised up on coffee and bread for breakfast, and, oh, it was a long time it went that way, during the weekdays. We never *saw* an egg, or maybe ham and chicken, till on a Sunday. All during the week we had this big bowl of coffee. Watered coffee and a little cow's milk. And sugar and French bread. At that time French bread was a nickel; five cents a loaf.

And all the week, for dinner *and* for supper, we had different kinds of beans. We had red beans on a Monday, butter beans on a Tuesday, white beans on a Wednesday, blackeyed peas on a Thursday . . . And my mother used to buy what they called "lights," which was some kind of scrap on a beef. It would become food for dogs and cats, but it was also good for human consumption. "Lights." It looked like liver but it was *not* liver. It was called "lights." And my mother would make the grandest stew out of that; you wouldn't imagine how good that tasted.

When I was about five or six years old I started school—at McDonough 24 on Hillary Street. I was considered smart for my age because even when I was four, I can remember, I could answer the telephone. *We* couldn't afford a telephone, but the lady next door, I think she had one. I could call up, too. Well, that was considered as smart for a four-year-old at that time. And I wasn't going to school, then.

One time—oh, I wasn't bad, but I was mischievous, you know—I was in the street, pitching rocks, and here came a great big old black limousine, about thirty feet long, almost. I *know* they were rich people. Lowerline was a paved street, so this big car came through there. It had about four people in it, with a chauffeur! And I'm pitching rocks. So, I pitched a rock clean through the back window and it went through the windshield—in the front! And when I did that, my daddy was just coming from work, and my daddy said, "Now I saw what you did, and you know you gonna git it." The lady stopped the car, and when the lady stopped it, I'm standing there—I'm trembling. I was more afraid of my daddy than the Devil's afraid of holy water. I'm telling you the truth. When I knew my daddy was going to whip me I'd pee all over myself, I was that afraid of him, because one time he like to killed me; he whipped me across my back with a wire clothesline and weakened my bladder and caused me to wet the bed till I was fifteen years old. That's how weak my bladder was. He was a mean man.

My daddy went to the grocery—the grocery was about a half a block from our house, on the next corner—and my daddy got a brand new rope. When the lady got out of the car, he told the lady, "Well, Madam, I can't afford to pay for it, but," he said, "I'm gonna give you some satisfaction, here and now." My daddy told me, "Giddown!" I got on my knees, put my hands behind my back, and my daddy beat me something awful in front of those people. That night I had welts on my back. I couldn't sleep laying down on my back. And my mother, she got a whipping, too, from trying to stop him from whipping me. All this used to be a regular routine that way.

During this time, when the First World War broke out in 1914, there was one of the biggest epidemics of the flu that I've ever known. I never did catch it—not at that time. I must've been immune to it because the lady next door, she used to get letters from her husband in the army in Germany, and she couldn't read or write. I was the only one who could read; I could read when I was seven years old. She would send next door for me to come over and read these letters for her. Well, *she* came down with the flu. She would knock on the wall for me to come over and I sat right at her bedside and read these letters for her from her husband. It was a miraculous thing that I didn't get the flu, being that close to her, because at that time they built houses with not much ventilation. They had maybe one window in the front room and one in the next room, and there would usually be one in the kitchen. Sometimes they didn't have *no* windows in the kitchen. Then the back door opened up on the back yard and on the side was the toilet. Fortunately we had plumbing—sewage—but you had to come out the back to go in the toilet. The toilet was on the outside because you never had enough room to build the toilets on the inside like they do today.

At about the time I started school my real grandfather, my daddy's father, came to stay with us. He'd come from the country because he was an old man, and my daddy took him to live with us. My daddy knew he was very sick with asthma and he was in the country staying by himself after my grandmother left him. I was my grandpa's right eye. My grandpa wouldn't let my daddy put his hands on me, but my daddy'd wait till he wasn't there, and he'd beat me up anyway. My grandpa lived with us for—I don't know exactly how many years—before he died.

I used to sleep with my grandpa, and when my grandpa would get an attack of that asthma I used to get up during the night. He'd always want to drink some hot water—just plain hot water. Look like that used to—I don't know—like it was something that caused him to sort of breathe correctly.

The night before my grandfather died my father was fixing to go out. He used to go out all the time—go out hustling women and stuff. Of course, when my mother would go out, when she'd come back, she'd get a beating. Anyway, he was fixing to go out and my grandfather told him, "Son, why don't you stay home tonight?" and he got my father to stay home. Good thing! I can remember, my mother had cooked dinner and she had made some cornbread, and my grandfather ate some of that cornbread that night. He got an attack of that asthma and while he was having difficulty in breathing, that cornbread came up and smothered him. He died in my father's arms on the back steps, where he was trying to catch some air. He died in my father's arms.

After he died, we got ready. My daddy got him fixed up beautiful for the wake that night. My grandpa was laid out on the cooling board. That's what they would use. It was an old ironing board on two wooden horses and planks, and they'd lay you out on that. There was no such thing as embalming at that time and you talking about bad! Whew! Dead people's odor is awful! They used to get a whole lot of flowers and stuff, and they had some kind of stuff that's similar to those sprays they use now. They'd sprinkle some kind of stuff. And the scent of flowers and that dead scent was enough to make you sick. I don't understand how those people could eat and drink coffee. I couldn't. I couldn't even stay in the room.

That night, at the wake, who came to the wake but my grandma! My daddy's mother. And my grandmother, in front of all those people, while my grandpa was laid out on the cooling board, she looked at him and got on her knees and said, "*Now* I got you." She said, "You dirty bastard!" That's the way she said it! "I'm glad you *gone* and I'm sorry you stayed so *long*. You should've *been* dead, you dirty bastard." And those people thought that was something, for her to cuss him out like that on the cooler after he's dead.

2

When the Roll Be Called in Heaven

When the roll be called in heaven,
I want to answer to my name . . .

MY GRANDMOTHER used to take me to church at least three times a week—weeknights and Sundays. Sunday was always the big day in the Baptist church. They had the most people, then. And I could sing! I used to write the words to gospel tunes and sing them in church. I was considered as a gospel child prodigy.

In those days, after the preacher would get through speaking—would get through his sermon—then they had what you'd call a Holy Rollers' meeting. Somebody would strike up a hymn and all the rest of the members would just fall right in. Sound like the Harold Johnson's Choir. That's something!

They didn't have all those pianos like they do now. The Baptist people, at that time, in their tradition, didn't use instruments. None at all. Now, they have drums, they have piano, and organ, and choir. But then, they didn't have that. All you did was start patting your feet and clapping your hands and just start singing. They didn't have a choir; the whole congregation was the choir—everybody that belonged to the church, that was in the church that Sunday morning, or whatever night it was they had regular services.

I was just seven years old and I was so small, behind those benches, the people couldn't see me. The benches in the church were so high. They could hear me but they couldn't *see* me. So, my grandmother used to sit me on her lap, and, oh, my goodness! When I'd start singing, "When the roll be called in heaven, I want to answer to my name!" Oh, way, after a while the sisters'd start clapping and stomping their feet and they'd start to fall *in*. The ones that knew the words, they would sing along. For them that didn't know the words, they would hum. And it was the most amazing thing you'd want to hear. All these beautiful voices.

Then, after a while, I'd start to reading from the scripture. Like this thing I did, I put in "When the Saints Go Marching In." Hoooo! Those sisters'd be jumping all along the benches, clapping. The preacher used to tell my daddy, all the time, "That boy is gonna *be* somethin," he'd say. "I never saw a young man that knows so much about the scripture at his age."

Well, that was my hustling. My "hype" you might call it. They used to pick up a collection—special for me—every Sunday. That used to be my spending change. I'd have enough nickels and pennies to buy my candy and snowballs and cake and stuff like that, like kids do.

That kept going for a while until I got a little older—about a year or two. Finally the Reverend got hip to me and told me, "Son, I'd like to talk to you."

I said, "Yes, sir?"

He said, "Now, you old enough to join this church, because you old enough to know *better*. Now, you got to either join this church or you cannot sing in here no more. And there will be no more collections picked up for you."

Now, *that* settled *that*, right there. That put a stop to it, because I didn't join the church. But that's where I got my start—singing.

Then, they used to have something going on every Sunday that they called an "excursion." They had a little, maybe two-coach, train and an engine. It would go, say, from New Orleans to Baton Rouge and back again. Or to the little town where I was born—but on the other side of the river—and back again. The railroad company would charge so much, round trip, for each person. They would advertise they were having an excursion on such-and-such a Sunday. It was considered as a lot of people going on an excursion, and for the colored people, in the Baptist religion, this was a big thing for them. It was somewhere to go, and they'd have a gathering of people and they'd have fun. For the Baptist people, singing *was* fun. It was just like a Baptist person was going on a picnic or something, or going to some festival, or something like that. That was the effect this excursion took on the Baptist people. They'd put on their Sunday-go-to-meeting—the best clothes they had—and look their sharpest.

The train used to stop at every little one-horse town—every little station. Sometimes what they would call a station was just one little bitty house on the side of the track. That train would stop there because sometimes there'd be people in the house, or standing on this little platform right there, to catch that same train. So it stopped at every one of these stops.

My daddy used to take me on these excursions. I used to write church hymns—spirituals—and my daddy would have them printed. They used to call them "ballots." My daddy used to have from a thousand to fifteen hundred of them printed in a printing shop. It didn't cost him that much at that time. It cost about a cent apiece. My daddy was a good gospel singer, too, and me and my daddy, we'd start singing on these excursions and the people in the coaches, they'd start clapping and going on, and my daddy was selling these "ballots." For ten cents apiece! And I ain't *never* seen none of the money!

In the Baptist religion, it was said, it was better for you if you started young in the religion. Then, you'd eventually grow up in it. And the Baptist religion, they were strict, because you couldn't use cursewords—that was a sin—and it was a sin to drink whiskey and it was a sin to smoke cigarettes. In other words, if you were a real true Baptist, you didn't smoke, you didn't drink, you didn't swear, and you didn't have sexual relations until you got married. That's how strict the Baptist religion was.

It was a sin to sing blues, too—or any song not pertaining to religion. Like any of those pop tunes. Most everything they sang spiritually really *sounded* bluesy but you couldn't get a strict Baptist person to go out in public and sing the blues. A record company offered Mahalia Jackson two hundred and fifty thousand dollars to sing the blues instead of spirituals, but she wouldn't do it. There's nobody sang spirituals like Mahalia Jackson, and she came right from New Orleans, out of a Baptist church in New Orleans.

A lot of people think the Catholic religion is strict, too, but the Catholic religion is only strict to a certain extent—at a certain time: between Ash Wednesday and Easter Sunday. It's said that during Lent, New Orleans is the most religious city in the United States. Most of the people you see come out on Bourbon Street during that time are tourists and visitors. The actual people that *reside* in New Orleans, during Lent there's seventy-five percent of them you won't see out there on Bourbon Street. But as soon as Easter Sunday comes, that night, here they come, boogity, boogity, boogity. From then on, they're going to pitch a fiddler's boogie woogie. It don't make no difference *what* they do as long as at the end of the week, whatever they did, they go to confession and they confess whatever sin they committed.

The Baptist people, when you were considered as a member in the Baptist church, you prayed for your sins and you prayed to the Lord to show you a sign. People'd come to church and when the preacher'd get through preaching he'd say, "If there's any sinners in the house that want to get on the right side of the Lord and be baptized, come forward." Then, maybe some young ladies, maybe eighteen, sixteen years old, they'd come up and get on the mourner's bench. And on this mourner's bench they'd have somebody—a deacon or somebody else—around to say a prayer for Jesus to guide these people in the path of righteousness, and anoint their soul, and all that. Then you'd go through *that* ritual.

Some of these people, they wouldn't come back to the church, but a lot of them did. A lot of them prayed and they saw the sign where they were fit morally to belong to this church. Eventually they'd learn all the habits of the people that attend this church regularly. The older members would teach the younger ones the fundamentals of the religion and eventually, when they learned all those things, they set aside a Sunday for a baptism—a warm day, because a lot of times they baptized in the river—the Mississippi River. Lately they've started baptizing in pools, but during the time when I was a kid, they would baptize you in the river.

Everybody would be all dressed in white. They were all members of this particular church and just for this baptism—for this occasion—they had a certain way of dressing. The sisters would have big long gowns—made not like a dress but like an actual gown—with white caps on their heads and a white piece over their shoulders like a cloak, but it was white, all white. The men had dark suits and probably a white band across their coat sleeve, and the preacher, he'd have white trousers, white shirt, and black tie, and he had one of those cloaks. When he'd walk down in the river, he'd walk as far as his shoulders and the cloak would float out.

So there wouldn't be any danger to the people of drowning or anything like that, or slipping in a hole, they had people go out there and inspect it with big, long poles, to see just how deep it was and how far they could walk out. They'd want it deep *enough*. When the preacher'd get through saying all these things in the Bible—he had the Bible in his hand—he'd give one of the deacons the Bible and he'd push you down. I mean all the way *under.* They'd hold your nose and you'd close your mouth, and when you came up like that you'd come up SHOUTING. And everybody would start up a hymn like "Walking in Jerusalem, Just like John." Some of them sang in unison and some, if they knew how to harmonize, some of them sang in harmony, and it was a beautiful thing to listen to.

And these same people, a lot of them right from this Baptist church, singing these hymns, went right out and sang the blues. Blues, rock and roll, rhythm and blues. Even today, half of them still sound like spirituals—like Baptist church hymns. They take the melody from a Baptist church hymn, change the words and put it into rock and roll. But if you go back far enough, you can tell, from the various phrasings of the blues, that it was similar to a lot of the gospel music that was sung in the Baptist church.

3 When Your Mother's Gone

When my mother was livin,
I could take this world at ease . . .

I WASN'T BUT ten years old when my mother left. She took my sister with her, too. My sister was just a kid. My mother couldn't take both of us so she decided to take my sister. She decided to go because she had met a man. He *had* been living in New Orleans, but he left and went back home. He lived in a little town in Louisiana called Oscar Crossing, and he gave my mother the fare for her and my sister to come up there where he was living, in the country. I never did know who he was.

When my mother got ready to leave, she waited till my father went to work and then she and my sister packed up. I said, "Come on, let's go. I'm gonna take y'all to the station." So, I took them to the station. We were out there in the morning to catch the train but I didn't know exactly what time the train left, and when we got to the station we had missed the train—that morning train.

The next train didn't leave till about twelve-something, but I didn't want to see my mother go back home and have my daddy catch her. I knew he would beat her up. One time he beat my mother around the eyes so much, till my mother went temporarily blind. And my daddy had a woman, then. She used to come to the house and I knew that was his woman. This woman had three hundred dollars in the bank and at that time, when you had two, three hundred dollars in the bank you were rich. She used to come there and my daddy'd know my mother couldn't see. That was the cruel part, right there.

So what I did, I knocked on some lady's door. I didn't know anybody around there, but I went around the train station there, around Saratoga Street. The First Precinct used to be there, then—on Tulane, between Saratoga and the next street, before they moved and built the new one on Tulane and Broad. I knocked on this lady's door and I asked her would she mind my mother and sister staying there till train-time because we missed the train we

11

were supposed to get and it'd be a few hours before we could catch the next train. I said, "We livin way up in Carrollton and didn't want to go all the way back home and then have to come back."

And the lady said, "Well, you're welcome to stay here."

So, we stayed there. But that wasn't the reason why I didn't want them to go back. I didn't want my daddy to catch them. We stayed there, and she got the train, and I went back home. And when I got home, when my father came home from work, he went all through the house and looked for my mother. He said, "Where's your mama?"

I said, "I don't know."

"You don't know?"

"No, sir! I don't know."

And he went to looking in the chifferobe and he didn't see any clothes! He said, "Boy! You! Where did your mother go?"

I said, "I *told* you, I don't *know*."

And he said, "She took your sister with her, too."

"She must've. I don't see her. She ain't around here."

So! He said, "You gonna tell me where she went!" And, boy, he was a jackleg barber at that time, too, and he had one of those razor strops that you sharpen those razors on. The kind that you see in the barber shop. They were thick and heavy, and boy, he used to always make me get on my knees all the time. Man, he whipped me. Boy, he whipped me. Had big old welts on my back. I couldn't sleep on my back. Slept on my stomach, it hurt so bad. Man! And I wouldn't tell him for nothing in the world. I just said, "Well, I'll tell you, Papa, you just gonna have to kill me cause I *still* don't know, and if I *knew* I wouldn't tell you."

He just whipped me till he couldn't raise his right arm any more. Till his arms got tired. That's true! But I wouldn't tell him. I said, "I don't care if you *kill* me, I ain't gonna tell you."

But he never *could* get it out of me. I guess he just said, "Well, that boy ain't gonna tell me, cause I know behind that whippin he mus don know where they is, cause he'd a tol me." When he saw he couldn't get it out of me he just took it for granted they had gone. And I never did tell him. From that day until the day my daddy died, he never did know from *me* where my mother went.

But I knew where they were, so I got the blues for my mother and my sister. My daddy had started bootlegging after my mother had left and he had this liquor around the house. He used to drive a horse and wagon full of groceries on the top and those quarts of whiskey under the bottom. I went with him one day to deliver whiskey to one of these big buildings around Canal Street and St. Charles. At that time they were big buildings because they'd just come up in the heart of town. He knew where he was going because he knew how to read. He had finished school in the third grade. My daddy'd get out and get down under the groceries and take those bottles of whiskey and anisette and gin and go up in the elevators in the buildings and bring his order and get that money and put it in his pocket.

Sometimes, he'd leave five or six bottles at the house. He used to sell some stuff called anisette and when I'd come home from school, man, that anisette was kind of sweet. Man, he'd come home, find me high as a kite, lying across the bed. He'd ask "What's the matter?" I'd just lay there, and he'd smell the liquor. He'd come smell the liquor on my breath and say, "You been drinking up my liquor."

And I'd say, "Well, Papa, I don't know. It taste mighty sweet to me. Tastes *good*." And I'd be crying, too, because I wanted to see my mother. One time he found me and I'm lying across the bed and he's trying to wake me up and I'm loaded. Knocked out.

After that he tried to pacify me. Tried to give me anything I wanted. But that didn't do any good. I wanted to see my mother, and I cried for days and days. I just cried. So, he tried to find out where my mother was. He wrote my aunt a letter and he told her that I wanted to see my mother so bad, he didn't know what to do. I just kept on crying every day and he said he was trying his best to find my mother. And *she* wrote and told him to bring me to *her*.

He told me, "Alright. I'm gon take you downtown and I'm gon buy you some clothes and I'm gon take you to your mother." So he took me. But he didn't take me to see my mother. He took me to see my aunt. She was in Willow Grove, and *she* took me to my mother, and I stayed there with her for a while.

4

Barefoot Boy

My shoes so worn out,
I'm back on my feet again . . .

MY MOTHER was living in Gramercy, her and my sister. She had left that man in Oscar Crossing, because the man, after he got her and my sister there, he was not the type of man he was cracked up to be, neither. And she found out that she had done jumped out of the frying pan into the fire! So, she took my sister and she went to Gramercy, Louisiana—across the river from Wallace. I don't know till *today* how she managed to find her way there because my mother couldn't read or write, and my sister was too small. She didn't know anything.

So, when I found out where she was, she had got this job working in the family house of the man that was the president of the sugar refinery company in Gramercy, which all my cousins used to work for, over there. She had a little one-room-and-a-kitchen house. She'd sleep in the bed and then she'd make us a pallet on the floor—me and my sister. For those days, for a woman, she was making a lot of money. She was making twelve or fourteen dollars a week—about two dollars a day. And when she got paid, she just brought us to the town. It was one of these little towns in there where they sell clothes, and shoes for kids, you know? That's when I got the first pair of five-dollar shoes I ever wore in my life! My mother bought them for me, because she was making good money at that time.

I stayed with my mother a good while during the summer months and then my aunt put me to work in the rice fields, pulling the grass out of the rice.

Those rice fields were something else, man. The rice was separated into acres, and they'd have it banked off with a little levee called a headland. They used these headlands like levees to separate it into sections and they had this pumping station for irrigation that used to pump the water from the river on the land—on the rice.

Well, the people'd work this way: they'd start at one end, grassing the rice, and as they'd go on down they'd get in deeper water, where the rice is growing rapidly. They'd usually start working from the back end and work toward the front, toward the farmer, the plantation owner. They were working toward his house, but they'd start way back in the fields. Way back where, when they'd start walking back there, the trees back there looked like little Christmas trees, just a few feet high, they were so far back.

They'd work so many acres. They'd have twenty-five, thirty, thirty-five, forty people strung across and they'd work from one headland to the other headland. That's supposed to be an acre. You could distinguish the grass from the rice because the grass and the rice looked different. The rice had blades on it—was sharp as a razor. If you weren't careful you'd have your hands all cut up by the time the day was over. You could tell the rice, too, from the little green seeds hanging on the branches, with the shells on it.

So, you're grassing. You're pulling the grass out of the rice. Well, these people, when they start, they're in this bent-over position so long, till a lot of times they'd have to straighten up and stand up for a few minutes to ease the strain off their back. And when they'd get to the other headland, then they'd walk over it and they'd start working in the next acre.

And these people! Only one person had to start singing and the whole bunch would fall in line. Now, these, in this section, they might be singing spirituals, and these, in this section, they might be singing the blues. Or just humming, not singing any particular words. Just a tune. And I used to be right in there, singing right along with them. And Lomax, the folk song collector, used to go around in these rice fields and cane fields, where a bunch of colored people were working, and record.

Now, in this rice field, they used to have these big water moccasins—snakes—running through the water. You could tell any time a snake was coming through, because you could see that rice part when they'd be crawling through there, and boy, there'd be twenty-five or thirty people running and screaming and getting out of the way! And you couldn't grass rice with shoes on; you had to be barefoot. With shoes you'd mash all the rice down. The only man could wear shoes was the foreman.

The foreman was a colored fellow. His name was Buddy Blue. He was so black that he looked blue when the sun shone on him so they called him Buddy Blue. He used to go around with those high boots and there was very little walking he could do through that rice. But when he'd see everybody break out in a run, he knew a snake was coming. He had a big old hickory stick and he'd get right close to that snake and hit him across the head, whop! Or break his back. He'd pick him up, throw him on the headland, stomp on his head and kill him and everybody'd go back to work.

One girl had one of those snakes run up her dress! Got in her bloomers! Boy, you talk about something! She was shaking and going on, trying to get that thing out of her! Boy, it was tragic, but it was something to laugh at, too.

When the rice would start getting yellow, then they'd drain all the water back off of it and that's when they'd cut the rice. They'd tie it up and fellows would come in big wagons with about six or eight mules. They called them mule tong. They'd put the rice on this wagon and take it to the mill where they'd thresh it—take the seeds from the shells. I worked in there, too.

But I missed all the kids at school. I'd seen my mother and I was satisfied. I wanted to come back home. And somehow or another my father came. He found out some kind of way and he came to get me to bring me back to New Orleans to go to school.

The next summer I went back out into the country. Stayed with my aunt in Wallace and worked grassing rice again. That year I stayed on past summer and went to school out there. Stayed till winter and that was enough for me. I'd grass rice in the morning and go to school in the evening. They didn't teach any further than the sixth grade out there and I knew more than the teacher was teaching me. I went to school for a month or so, but when the teacher found out I knew everything, I had to get out of school.

Then I started cutting sugar cane. I worked in the fields. All that land was owned by a Mr. Toussaint. Mr. Toussaint owned all that land and owned that plantation. On this plantation, the boss would tell you, "I pay you a dollar a day, you eat meat; dollar-and-a-half a day, you eat yourself." In other words, they'd feed you for a dollar a day, and for a dollar-and-a-half a day you'd feed yourself.

But, we didn't get paid in money on the plantation! They didn't pay you off in money! They'd give you a book, with coupons in it, called a coupon book, and in this book they had coupons for five cents, ten cents, twenty-five cents, fifty cents, and a dollar, and if you used up that book before the weekend, that's all she roll. They had a company store on the plantation. They sold everything from soup to nuts in that store. You could buy anything. They had a section for hardware; fellows that wanted to build a chicken coop or hog pen or something like that, they'd sell nails and everything. They'd give you these coupons and whatever you'd want to buy—like if I wanted to buy some candy or soft drinks—I'd just give them a coupon.

They paid *cash* at the refinery and my aunt's two oldest sons used to go across the river and work there. My aunt had her own house and her two oldest sons stayed with her and worked at the sugar refinery—the Gramercy Sugar Refinery. They got paid better money there than in the fields. When you worked at the sugar refinery, that was the highest paying job in the country at that time. If you could get a job in the sugar refinery you were a big shot.

My aunt used to feed me. We used to bring a little bucket. We had a little tin bucket with a little top in it, and we'd put our dinner in that little tin bucket. My aunt would cook beans and rice and stuff like that. We'd put beans and rice in the bucket and bring it with us. And she made homemade bread. They called it rising bread, at the time. They made their own yeast with flour and something else—I can't remember what—and they used to let it set a long time. Then, they'd mix that with this bread and they'd put it in the oven. They'd have it in sections and it would come out looking like biscuits. But it wasn't biscuits—it was bread. So, we'd have this bread, and these beans and rice, and fatback or whatever, because my aunt used to kill a hog every year. And we'd eat that.

Around ten o'clock we'd get a break, because you had to get up at three o'clock in the morning. You had to be out in the field when the sun was rising. You had to be out there around five o'clock. When you'd get there, they'd put everybody in a big mule-and-a-wagon, because they had thousands and thousands of acres of land. It took the mules and wagons—with about ten of us in there—took them about almost an hour to get where we had to start working at. That's why we had to get up so early. They had a whole lot of mules and wagons to haul everybody by groups because a wagon would hold just so many.

And then we'd all get out there. Sun was coming up over the horizon and you could see that red reflection against the sky just before it peeped over the horizon. Everybody'd get out of the wagons and they'd say, "Hit the headlands!" Well, first there's the headland, and then, there's a little ditch and the sugar cane field starts. And as far as you could see, everybody's lined up. When everybody gets lined up then the foreman, he hollers, "Alright! Let's go!" And you start. When you started from the back end, coming this way, coming toward the front, all you could see was sugar cane, sugar cane, sugar cane. All you could see. All the way. And he'd say, "Don't forget, now, high top and low bottom." In other words, when you'd reach up and get that stalk of cane, you had to hit it with your cane knife from the high part and then you had to dig your cane knife in the ground till when that cane'd be cut down you could see the roots, through the cane. They didn't want to lose *nothing* on the sugar canes; didn't want to leave anything in the ground if they could. Then, you'd just cut it, throw it across there, and they'd have men come out there in this big wagon and take it to the sugar refinery.

They had a foreman. A white fellow. He was the *big* foreman. That fellow with the stick and the boots in the rice fields, he was just a straw boss. He was a boss over *us*, but the foreman, that Mr. Shep, he was the boss over *everybody*. Over fellows like Buddy Blue and everybody else, too. He'd ride on his horse and, man, they'd have people working in that field as far as you could see.

I stayed on there until winter caught me there. That's when I got mad. Everybody out there cutting sugar cane. Man, it was so cold you couldn't stick the cane knife in the ground because it was frozen stiff. I'd go to light a fire and I couldn't close my hand enough to strike a match. My hand was like it was frozen open. I couldn't close it. Out in those wide open spaces, the wind'd cut you a brand new frock! And I was only about twelve years old.

I just took the cane knife, man, and threw it down and walked off the field. And Mr. Shep—the foreman—said, "What's the matter, there, boy?"

I told him. I said, "Look, mister, I ain't used to this kind of work and it's too cold for me. I'm goin home."

So, what he did, he said, "Well, come here, son. You don't have to go home. I can understand. You from the city." They didn't say New Orleans. "You from the city and you ain't used to this kind of work. You soft." He put me on his horse till I got warm, but that didn't do any good. I was going anyhow.

I hit the headland and I walked back. I walked back home and my aunt told me, "What's the matter?"

I said, "Aunt Martha, look, I'm goin home. I can't stand that kinda work. I ain't used to that. It's too cold for me."

"What makes you more different from my sons? *They* still out there."

I With friends, on the porch of an old gambling house in Willow Grove. (Holly Miller)

They had a little gambling joint where they used to gamble against one another. It was like a family affair, because everybody lived in this little community and everybody knew one another. . . . (p. 20)

"Yeah, but they *used* to that. Not me. And, Aunt Martha, I'm gonna tell you the truth. I'm leavin here." And I wrote to my daddy to send me the train fare to come home—about two seventy-five, I believe.

My daddy sent me five dollars in an envelope but I didn't wait for the money. They had a little gambling joint where they used to gamble against one another. It was like a family affair, because everybody lived in this little community and everybody knew one another—just like one happy family. They'd leave all their doors open and nobody'd take anything.

I was too young to be in the gambling house but my cousin, Yurt, he was running the games there. My cousins, they were kind of "tesh hogs"—kind of rough. They had a cat in there, didn't do anything but play "coon can." He was supposed to have been the best around there. When he told me I couldn't come in there because I was too young, then my cousin told him, he said, "Now listen, that's my cousin and if he don't come in here, you got to get out."

Now! Cat said, "That's alright, man." His last name was Zeno. "That's alright, Zeno." Man! So, I came in.

Well, right by the step—as you go in—I found a rusty nickel. Right down by that step. I picked it up and put it in my pocket and I went in there. They're playing coon can. I knew how to play coon can *long time*—from when I was a little boy, watching the big boys and the gamblers in New Orleans. And I'm sitting down in there and I'm watching this cat. He had beat everybody in the house, so he looked at me and he said, "What *you* know how to play?"

I said, "Well, I don't know how to play *nuttin* too much."

And he said, "You mean to tell me you a country boy, you don't know how to play coon can?"

"No!" I said. "I play a little," I said, "by watching people, but I don't know that much about the game, and I don't have no money anyways. All I got is a nickel."

He said, "Sit down! I don't wanna see you with *that!*"

I said, "Okay."

By the time he was trying to win a *game* I had won my bus fare home! And I came out. I said, "Well, nice knowing you, my friend."

He said, "Nigger, if you tell me you didn't know how to play this game again, I'll kill you." He said, "Where you learn how to play like that?"

I said, "Well, you see, from the sidewalks of New Orleans, my friend. You see, you never judge the book by the cover till you read the pages."

And I hailed that bus right there. I went right outside and hailed that bus. And I beat that money there. When I got home my daddy said, "You got the money that fast?"

I said, "Nooo, daddy, but I tell you what I did. They gonna send you your money back because I *won* my fare back home with a rusty nickel. And," I said, "I don't never want to go back there no mo!"

And I didn't go back any more. From that day till today. One thing I didn't like about the country was they didn't have any electric lights, and if the moon wasn't shining at night you couldn't see where you were going. Those people out there, they were like night owls. They could see in the dark! Their eyes were accustomed to that. They could see in the dark. And when the moon would shine, oh, they'd be out there on the levee, playing ball and all that kind of stuff—at night, when they weren't sleeping. But during work time, they had to get up early in the morning and they'd have to go to sleep early.

But after that I never did go back there.

5

I came here with nothin,
I'm gonna leave here with nothin,
Cause I ain't got nothin to lose . . .

NOW, WITH my mother and my sister gone, and my daddy bootlegging, my grandmother didn't think it was a place for me to be—with my father. I was old enough, then, to caddy at the Audubon park on Saturdays, when I didn't have school. On Saturdays you'd carry those bags for nine holes for seventy-five cents. But I was my grandmother's eyes—my grandmother couldn't see anybody but me—so she came up there and she got me and brought me down to live with her. She lived down across the street from Valena C. Jones school, on Annette, between Galvez and Miro, and she enrolled me in Valena C. Jones. I was right across the street from the school. And, do you know, I'd be late for school. House was right across the street! It sounds funny, but it's true.

Valena C. Jones was a wooden school but it was built like a double house. It was just one building but it was long and it had two sides. The first grade started on one side of the building. Then you'd go to second, third, fourth, fifth, and when you got to the last room at the next end of the building, you'd start your next grade—sixth—on the other side. Then you'd work your way on back to right across from where the first grade was.

Miss Fannie C. Williams was the principal. You had two semesters in each grade: The B and the A. I was up to the sixth grade in "24," so they enrolled me in the sixth grade in Valena C. Jones. I started in 6-B and then I was promoted to 6-A. Then, I was so smart in 6-A, they skipped me from 6-A to 7-A—skipped me a whole grade. From 7-A I went into the eighth grade and I finished the eighth grade with top honors. So, I went through Valena C. Jones school.

Times was so *hard* then. My grandmother used to work in a bake shop where they sold this long French bread. When she used to come home, they'd give her all this stale bread—bread a day old.

They'd bake fresh bread and give her that hard, day-old bread. My grandmother would bring a whole big bag of it home. That bread was so hard, I used to take the hatchet and chop that bread on a little piece of pavement out by the back door. Then I'd soak it in sweet water. Soak it in water and sugar and eat *that* for my lunch. And you know where they cook that steam-cooked rice? Well, the bottom of the pot—the crust of the rice—we used to put condensed milk in there and eat *that* for lunch, too.

While I was in Valena C. Jones school I bought me a ukelele. I can't remember exactly what inspired me to play the ukelele, but I always figured that if I tried, I could play it. I could always sing, see, and the ukelele was a sort of complementing instrument if you could sing. But in order for me to try it I had to buy one, so I went to Werlein's and I bought me a ukelele for a dollar and seventy-five cents. It had catgut strings. I started fooling around with it, and I learned how to play from my singing.

Actually, at that time, ukeleles had a tune, alright, but if you played it something like they play a drum, and the drum was tuned in the right pitch—orchestra pitch—then you could sing with it and it would still sound alright. See, you don't hear any *lead* tune on a drum but if nobody was playing it but you, you could play drums and sing with it. Well, at first, the ukelele was the same way, to my idea, as a drum. I kept fooling around with it. Whatever position I would put my fingers on, I'd fool around with. I'd fool around till I'd find some kind of change which corresponded to what I was singing. I just kept fooling around with it like that, until just from hearing the tone of a different chord I could tell I could fit that chord with my voice.

Alright, now, I kept fooling around and I used to listen to records on these old victrolas that you wind up. I used to listen to Freddie Keppard and Louis Armstrong—well, Louis Armstrong was my idol at that time. In fact, he was practically everybody's idol, in a way of speaking, because he was the hottest thing going at that time. So, I used to practice singing a lot of his songs I'd hear on records, like "Confessin That I Love You," and "Nellie Gray," and "Everybody Loves My Baby"—a lot of tunes like that.

I got to be pretty good at it, and then I used to take it to all these school football games and to supper parties, too. I was too little to play football. I wasn't big enough. I played *baseball* with the school. I was a pitcher on the baseball team. We won five silver cups for the school in succession and I was on the pitching staff. We played

Marigny school in the Eighth Ward, we went to Algiers—it was sandlot baseball. But then, when they had football, I was too small to play, so I'd be in the grandstand with my ukelele. Playing. Girls all around me. Just singing and going on. That's what made me so popular with the girls at the football games. I'd play something and all of them would be clapping and singing—singing along with me, just having a good time.

That was back at the Crescent Star Park. All that ground, that whole square block and across the street, too, belonged to a colored fellow, name of Mr. Blackburn. He leased this ground to the baseball players that had to have a park. See, at that time, there were baseball leagues that used to play there. They built the park there, and they called it the Crescent Star Park. The name of the team was the Crescent Stars. And around that area there were rows of houses. Each row had a name, like, "Bucket of Blood" was between Annette and Allen; every Saturday night they'd kill someone. "Billie Row" was on Tonti, around the corner. It had "gown men," who dressed in a long black robe and used to carry knives and swords. Each of these rows had a baseball team, too. They were like professional black leagues.

Well, we from Valena C. Jones school, we would rent the Crescent Star park to have our football games. After the football games everybody would go home. Kids were disciplined then. They weren't like the kids now. Just had a lot of fun. Never had sex or anything like that on their minds. The girls, and even the boys, we just had a lot of fun, and this was for the simple reason that the boys knew the girls were shy. They were afraid that if they'd approach the girls, the girls would go tell their parents, and that would make a big humbug because the girls were still in school and they were all underage, you know.

I got so popular with the ukelele until every time somebody would give a supper they'd come for me. Most every Saturday night they'd give a supper. A supper'd consist of fried chicken and gumbo and home brew. They didn't have any beer then—they made their own beer. Made home brew and they put it up in bottles and they sold it.

They'd come and get me at my house and they'd say, "Bring the ukelele," and I'd say, "Alright," and I'd play for them for free, just to be there among the girls. And then, if I say it myself, I was a pretty handsome young cat. My daddy used to dress me up. Boy! I used to be sharp. One thing I can say about my daddy—he gave me everything I thought I wanted. I was one of the best-dressed cats in the school. My daddy had his ways but he saw that I had what he thought I should have. And the teachers used to admire me because I used to dress so nice. And girls! Whew! I had more girls than Carter had liver pills. I'm telling you the truth. Had two during the week and three on Sunday. That's right. My mother used to have to run them from my door. They'd come and they'd be looking for me.

See, my father and my mother had got back together. I think it was after that first summer that I spent grassing rice. When my father came out into the country to bring me back to school I think is when he brought my mother back, too. I can remember when he came there, to where my mother and my sister and I were staying in Gramercy. I can remember he stayed that night. He slept that night, and then the next day we caught the train and we came back home. I think he brought my mother home with us, too. My mother always did love the man. She always did. As cruel as he was, she still loved him. They married when she was fifteen years old and she still loved him, no matter how bad he treated her.

Anyway, she came back and when she came back, that's when my father moved from uptown down on Annette, near where my grandmother was living. My grandmother was living on Annette between Galvez and Miro, and my father and mother moved to Annette, between Miro and Tonti.

My daddy, he always could cut hair, so he bought him a chair and opened up a barber shop in the front of the house. The rest of the house was living quarters. So then I left from staying with my grandmother and I went back to my father and my mother. When he opened up the barber shop there everything went on alright.

6

Fly Hen Blues

The rooster crowed and the hen ran around,
If you want me, baby, you'll have to run me down . . .

I FINISHED the eighth grade at Valena C. Jones when I was about sixteen or seventeen. Then I was promoted to the ninth grade, which was called junior high. I was promoted to Joseph A. Craig school, which was between Bayou Road and Esplanade. I don't know if it was exactly on Claiborne, but I know it was between Bayou Road and Esplanade or *on* Bayou Road near Esplanade—right up in that section there. The school belonged to colored at that time. They had an elementary school downstairs and the junior high was upstairs.

So I went to junior high. My history teacher was Professor Long and my math teacher was Professor L. B. Crocker. I finished junior high, but I was sick for most of the term and ended up having to do three months' work in three weeks' time so I could pass to the tenth grade. I went to school, got my papers and I did the three months' work I was absent. I did the three months' work in three weeks and I passed. I was promoted to the tenth grade.

I was supposed to go on to McDonough 35 for high school. Rampart and Julia, I think it was, or somewhere around there. It was right near the railroad station. Somewhere around there. McDonough 35. All the kids in my age and classes had graduated and a lot of them went to McDonough 35. After they finished there, a lot of them went to college and all that stuff. But I didn't go. My father, he was a rounder, in a way of speaking. My mother called him a whore-monger. My father, he spent a lot of money on outside women, instead of being interested in sending me to high school and college. And my mother was *so* good—until anything he did was alright with her. His women would come in the barber shop— stop in—and my mother would leave and she'd go in the back and stay back there. She was so good and trustworthy and everything. In fact she just loved the man, and no matter what he did, was alright. And they used to fight and he used to beat her up and everything.

Besides being a barber, my father was a hod-carrier for the plasterers. About that time, he closed up the barber shop and got a job in Baton Rouge as a hod-carrier. They were building Louisiana State University at Baton Rouge and my daddy went to work on those buildings. On the Capitol Building, too. My daddy worked on all those buildings, and he took me to Baton Rouge with him.

Where my daddy was rooming at, in Baton Rouge, in the front room there was an upright piano. My daddy was working and he couldn't take me on the job with him, so I'd be there all day by myself till my daddy would come in the evenings. That's when I started fooling around with the piano. I started playing around with this piano in the front room. I had played blues on the ukelele and I'd played pop tunes on the ukelele, but that's the first time I played the piano. But from singing and from my ear, I learned how to play the piano, too.

That was all cut short, because what happened was my daddy had a girlfriend around there, and she fell for *me*, hook, line, and sinker. Every evening, he'd come home, he'd find us, me and her, sitting on the swing on the porch. I was supposed to be a pretty fair looking country boy at that time. Young, full of pep, vitality— ready at the drop of a hat. When that happened, my daddy hurried up and brought me back to New Orleans. Didn't let me stay there. He sent me back home and I went back on the ukelele.

But my daddy stayed in Baton Rouge, and he wasn't doing anything for my mother and my sister. That's what made me get mad, and I quit school and I went to work. I was over eighteen by then and I could do what I wanted. To be a *real* man you had to be twenty-one, but I figured if I was over eighteen I was man enough to make my own decisions. So I just up and quit school and I went to work to help my mother and my sister.

I went to work with the plasterers in the Seventh Ward. On my first job I worked carrying mortar in a bucket for the plasterers. The contractor was named Mr. Rousseau. He lived the next corner from our house—which was where my daddy had the barber shop—on Annette between Galvez and Miro.

In the Seventh Ward there were a lot of very skilled people. They were plasterers and they were electricians, and bricklayers and carpenters, but during that time they didn't have such a thing as you had to have a license to be *this* and a license to be *that*. If you knew what you were doing you just knew your work, that's all.

They'd help build one another's houses and everything. They all were like one big happy family. They worked together. Every Sunday they were off, they would get together—all the builders. The one whose house they were building, it wouldn't cost him anything. All he had to do was furnish the materials and they'd work on his house—every Sunday. They would have a great big old iron pot of red beans and ham hocks in the yard, and a big old pot of rice, and a couple of half-barrels of beer or a big barrel of wine, and they'd eat and drink a while, then they'd work a while. I'd bring my ukelele, too. Every Sunday they'd work like that until that house was completed. I mean, if they had to put the foundation down, the bricklayers would be there to put down the foundation and everything, then the electricians went over and put all the electrical work in, then the lathers put the lathes in, then the plasterers came over with the rough work, and then the pros came in with the smooth work.

The work I was doing with them was carrying the mortar in a bucket. In *two* buckets. I wasn't heavy enough to be a hod-carrier, so I used to carry the mortar in the buckets for the plasterers to plaster on the wall. That's the first time I ever had blisters on my hands in my life, because I never did do any hard work like *that*. But I *did* it, and I was making good money. And I was learning to be a plasterer.

At first I was an apprentice—for the first year. Then, the second year, I bought a trowel, and I started learning how to put the rough coat on. The *real* plasterers put the smooth coat on. Then I used to have a float to smooth it off. When I would finish that, they would give me this buffer to smooth off the wall, but, now, when they came to all the cornicing work and all the professional stuff, well, they did that themselves.

I was doing pretty good. I got good enough that they were paying me five dollars and twenty cents a day! They were paying me as a plasterer's helper, instead of an apprentice, and I could start taking care of my mother and my sister. Everything was okay because there was some money coming in.

I had kept on playing my ukelele. A bunch of us used to play ukelele in the Seventh Ward. They had a *bunch* of ukelele players. There was me, Danny Barker—I believe Danny played the uke— Joseph Francis, and a little bitty brownskin fellow. Good looking little boy. He died young. I don't know what he had—whether he died of pneumonia or what.

Well, way after a while, people used to start to *hire* me to play at fish fries. At that time, people weren't making much money so they'd get together and have fish fries and things like that. In the Seventh Ward they had a bunch called the Boozan Kings. Boozan, that's a Creole name for booze—liquor. Boozan Kings. Danny Barker belonged to it and Louise, too. So all we had was a little club and everybody, they would give a fish fry on a Saturday and they would hire me to play. They had all the girls, and all I wanted to eat and drink, and oh, I was something else. I'd play and they would give me fifty cents for a night. I had me a ball!

I couldn't stand that plastering, though. It was a little bit too hard for me. So I quit that job and I went to work at the Economy Dental Company, on Canal between Burgundy and Rampart. They were right next to Grant's Store. I worked there for about two years. An old white lady there—she was kind of sweet on me. She'd buy all my clothes for me. Her son-in-law owned the Jackson Brothers Clothing Store and she'd write a note and tell them to give me what I want. Sometimes I'd get two suits. I'd be dressed up like a big wheel. But I lost that job, just as soon as I got married.

7   **Death House Blues**

I've been ordered to the death house,
There's no need to cry,
I murdered my woman,
Now I'm condemned to die . . .

I WAS a virgin when I got married. That's right! Broke my maiden when I got married. That's the truth. And the funniest thing—it was just the opposite way around. I was a virgin and my wife wasn't. That sounds funny but it's the truth.

I was eighteen. The girl I married was sixteen. She was from uptown—around First and Liberty. We stayed together about nine months and that woman made me see stars. I'm telling you the truth! If I wasn't a level-headed fellow I'd probably've went to the penitentiary. I probably would have killed that woman. But I thought about my freedom and I said, "No. If you can't agree, it's the best to disagree." So I put her out of my house and I swore I'd never marry another woman as long as I lived.

Oh, I was fooling around with a whole lot of women, because those times, playing at those fish fries every week, that gave me a chance to pick up on all the girls. I could pick them out. I really could. If I felt like I wanted to have sexual desires—sexual inter-course—I'd just call, and it was like I had magic in my voice. When I called it looked like she'd just turn around, no matter what she was doing, and just come to *me*. And I'd just tell her, "When I get off, wait for me." Then we'd go ahead on out and get *that* over with. You talk about a man oversexed and that was *me*. That's right. But, you see, when old man time catch up with you, and when you can't come if they call you, that's *it*. It's all over but the shouting and that's over, *too!*

I'd lost my job at the Dental Company when I got married. I had to do something else, so I went to work in a sugar refinery down in Chalmette as a sack-turner. The fellows come with those hundred-pound sacks of sugar; after they dump it out, they throw the sacks on the side. I had to turn the sacks inside out and shake them and stack them up. Every week they'd wash all these big stacks of sacks to reuse them again. So I was a sack-turner for a while.

Then I met another woman. She had a husband. I was small. I was the right age but I was small for my age. And this woman was big. Her husband ran on a ship and she was calling herself taking care of me—giving me money and everything like that. We went uptown, to a friend of mine that ran what you might call an immoral house. Nobody knew about what went on at night there because everybody got out of there before daybreak. And everybody left one at a time. One went one way and the other went the other way—so it wouldn't look suspicious. I think she was paying off, though, because they had a precinct not far from there. Nobody ever bothered her, so I guess she'd been paying off.

After a while I got a job at the Kit Kat Restaurant on Royal Street, between Canal and Iberville. Washing dishes—pots and pans and things like that. A big fat lady was the cook, and she'd have me cutting up onions and garlic and stuff for the seasoning. Then, I had to deliver orders.

One day I delivered an order to a hotel on Bienville and Dauphine, called the Planters Hotel, and I met this girl. It wasn't the *first* time I met her. I'd met her before, when I was working at the Economy Dental Company. I'd met her at parties a couple of times with her step-father and her mother, and she and I were, you might as well say, courting. Or something like that. We weren't intimate sexually, but we went to a couple of parties together. But then I had got married to this other woman and then she—I don't know if she did it for spite or what—she got married, too.

Anyway, I didn't see her for a while—it was about three years—and then I saw her on this day. She was working as a maid in this hotel. Changing bed sheets and everything, after the people checked out of the room, to have the bed ready for the next people that checked in.

I looked at her and she looked at me, and right away I saw the sparkle in her eyes. I knew she still had something for me, so I spoke to her. I never will forget. It was on the day before Easter Sunday so the next time I was out on a call I stopped and bought her a nice big Easter egg and I brought it to her up in the hotel. We started talking about old times and she told me her and her husband were separated. I told her, I said, "Me and my wife's separated, too." So, from one conversation to another, I told her, "I'll see you." And I left.

Now, she and a friend of hers happened to be living up over this building and they had a little sweet shop in there and they used to have a bench out in the front. I'm sitting on this bench and I start singing this song:

Sweetheart if you should stray a million miles away,
I'll always be in love with you.
And if you should find more bliss in someone else's kiss,
I'll always be in love with you.
I can't do any more, I tried so hard to please,
But let me thank you for all those sweet and tender melodies.
I wish you happiness, but as for me, sweetheart, I guess,
I'll always be in love with you.

And she fell in love with me on that tune. She was still married but we got together.

The first night we went out was when she and I and her mother and her mother's man, we all went to the same place. They had a little couple of houses in the back of a garage on Claiborne, near Esplanade, and that's where we spent the night. We went there and we laid out there. And that's where she taught me. She was the one that really taught me what to do because I was ignorant. I didn't stay long enough with my first wife to know her *name.*

About that time I started making money shining shoes in a barber shop on Dauphine and Iberville. *Good* money, too. The man told me, "All you have to do is keep the barber shop clean. You got your brushes and everything here. You buy your polish, and all you can make, all you can make is yours. Just keep my barber shop clean."

I said, "Alright, sir, when do you want me to start?"

"Start tomorrow."

"Okay." Went there the next morning and I'm cleaning up. Sweeping those nice tile floors. It's a high-class barber shop. White barber shop. Had all white barbers in there. One in there was called Mr. Matt. He was a master. And he was a racehorse player. The bookie joint was right around the corner. I didn't know anything about playing racehorses, but every time these fellows would make a winner, they'd get two or three dollars worth of change and just throw it in there on the *floor!* I'd pick up all that change and put it in my *pocket* and I was making ten, twelve, fourteen dollars a week! And at that time, that was good money.

I bought my first tailor-made suit, then. On Rampart Street, at the National Tailors. I paid twenty-five dollars for that suit and it took me about three weeks. You know, you put your five dollars down, and they take your measurements and things, and you show them what you want and then you go on, until they get through with it. It was pretty. Blue pinstripe. Boy, was I sharp. I never will forget that.

This girl, the same girl who I met in the Planters Hotel, she came out there to the barber shop to talk with me. She was going with a man that was an ex-policeman, and he was giving her four and five hundred dollars a week. So she came to me at the barber shop and she told me, she said, "Listen, honey."

I said, "What?"

"You got a break."

"What's that?"

"Well, honey, you don't have to be smellin these white folks' feet no mo," she said. "I'm takin you out of here, cause I got a good thing goin, to take care of me and you *both*. Quit now and come with me."

I said, "Okay."

So, she gave me some money and we went on out to dinner and after that, every Monday around twelve o'clock, like clockwork, we'd meet at the corner of Canal and Rampart. They had a shoe-shine parlor there called the Square Deal and they had about six or eight chairs in there and these cats used to make a lot of money. All the fellows in this shoeshine parlor had a club, and every year they used to give a parade. They'd wear all yellow trousers and yellow silk shirts and everything, and they'd just parade all around the Seventh Ward. That was their big day. One day a year they'd give this thing. The Square Deal Shoeshine Parlor.

Anyway, every Monday I'd wait for her right on that corner and when she'd come, oh, she'd be switchin! She was built like a brick shithouse! I'm telling you. She was neat in the waist as a wasp and spread out round her tail like a throughbred racehorse. Beautiful. Beautiful. The cats at the Square Deal used to get together and start whispering, saying I was a pimp, a hustler.

She'd say, "Come on, honey, let's go."

I'd say, "Okay." And we'd go around the corner to the stores.

She'd get me a pair of shoes, she'd get me five or six different colored silk shirts and a couple of suits and everything, and then give me some money to put in my pocket! I really was living on easy street then.

Every Sunday we'd have a Sunday dinner together. This policeman that was giving her the money, he didn't know me and her were going together. Her mother knew, but he didn't. He's sitting at *this* head of the table, I'm sitting at *this* head of the table, her mother's on the other end with *her* husband, and she's on this end. We'd all have Sunday dinner together and he never knew. I guess, he being an expert, if he'd have guessed, he'd have killed me. But he didn't know it; that she was spending *his* money on *me*.

She had a friend, a big black fat woman, who was living upstairs, on Annette, between Galvez and Johnson. When she wanted to see me, we'd go by her friend's house and we'd lay out. Her friend was going with an old white man that used to work at the Pickwick Club on Canal Street; a big, high-class club. They didn't allow any niggers in there *atall!* Unless you were a porter with a white coat on. The friend also had a young Italian white boy, and the money she'd get from the old man, she was dressing up this white boy. Buying him silk shirts and things. He used to come lay out there while the old man used to work all night, and he'd get out of there before morning.

I saved him one night. Me and my woman, we were right next door to them, and one night he was in *this* bed with her and I was in *this* bed with my woman, and I happened to look downstairs and I saw the old man coming up the stairs. I knocked on the door and said, "Man, get out of there and come over here right quick, cause that old man's coming." So he got out of there and he got in the bed with me and my woman and that's what saved him.

Then, I had another girl. Her name was Lucille. Lucille Honoré. She was fourteen years old when I met her but somehow or other she fell in love with me. Her and my sister were good pals and we used to go to the Ivy Theatre, which was on Annette and Villere. I'd sit between her and my sister and I used to try and make like I was resting my arm on the seat, trying to put my arm around her. She was kind of shy at first. I'd sneak my arm around her and she'd take my arm off. I worked a long time before I could get next to her.

The first time we had a date, we went to a friend of mine's

house. I can't call his right name but we used to call him Brass for a nickname. He had a color like brick—a brassy looking color. Not too light and not too dark, but brassy. That's why we used to call him Brass. His hair was the same way, too. So, we went to his house and that's the first time she ever had intercourse—with me. She was a virgin but, fortunately for me, she didn't get pregnant or anything like that.

We kept going together. We used to meet in the theatre. They had a little theatre they'd built on Annette and Miro. A colored fellow, named Mr. Marchese, used to run the theatre. He was the boss. He was one of the bosses in the grocery store across the street, too. The first time I played my ukelele and sang on the *stage*, in public, was in that theatre.

We used to go in there and sit way in the back—*way* in the back of the theatre. They had a little bitty old screen and it was *dark* in the back. We'd be hugging and kissing and swapping spit and all that kind of jive, and I'd be using my hands, feeling up on her and everything, until . . . In the back, they had a men's and a ladies' toilet. A men's on this side and ladies' on this side, but you could sneak out of the ladies' toilet into the men's toilet, or the man could sneak out to the ladies' toilet. So we'd go back there. She'd go on back like she was going to the ladies' room and I'd go behind like I was going to the men's room and first thing you know, she'd cross over to me and then we'd knock off a piece right there and go on back in the theatre.

One night we stayed back there so long everybody was almost gone and the theatre was almost closing up! When we finally got out, on our way taking her home, on the same street where she lived with her mother, they had a house with a little alley under the porch steps. We went back in that little place and we did our thing right down there. The theatre's closed and her mother's looking all over for her because it's after twelve o'clock. We were laying down on the pavement back in there, goin to town! Her mother passed right by us. Her mother passed by on this side and then she went on back and she passed on the other side. I was so scared I didn't know what to do. I thought she was going to turn around and see us. But it was so dark! They didn't have but one light on the corner. Then, when her mother got out of sight, around the corner somewhere, then we got up and we ran on home. She never did catch us.

Finally, we were inseparable. Everywhere you'd see her, you'd see me. When her father found out, he wanted to kill me, cause she was underage. She was fourteen. Her father and mother knew I had been married so they didn't appreciate her going with me.

Her father and my grandfather used to drink wine in this place right across from the theatre; right there on Annette and Miro. My grandfather used to shave his head, and his head was so hard, he would bet anybody that if there was a brand new board in the place, he could bust that board to pieces with his head. Well, her father was saying what he was going to do to me and he told my grandpa, he said, "I'm gonna kill that little nigger." He didn't know that was my step-grandfather. And then, when he started describing who I was, and he called my name, my grandpa said, "Now, look. That's my grandson you talkin about and if you mess with *him*, then you gonna have to deal with *me*. The best thing you can do is keep your daughter away from him. He ain't forcin her. You keep her away from *him*."

But no matter what they'd do, they couldn't keep her away from me. After her parents found out they couldn't keep her away from me they agreed to let us stay together. So we lived around the corner on Tonti Street. Her mother's sister had a double house. She had one half of the house and she rented us the other side. And my mother gave us a bed and a stove and chairs and tables and everything, and some pots and pans and all kind of stuff like that, to get us started off.

Where all the trouble came was the night they had a dance, called the Fathers and Sons. It was on Allen, between Miro and Tonti, at the bottom of one of those duplex houses where you go up the steps and the living quarters are upstairs. Downstairs was like a hallway. I told Lucille, "Now, you comin with *me* to the Fathers and Sons." But she was taking her own time and the thing started at nine o'clock. She kept telling me she had somewhere to go before it was time and she wasn't ready yet. I think she was waiting for her girlfriend.

I was still going with this other woman that was giving me the money and *she* was going to be there, too, so I said, "Well, now listen. If you ain't comin with me, I'm goin by myself. I'll meet you over there." And I left and went by myself. When I went over there, my father was there, and all the other fathers and sons were there and other people were there. And then this girl came in. She came in there, her pocketbook chockablock with money, and we went and sat down together.

Me and her were sitting down in there and the music was play-ing and everybody was having a good time. We were just sitting. Sitting on the bench together. We were sitting together when Lucille walked in, and she came and stood up in front of us and said, "I wanna talk to you."

"I ain't got nothin to say to you," I said. "I told you, you were supposed to come *with* me and you didn't come. So that's it."

Oooohhh, and my girlfriend there, the money girl, she said, "How much money is you givin him?"

Lucille said, "I ain't givin him *no* money."

"Well, everything you see he got on there, I bought it for him. Those silk shirts you see him wear? I bought em. He's my man. I gives him anything he wants. And when you think you able to give him what *I* give him then you *may* have a chance. Now, we leavin here and we goin to the room and we goin to bed. He's comin home with *me*. If you want to come, and come in the room and watch, that's alright with me. Or, If you want to sit on the step and wait till he gets through with me, then he'll go with you." That's just the way she told her.

Ohhhh boy! When she said that, then Lucille—I don't know where she got the knife, but she had a little knife, and she stabbed that at my throat. I leaned back and she hit me on my right shoul-der and came down. All I saw was the blood. My shirt was split wide open; she ripped that silk shirt. I looked down and saw my blood and everything, and her father and my father and everybody gathered round in. That's when she let them know.

She told her brother, "Turn me loose. Turn me loose! That's my man and I love him and I'll kill him fore I see anybody with him."

So we all broke up that party. We all came on outside. Lucille's people took her home, and I went home with the other woman. I took her to that house that we used to go to. When we got upstairs, she started talking her fly talk and everything, telling me about, "Ain't you gon take off your clothes?"

"No, not tonight."

"Well, what's the matter?"

"What's the matter? I'm going home! By my girl's house. Where I stay at. That's my girl, see? That's my love and I'll tell you, I live with her and that's where I'm going."

Now, *she* started raising all kind of hell. Dope-popping and gang-busting, you understand? She said, "You mean to tell me you goin to that whore's house?"

And the minute she said that, I hauled off and hit her a left hook. I'm not a violent man, but she made me so mad I hit her in the face and I split her cheek bone open. Her cheek split wide open. My man, there, this old white boy next door, Bo, he came over. He had heard the noise. He said, "Man, you crazy? You gon mess with your livin like that? That woman is your livin, man. What you want to do that for?"

I said, "Well, I don't give a damn, man. She can keep her money. I ain't takin anythin," and I left there and I went on back to Lucille. I went back to the house.

After that, she came to my daddy's barbershop looking for me. She didn't want to come to my house, but I had a good friend of mine; he and I were like brothers. He used to eat and sleep at my house. Anything he wanted, he could come and get from my mother and my father because me and him were just like two brothers. His name was Fred Ford. She went to Fred's house about eleven o'clock at night that next night, and she told Fred to knock on my door and call me. Fred called me and said, "Say, man."

"What?"

"Broad at the corner, man. She waitin for you."

When I saw her, she was in the shadows because she didn't want me to see that black eye she had. She grabbed me and hugged me and kissed me and told me everything was alright. Her mother had been looking for me to kill me, but she had told her mother, no, that she was in love with me and it was actually her fault and that settled that. So we got back together for a while, and I kept on seeing her.

Me and Lucille finally broke up. She started going to Rampart Street and everything with a girlfriend of hers. That's where everybody used to hang out—around the Astoria on Rampart Street. I got tired of that and I got tired of fighting with her and we separated.

But, now, from all that commotion at the Fathers and Sons dance, my father heard about me and this woman that was giving me the money. So, what happened was, now me and my *father* got into it. My father told me, said, "I don't want you to go and see that woman no more. That's another man's wife and you gonna get yourself in trouble." See, she was *still* married to her husband. They had separated but they hadn't divorced yet.

I didn't pay him no mind. I didn't pay him no rabbit-assed mind. I was going to see that woman any time I got *ready* because she was the one that had the *money*. But he didn't understand that because I didn't tell him that.

So, to make me *know* he didn't want me to go down there, he took my ukelele and smashed it up against the post—broke it all up in little bitty pieces! And I told him, "Well, I'll tell you, Pops," I said, "I don't give a damn what you do, you ain't gonna stop me from seeing her." "And," I said, "next question. I'm gonna buy me another ukelele, and you can't stop me."

He was surprised, because I never did talk back to him before. But I told him, I said, "I don't give a damn if you kill me, cause you sure can't hit me, that's one damn sure thing. And," I said, "I ain't taking nothing off you any more like I did, cause I'm eighteen years old, now, you understand? And I can take care of myself." He didn't know I was getting money from this woman, see?

So I left there. I took my clothes and I went back and stayed with my grandma, in the next block. Then I went and bought me another ukelele, a better one than what I had, and I stopped speaking to my daddy for a whole month. I wouldn't walk on the same side of the street as his barber shop.

My daddy tried. He'd come where I'd be with the rest of the boys. I had a friend of mine, lived right across the street from my daddy's barber shop. A family called Julouke. There was Richard Julouke, there was Joseph Julouke, and oh, they were bad. They were bad cats. Then there was a fellow, used to be an insurance man for the Unions Insurance Company, married one of the Julouke girls. His name was Eddie Robinson. Well, they had a fine double house, right across from my daddy's barber shop. It was made out of brick, with a paved porch and everything. We'd sit out on their porch over there and we'd play cards—five up, coon can, pitty pat, and everything. On the porch. Me and Fred Ford used to be partners. We used to play for money and we used to give signs and everything. Like, I could put my five fingers down and that meant for him to play clubs, or I could give him a sign that meant for him to play hearts. We had a way of doing it, and those cats didn't ever pick up on what we were doing.

So, here comes my daddy. I still haven't said anything to him. He came standing up there, looking at the game. I *still* didn't say anything. He'd sit down and try to get me to talk to him. But I wouldn't say anything to him. He wanted to talk to me so bad he didn't know what to do. But I was determined. I wasn't going to speak to him any more, and that hurt him to his heart. That hurt him till he could cry, and I knew it. My daddy never did talk rough or harsh to me ever since that day. He realized that if I was man enough to defy him, then I was man enough to take care of myself.

Me and this woman, we went together for a while, and all the time we went together, this same cat was giving her all that money. Then something happened and me and her separated, too. She was going with another cat around there, and then she finally met another cat from the Ninth Ward and the last time I heard she was staying with him. I didn't work for a long time while I was with her. But when me and her broke up, I went to work.

8 Box Car Shorty and Peter Blue

Here's what Box Car Shorty said to Peter Blue,
"You done took my money, now I've got it in for you" . . .

GOT ME a job at a shoemaker's shop—the Busy Bee, on Rampart across the street from the Elite Restaurant. But first, I bought me another ukelele—a better one than what I had. It was sort of a "banjo-uke." It was made like a banjo, but it was tuned up like the last four strings on a guitar. I could always sing, so I complemented myself with that.

Then I got me a piano player. Oh, what a piano player he was! Mitchell Frazier was my piano player. That man had the best left hand since Fats Waller. He could span, with his left hand, tenths and twelfths and notes like that. He didn't have to jump them. He'd just open his left hand like that and hit them right on the head just with one hand. That's how big his hands were. He'd play those basses with that one hand. He was a master on the piano with both hands, but he had the best left hand since Fats Waller and I think Fats Waller had the best left hand in the business. He was a tall, brownskin boy.

We went around, making it our business to play together at those fish fries. We got this one gig—a band of racketeers sent for us to play for their party they were giving. They all had to serve time, but they were having a party before they went to jail. What happened was, we went down there. It was down on the lakefront, in one of those cabins that sits about a hundred yards out. You walk on a platform from the beach to the cabins out there. And in these cabins they had a whole gang of officials and policemen and everything like that, keeping an eye on these racketeers. And women. Skinny-dipping, jumping in the water stripped naked and everything. The camp had rooms on each side and every once in a while you'd see one of them going in with a woman—in a room—and another one going in with a woman—in a room.

Now, when we were playing, there was one officer out there, who didn't like the idea of me playing and watching all these naked

41

women jumping out of the water and jumping on the dance floor. He wanted to make me turn around and face the wall! He hit me on the leg with that stick of his, but they had a great big black guy— about six feet four—he weighed about three hundred pounds, and he had a ham knife in his hand from when he was slicing the ham. He walked up to that officer and said, "Now, if you hit that boy one more time, I'm gonna take your head off with this knife!" Then another one said, "Now, you get outta here. Now! Before they find ya in the lake with a cement overcoat. Just git out. Now! And," he said, "I'm gonna be sittin right here and you can come back with the whole police force if you want to, I'm gonna stop em before they hit that platform down there. I'm gonna stop all of em." *He* was sitting by the door with a whole boxful of bullets and a rifle. He had one of those boxes that milk cans come in full of ammunition—bullets. I was so scared, I didn't know what to do. But after that, we all drove back. They drove us all back home.

Then Louis Armstrong came back to town. He had been gone for nine years and this was the first time he had come back to New Orleans so me and a friend of mine from school, named Lionel Torregano, went to see him, to try to get a break. Lionel played ukelele, but he was left-handed. He played left-hand ukelele and I played right-hand and both of us could sing. We made sort of a duet-like. We had an act. We used to go around hustling in all these places on Bourbon Street on what we could pick up. We went up to see Louis Armstrong, to try to get a break with Louis.

Louis was playing at the Beverly Club, out in Metairie. He played out there, oh, about a month. And every night, Louis Prima would invite Louis Armstrong to his house for dinner and everything, and tell him to bring his horn. Louis would bring his horn, and that's how Louis Prima got his ideas—from Louis Armstrong. Then Louis Prima went to the Famous Door in New York and tore it all to pieces with that stuff he got from Louis. Of course, I give him credit, too. Prima was a good entertainer—a great entertainer—before he was playing the trumpet. But it was from Louis that he got the idea of playing his trumpet *and* singing.

So Lionel and I, we went up to the Page Hotel, on Rampart Street. That's where Louis was stopping at. We walked up there, from way downtown. We went and talked to Louis and played some ukelele for him and I was singing some of his songs. He was glad to see us. Glad that we were interested in music because that's how he started out, back at Jones's Home for Boys. He was always interested in kids that were interested in music. We had walked up there because we didn't have any money for carfare—it was a nickel carfare and we didn't even have a nickel—but he *gave* us a dollar to get back! He gave us a dollar apiece.

On our way to see Louis, walking up Rampart Street, we had stopped at this shoemaker's shop with a shoeshine stand. An old Russian fellow, or a Dutchman, had the shop. It was called the Busy Bee Shoe Repair Shop. On Rampart Street, near Canal. Right below Soulé's. Right next to Moler's Barber College. They hadn't built the Loew's State Theatre yet, but they had dug down in the ground and they were pile-driving the posts and everything, and I used to stand on the rail and look at that, before they put the foundation down. Across the street was the Elite Restaurant where you could get all the beans and rice you could eat for a dime! And then anytime you wanted extra bread all you had to do was ask for it.

Well, this old man stopped me on my way up to see Louis and asked me did I want a job shining shoes? On the way back, after me and Lionel had gone to see Louis, I stopped back at the shoemaker's shop and the old man, Mr. Gus, he told me, "Son, shoeshine stand he's-a yours-a if you want him."

I said, "You mean I got the job?"

He said, "Yeah!"

"When you want me to start?"

"You can start-a right now if you want-a."

And I said, "No! I'll be back tomorrow."

And he said, "Alright."

Lionel and I went back home and the next morning, when I came there, I had the shoeshine stand. That morning I went there and cleaned up the place, and then I got to polishing all that stuff and I straightened up everything on the shoeshine stand, ready for business.

I was doing pretty good at the shoeshine stand. I used to have a little book, and every shoeshine I'd make, I'd write it down in the book and put the money in the cash register. At the end of the week, whatever showed in the book, he'd give me the money for it. I wasn't making a salary but I was making all that money shining shoes. About ten cents for a shoeshine.

Then, I didn't have a written contract or anything like that, but I had the opportunity to be the one to dye the ladies' shoes for Chandlers'. Chandlers' Ladies' Shoe Shop on Canal Street. The ladies would buy shoes made out of—not leather, but canvas-like—some kind of cloth, and I had the kind of dye for that. If they had a pink evening gown and they wanted their shoes dyed pink, all I'd tell them was, let me see the dress. Then I'd go buy the dye and dye their shoes. It'd be all day by the time their shoes were dry. Then I'd just take the paper out of them, and I'd clean the soles around the edges if it were necessary, and I would deliver them. I would deliver sometimes eight and ten pair of shoes in a day. When they found out I did such a good job at dying shoes, I used to get all the acts from the Sanger Theater. That was right around the corner. They used to send me shoes or I'd go get them. I'd go get them and I'd bring them back. Sometimes they'd give me a quarter. Sometimes, when I'd dye shoes, they'd give me fifty cents, so I was making pretty good change there, too.

There was a colored shoemaker in the back, named Walsh Lundy. This shoemaker back there, he told me, "I'm gonna show you how to make some money," and he had me put down extra shoes. If I'd shine one pair of shoes, he had me put down five pair. On a Saturday, sometimes, I'd put down fifteen or thirty extra pair of shoes I shined and I'd get paid for that! The old man didn't know any better. He used to have so much stock—used to buy so much leather. There wasn't any such thing as taking inventory and all that. He didn't know anything about that. I mean he could just barely talk English. He had just come to this country and he was kind of dumb. He wasn't "hip to the dip." He had a young woman and she used to jive him. He was an old man and she was a young woman and she used to come in there any time and hit the cash register and take as much money as she wanted out. Maybe kiss him on his bald head and go on out.

Walsh Lundy was one of the best shoemakers I've ever seen. He was a genius. That man could make jockey boots for the jockeys riding out at the Fairgrounds. Anytime anything'd happen to their boots they'd bring them to him. And you know how thin you've got to make those soles! He'd cut that sole down so thin, by God, you could almost read through that rascal. He was a master. This man was so great in women's shoes, he *glued* the soles on the women's shoes—didn't use nails. He was perfect. People from everywhere would bring their shoes there.

He had lost his leg hoboing. I think he slipped on a freight train and had his leg cut off way up at the thigh. He always wore a crutch under one arm—one crutch. Walsh's regular customers that would come to get their shoes fixed—if he'd half-sole-and-heel one pair of shoes and put just rubber heels on another pair—he'd just put the price of the rubber heels in the cash register and put the half-sole-and-heel in his pocket.

One day I was sitting on the shoeshine stand. Nothing to do. Walsh picked up a piece of leather and turned and hit me and said, "Get up from there, boy, and come back here and learn something. You may be a shoemaker someday."

"Okay."

So I got up from there and he taught me. First, he started me off with taking the old heels off the shoes, preparing them for him to put the new heels on and fix them up on his machine. Then he taught me how to use the machine—the buffing part. After he'd get through sewing the shoes, and the soles on the shoes, and everything, then he had me working the machine to round out the soles. I'd put a little stand on them and put them on the buffing machine. I got to be real good! The only thing about it is, those knives were so sharp that cut the leather, if you weren't careful you'd be cutting up your hands! That went on for a while until the old man sold the place to another fellow. Walsh told *this* man I was a shoemaker! I started getting paid for working behind the counter with Walsh, and for shining shoes, too.

Then I met a woman—you couldn't tell her from white to save your life. Her daddy was Italian—he was white—and her mother was French, but *my* color. She was beautiful, with long black hair. The first night I met her I was playing ukelele up on a place near Napoleon Avenue, somewhere. At some house party. She and her husband and her cousin and *her* husband were at this party. I was playing. They were serving liquor, and I was playing in the kitchen. They had a big kitchen and they were eating and drinking and I was playing for the party—in the kitchen.

She talked to the landlady that had the house. She gave the landlady some money and told her to bring a bottle of whiskey up in the front room, and she told her to tell me to come up in the front room behind it, because she had fallen in love with me. The husbands stayed in the kitchen, but her cousin had to come with me. We went up in the front room, and when I got in the room, she told the landlady, "Close the door." The landlady closed the door. She looked at me and I looked at her, and she told her cousin, "He looks at me like he don't like me."

I said, "Why shouldn't I like you? Sure I like you."

"Look," she said, "where you work at?"

"I work at Canal and Rampart."

She talked to me. She sat on the bed and she said, "Come sit down here by me. Don't be afraid."

I was scared. Her husband was right in the back and I didn't want to take chances. Her husband was bright—light color with straight hair. He looked like a big Spaniard. Tall—about six feet two. Big! He weighed about a hundred and eighty-five pounds. He and she had had an argument and she had shot him. She didn't kill him, but she put him in the hospital. He was mean. He used to beat her up. He wouldn't hit her in the *face*, but he'd beat her with a broomstick till she had welts all round her *body*. She was beautiful. She was fine.

When I told her where I worked at, she found the telephone number in the book the next day, and about six o'clock that evening she called me up and told me to come by her house. Now, I got off at six and her husband got off at seven. He was working at the Jung Hotel, on Canal, in the next block, and she was living on Burgundy and St. Peter. When I got off I stopped at the house and she told me to come on in. When I came on in, she had the most beautiful silk Japanese robe you've ever seen—and nothing under there—and she told me, "Come on in." I went on in, and she had the lights down low. Pretty lights. She was working at the Roosevelt Hotel and made a whole lot of money. Her cousin was the pastry lady in the Roosevelt Hotel. They both made a lot of money. She made me go to bed with her right there, knowing her husband would get off at seven! The man could have caught me in bed with the woman. But me, I didn't have any better sense. Pussy crazy, I mean. And then, she looked like white, anyway, and was beautiful at that. So I just took a chance. What the hell. We knocked off a piece right there and she gave me some money.

After that I wouldn't take chances like that any more! I made her come down to *my* house. Come *my* way, so he couldn't blame anybody but her, because I couldn't *force* her to come down there. I was living with my mother and them, then, on Annette Street. She started coming to my house. As soon as she could get off on a Friday and get her money she'd get a taxicab and come down there. She used to come down in a *Yellow* Cab. The Yellow Cab drivers were white and they didn't know whether she was white or black. She used to come down there with buckets of food, with cornish hens—those little chickens with their legs all flicked up there— with all the finest kind of food, beautiful Rogers Brothers silverware, and all that stuff. She had access to all that, and she used to bring some of that to my mother. My mother thought I was stealing. I swear. From there we'd leave and we'd go rent a house on Havana Street for the weekend. She'd rent the house and she'd pay the woman to cook for us, because she wouldn't go back home till that Monday. All we did was eat and screw, eat and screw. And her husband never knew where she was.

She'd bring her cousin with her. Her cousin had to come with her all the time, for a shield, so her husband wouldn't think she was meeting a man. And I know her cousin wanted me to do it to her, too, because she'd get in the bed, just in her slip, and lay on this side of us. And we're going to town! I thought about it and I said, "Now there I was, I coulda had *both* of em." But I didn't know how *she* was going to feel about it, and *she* was giving me the money.

I mean brand new money. It would crackle when you went to spend it. She bought me—I never will forget—a blue suit, a white silk shirt, a tie, and a pair of black shoes. She bought me a pair of gray spats—at that time they used to wear gray spats—with buttons on the sides. Pearl buttons! Oh, I was sharp, I was sharp! Pocketful of money.

Me and her went together for about a year. But she fooled around one time and got a *black* cab driver. This black cab driver, I think he knew her husband and he told *him* where he dropped her off at. At my house. So it happened that he came to the corner of my house, trying to wait to see if his wife came out. I had taken her to meet my friends across the street and I could peep through the blinds and see him standing out there. He couldn't see us, but I believe he would've killed me. He waited there a long time. He waited till he got tired and he left. When he left, I sent one of the cats out there to take a walk to the corner and see which way he went. Then we hired a cab and went on to Havana Street and she didn't come back till that Monday.

Coming back, we took the bus. She had one of those white ermine jackets on. She was sharp! Dressed to kill! Beautiful! And I was sharp, too. We got on the bus, and the bus driver said, "Hey! Joe. How ya doin?" You see, when I was working at the shoemaker's, the bus drivers, they used to wear boots, and I used to shine their boots and stuff, so they all knew me. I said, "Alright."

At that time they had a screen on the bus and the black people had to sit behind the screen. I went to sit in the back and she came to sit back there with *me*. The bus driver called me to the front. "Hey, Joe, come here," he said, "Ain't that a white woman?"

I said, "Man! You crazy? That ain't no white woman, man! That's a colored woman. That shows you, see? Shows you how much you know." I said, "They got a whole lot of half-white and free-born down here, man!" I said, "She's Creole! Her mother's dark as me! That ain't her fault cause her daddy was white."

He said, "I just wanted to know, cause she even look like a white woman to me."

I said, "I know, but she ain't."

I got off the bus a block before I got to her house and she got off the bus at her house and the next time I saw her, she told me her husband had beat her black and blue trying to make her tell him where she was and she wouldn't tell him anything.

Then, one night, we stayed at her cousin's house. Her cousin and *her* husband went out. Her husband went home and didn't find her there and *he* thought she was around *there,* so he knocked on the door and asked her cousin's mother where she was. She told him she didn't know. We were in the front bed! Laying out! And we could see through the blind! He was standing outside again, and we're laying out! When he got tired of waiting he left, and we screwed the rest of the night. Then I came out first, went on about my business, and then, when the coast was clear—when her cousin's mother told her the coast was clear—then she got out and she went home. Got another beating, I guess. But it shows you. I mean, when you're young and crazy you take all kinds of chances.

How me and her fell out was, she had gone in the hospital for something. I think he broke her jaw or something. He beat her up and she was in the hospital. We broke up because I didn't go to see her! When she got out I met her in front of the Municipal Auditorium. In that open space there. She had one of these big collie dogs and we were sitting out there on the grass and she told me, she said, "Well, if you didn't think enough of me to come see me, we'll just have to call it a day, because you don't care nothin bout *me.* You just care about what I can *do* for you." Now, I know she couldn't have been expecting me to go see her with her husband there, too! I'd have given everything away! But I've never seen that woman from that day till today!

All this time I was still playing the ukelele. What really started me into music professionally was, I used to bring my ukelele to the shoemaker's shop. On Saturday mornings we had a lot of work to do, but during the week, in the mornings, I used to bring my ukelele up there and when I didn't have anything to do I'd sit down and play. Walsh Lundy, after he found out I could play the ukelele, then just to pass the time he and I would sing harmonizing. All the people would come crowding in front of the door. People used to be in front of the place like *that!*

Oh, I could sing like a bird, then. I never drank anything. I didn't have that whiskey voice like I've got now. I mean I had a beautiful voice then, and I could really sing. I sang pretty songs, too. "Sweet Adeline" and all that kind of stuff. Different songs. All those songs they used to do. Community singing, like "I had a dream, dear. You had one, too." Sang the blues, too. And everything else—spirituals and all that. We used to harmonize, and Walsh could sing a good second to me.

So, here came these two boys. One was named Hats and Coats, and the other was named Green. They were the two best dancers in the city—Hats and Coats, and Green—just like you see Pork Chops and them, nowadays, dancing on the sidewalk and passing the hat and all that. They came to get some taps put on their shoes, and I was playing the ukelele. They heard me playing, and they looked at me, and Hats and Coats was the first one who approached me.

He said, "Say, man. What you doin in this place cuttin up your hands? You ain't got no business shinin nobody's shoes, man, with all that talent. The way you can play and sing, man, you could come with us and make a lot of money. Playing for us. I tell you what you do," he said. "Quit that job and come on with us and make some money."

I said, "What y'all do?"

He said, "Well, man, we dance."

"Yeah? What kind of dancin?"

"We're tap dancers." So to give me an idea, they said, "Hit something."

So I did, "Plink, plink, plink, plink, plink."

And they, "Doo, doo, bippity-bop, whew, shi-bop, prrr, bop, ta-taa, do-bah!"

I looked at these cats and said, "What! Them cats is real gone!"

So I went with them. I quit the old man. I told him, "Mr. Gus," I said, "I quit." And I quit the job and took my ukelele. Just like that! I didn't tell him anything. I just left.

I went with them and we started just like those dancers do out on the street on Bourbon Street. Passing the hat and all. We had special places we used to go. Wherever they played at, where they had a band, if they made any money, they had to split it with the band. If they picked up ten dollars, that was five dollars for the band and five dollars for them. If they didn't pick up but two, three dollars, there was three of them—little Earl Palmer was a dancer with them—then the band would say, "That's alright." But if they'd pick up over ten dollars they'd split it. When they got me to play the ukelele, they didn't need the band.

Earl Palmer was about nine or ten years old, but he was one of the greatest tap dancers in the *city*. His mother and his aunt, they were choreographers for the chorus line. They were the two best feminine tap dancers in the city. Thelma and Anita Fairfield. The Fairfield Sisters. They were teaching choreography. They taught dancing steps to the chorus girls in the shows—at the Lyric Theatre and at the Lincoln Theatre and places like that.

Earl's mother used to dress him up so cute. She used to make all his clothes. She used to make him white tails. White tux, tails, white satin shirt, white tie, and white shoes. And dance up a storm! He could outdance all of us. He was the cause that we could get in these big white nightclubs and do our number and pass our hat—pick up the money. The minute people'd see him then they knew him.

So we gave ourselves another name. Hats, Coats, Pants—I was Pants—and Earl Palmer was Buttons. I was playing for them. Earl Palmer became one of the greatest drummers in the country. He's got a big home in California, a big swimming pool and all that jive. Drives a big cadillac and everything. And I used to carry him on my back. His mother wouldn't let him go with anybody unless he'd be with me. I took care of him, and I saw that those cats didn't steal his money, too.

We started in 1931, before liquor had come back. That was when Louis Prima and his brother had the Beverly Club—Louis and Leon Prima. Leon Prima had the 500 Club, too, and he played there for many years. He was playing trumpet at the 500 Club and his brother was playing trumpet at the Beverly Club with his band. We'd go out there and we'd dance. We did so good out there, we started making so much money, that we used to hire a taxicab to drive us around. We got tired of walking around to the different clubs and getting streetcars and all that, so we hired a taxi. We hired a fellow from around Rampart Street. His name was Louis Henry. Later he got to be a big wheel. When I met him in New York he had diamonds as big as eggs and he was running a joint called the New Orleans Club in Harlem. He was a porch-climber, too. He'd get Christ off the cross and then go back and get the cross! Louis Henry was our cab driver. He used to drive us around. We used to pay him so much a night, and he could make more money off of us, driving us around at night, than he could just driving cab. He was driving a cab independently. There wasn't any such thing as a C.P. & C., and all that kind of jive. If you had your own car and you wanted to drive cabs, you could just drive around. Or sit in your car on a corner and see somebody and say, "You want a cab?" So, we got him to drive us around—for the night.

We had another place we used to go on Tulane Avenue, across from the brewery. There was a club and we used to go there. This fellow used to get the beer by the crock. Not in the bottles. By the crock. That crock had a spigot on it. A faucet, like. He used to have it up in the storeroom, and we used to go up there in our "dressing room," in our room back in the back. They didn't allow you in the club after you got through with your dance, so we went back in the back and we could drink all the beer we want. Just open the spigot and get you a can, and drink all the beer you want. Every Friday night they had boiled crayfish, boiled shrimps, boiled crabs—that they'd give away. You'd come in there to buy beer and drinks, and they'd give you a portion of boiled crabs or shrimps or something like that. If you wanted any more, you bought it, but they gave you the first order.

In the next morning we'd go to the Entertainer. Now, that was a place that the blacks called black and tan. It was around Iberville and Marais. Right back of where Krauss is now. Back there. In the red light district. The man that owned the place, his name was Pete Lala. He owned the Entertainer and he had a fat black bartender named Big John. That's what we used to call him. That's the first place that I saw in this town that was integrated. White and black came in there. Black women dancing with white men, white women dancing with black men and nobody said a word. Nothing! Nobody said a word. I mean it was just—you talk about integration, they had integration *then!* That's right. This was during the real segregation time, but in the district it didn't make any difference. Most of them were prostitutes, anyway. The white whores hustled Negroes just like they hustled the whites. Fifty cents a crack. And when the whores would get through, they'd meet their pimps and everything. The pimps would bring the whores to the Entertainer, and they'd come there and have a *ball.* That was the best—that's why they called it the Entertainer—the best entertainment in the city at that time.

All the greatest musicians that'd come off the boat—off the

steamer Capital—like Fate Marable and all them off the boat, when they'd get off, they'd come to the Entertainer in the mornings. Joe Robichaux had one of the best little bands in the country at that time—playing in there. Joe Robichaux, the piano player. He and I played together for a long time on Bourbon Street. That was the hottest six-piece band, I think, in the *country* at that time. Because, first of all, Earl Bostic was his alto player. And then he had a tenor player named West. And he had a little drummer, used to have to sit on two boxes, with a pad, cause he was short, but *boy*, he could play. Most of the boys who played with Joe Robichaux wound up with Don Redman and Duke Ellington and Cab Calloway. "Little Walter," Walter Williams, was playing guitar with Joe Robichaux and he wound up with one of the greatest trios in the country, the Three Peppers. Then he stopped playing guitar and he played bass. They had a bright boy up there, his name was Bell, and he played the guitar. He got lucky with a white woman and she gave him twenty-five thousand dollars and opened him up a place of his own, a barroom of his own. Then he played in his own place.

Anyway, we used to wind up at the Entertainer and we would get in a corner way in the back and come out of all those pockets with all that money—all the change and money we'd collected all night. We'd get back in the corner and split up the money right there. I'd say, "Now, look. Y'all split that money four ways." When we'd split up *aaaaall* the hats full of money, we'd give everybody equal. I'd count out how much we had apiece and out of that all four of us would put together and pay off the cab driver.

I'd take Earl's share *and* mine and put it in my pocket. I used to see that those cats didn't steal his money. I'd take his money and I'd bring him home. It would be around four o'clock in the morning and sometimes he'd be up on my back, sleeping, poor little fellow. He wasn't any more than about nine, ten years old. I'd put him on my back and he'd ride piggyback and his little head would be sleeping on my shoulder, like that. I was living on Lafitte, between Claiborne and Derbigny, and his mother was living on Claiborne between St. Ann and Dumaine. I used to walk there. I'd knock on the door and Thelma would come to the door and I'd say, "Here's your son, Thelma."

She'd say, "Oh, my poor baby."

And I'd say, "Here's his money, too."

I used to take care of him. He was small, but he remembers some of it. He was down in New Orleans not long ago. He came down here to play at the Fairmont Hotel with Peggy Lee and he came down on Bourbon Street. I didn't know him, he had gotten so big and tall. He stood up there and looked at me and I looked at him. Then he said, "Nigger, don't you know your partner? I'm Earl Palmer."

I said, "What! Oh, man! You got to be kidding. Boy! You grew out of my eyesight. I ain't even seen you since you was a little boy!"

Then we went up to Mason's Americana and we had a talk and everything and he was telling me what he was doing. He's a studio man. He writes and arranges and all, and then he plays the drums on all the sessions with Lou Rawls and all those kind of people. He makes around a hundred and seventy-five thousand dollars a year. You know he's a big man. He's one of the greatest drummers in the world, and he used to be one of the best tap dancers in the city.

I learned to dance from him. From Hats and Coats and Green and him. But when Earl Palmer stopped dancing and started playing drums, well, I became better than both of them. That's right. I became one of the best in the city. Later on, when I was dancing at the Gypsy Tea Room, I had dancers who used to come from New York and Chicago. They'd come down to New Orleans. They'd come to the Gypsy Tea Room and I'd take care of all of them. Take care of them *all*.

9   **Little Eva**

Little Eva, Little Eva,
Don't you hear me callin you . . .

NOW, WHEN the time came when liquor really came back, in thirty-three, I was still working with Hats and Coats and Green and Earl Palmer—Hats, Coats, Pants, and Buttons. We were dancing at these white clubs around town for what we could pick up off the floor and when we'd get through, we'd go down to this place on Claiborne, between St. Ann and Dumaine, where they were selling wine for twenty cents a quart. That's right. Wine, twenty cents a *quart!* Beer was ten cents a bottle and white lightning was ten cents a half-pint. Coca-Cola was five cents a bottle and then, if you'd get a half-pint of that white lightning they'd *give* you a Coca-Cola. That's during that time that liquor had just come back. They sold more wine than anything else because it was almost during the depression time and the cats didn't have that much money. I never will forget that.

That's were I met Eva Soule. She was tending the bar in this barroom on Claiborne Street. We used to stop there and drink wine and she'd wait on us. She was the cutest reddish brownskin Indian-looking gal I'd ever seen. Beautiful. Pretty as a picture. She was pretty as a speckled pup on a July day, hitched to a wagon with the tongue painted blue. She didn't weigh but a hundred pounds, but "them pounds was scattered round." She was little but she was built nice. Pretty. She looked like an Egyptian. Her hair, her real hair—long, pretty black hair—went way down to her posterior. She was Indian, Spanish, and Portuguese. She wasn't black, and she wasn't white, and she wasn't a "nigger." Indian, Spanish, and Portuguese. Her mother was three parts Indian and one part Spanish; she was brownskin—a reddish-brown-like Indian color—and she had those high cheekbones. Her daddy was Spanish and Portuguese. He was white.

She was seven years older than me and she fell for me! She fell for me, and I fell for her. She'd ask me to come back down there to see her, so I'd just go there every night. Every night, I'd go down there and talk with her. One night, I waited till she had time and then I asked her, "What time you get off?" She told me when she got off. There was a place around on Orleans Street; I don't remember the name of that place, but it was one of the hottest joints around there. They used to sell fried oyster sandwiches and fried chicken and hot sausage—which they used to call "chorice"—all the real good stuff, on French bread: "po-boy" sandwiches with ham and cheese and tomatoes and all that. They used to stay open all night. I waited for her and when she got off, we went over there. We had something to eat and had a couple of drinks, and she took me to her house. She said, "Come on, take me home," and I said, "Okay." So I went to her house.

She was living—this was on Orleans—she was living on La-fitte, between Claiborne and Derbigny. By the railroad track. I brought her home that night and she said, "Do you have to go home?"

I was still living with my mother so I said, "No!"

"Well, you can stay here with me."

"Okay."

So I stayed there, laid out there, and slept there that night. She and her husband were separated. She had three kids and she was going with Lester Santiago, the jazz pianist. His brother, Burnell Santiago, was one of the greatest piano players in the city. I mean, I took him for Earl Hines to hear him, I took him when Duke Ellington was in New Orleans, to hear him play, but they said, "If he could only read . . ." He said, "I can't read but I can play anything I hear." And he could.

Lester was playing at a club over a drugstore or something on Canal Street and St. Charles. Upstairs. He was playing the piano there. And Eva was going with him. But when she met me that was all for Lester Santiago. I stayed there that night, and then I stayed there a whole week!

One day, Lester came in there. We were laying down in the back. Since it was summer time, we had made a pallet on the floor in the back room, and we were laying down there. She had a thirty-eight Smith and Wesson Special, because she was afraid of Lester. She gave it to me and I had it laying right under the pillow. He came in. He didn't even knock on the door. He just came on in. He had come through the side door while we were in the back. Well, Lester knew *me* and I knew *him*. When he walked in and he saw it was me, he started talking and walking around and all that. Walking around.

I said, "How ya doin, man?"

He said, "Alright," and then he told Eva, "Hello. How ya doin?" She said, "I'm doin alright."

He asked if she had anything to drink and I told her, "Get up and get him what he wants." So she got up and gave him a drink. She was selling bathtub gin—alcohol and water—and she used to have all the porters off of trains. They used to come there when they would come in town. They'd stay in the coaches at the Union Station—they had special coaches with sleepers—and they'd sleep there. They used to come to her house because she used to go with one of the fellows that was a chef on the train. She was going with Lester at the same time, and when this fellow would leave to go on his trip—he'd be gone for three, four days—well, Lester would lay out there with her. When it was time for him to get back, Lester would go away.

So I did the same thing to Lester that Lester was doing to *that* fellow. He ain't had no kicks when he found *me* there.

After that, she straightened him out and she told me to go get my clothes. I went by my mother's and got my clothes and *lived* with her. Me and Lester have always been good friends. We never had any difficulties or anything like that. He just eased on out. He never did stop speaking to her that night and he never stopped speaking to me. We never broke friendship. But if he'd have started something I *might* have shot him. I didn't *give* a damn then. I was young. Foolish. You know what I mean. And she was so pretty it was pitiful.

She was thirty-five years old. Thirty-five? No. She was thirty-two. I know she was seven years older than me. She was thirty-two and I was twenty-five. She had three kids. She had a beautiful little girl and two boys. Everybody thought that she was robbing the cradle. I looked so young for my age. Even Vivian, her little girl, told her, said, "Mama, you robbin the cradle." Small as she was! Even now, people don't think I'm the age I am and at *that* time, when I was twenty-five I looked like I was seventeen. Had all my pretty white teeth. Beautiful! Every time I'd smile you'd look at me and you'd melt in your place! I was a lover from my heart. Vivian is still as beautiful as she was when she was a little girl. Her brother, Benny, took after his grandfather. You couldn't tell him from white to save your life. He was light complected with straight dark brown hair.

I *raised* those kids. Eva and I stayed together for seventeen years and I raised those kids. She and I. Her mother was living with us, too. A lot of times we did without eating so *they* could eat but we got along. We stayed in the house a whole year without paying rent because nobody knew who the house belonged to. Nobody came to collect so we didn't worry about paying. Somehow or another, Carriere's and Sons found out. I don't know if they found out where it was, or if they just *took* the property, but they took over the house and they started charging us: twenty-one dollars a month. But we *didn't* pay rent for a whole year and that helped us a whole lot.

Eva is the one who got me a job. She left her job on Claiborne and she went and got a job around by a place on Orleans Street. At first they called it the Sazerac but they had to change the name because the bartender at the Roosevelt Hotel had invented a drink called the sazerac. They changed the name of the place, but I forget the name they changed it to. An Italian fellow was running the place for a big politician.

Wherever Eva went and got a job, she talked for *me*. She's the one that actually started me into playing professionally—for *money*. She'd talk to the man for *me*. When she talked to *this* man for me, and the man said he'd pay me a dollar a night, I quit Hats and Coats and them. I quit *them*.

Now I was playing for a dollar a night. Eva was getting two dollars a *week*, but she was making more money than me. She was making all the tips and everything—ten, fifteen, twenty dollars a night in tips—because she was cute and the fellows liked to talk to her. I was extremely jealous. All the railroad porters knew her, and all the cats who worked at the New Orleans Athletic Club—all the colored boys who used to work in the rubdown, the masseurs, over there—they all knew her. They all used to come and *wait* for her to wait on them and they'd tip her real good. When they got ready to go, there'd be eight or ten of them together, they'd come up with fifty cents apiece, a quarter apiece, or a dollar apiece sometimes. Sometimes she'd pick up seven, eight dollars just off that one party. They came in at night when they got off from work.

They liked *me* because I played the ukelele. I was playing ukelele and I used to dance. They used to have sawdust on the floor and I used to wear my tap shoes. I'd be playing my ukelele and then, at a certain time when they'd have the crowds, I'd take a broom and sweep the sawdust out of the way. The taps wouldn't make any sound on the sawdust; they made the sound on the pavement—on the solid marble—so I would sweep the sawdust aside and do a tap dance routine with the piano player. The piano player was a little black fellow, called Catsy, and that was the floor show we had. I drew crowds around there! When I'd get ready to do my dance all the cats used to come from the New Orleans Athletic Club.

I worked there a while with her and together we kept the kids in school and dressed them up and everything. Finally we thought to make me a little money, so I left there and went and got me a better job around on St. Peter, at the Plaza. St. Peter and Villere. I got a dollar a night there, too, but a better class of people came there and I made a lot of money.

And just like Eva got *me* a job at the Sazerac, I got *her* a job at the Plaza. I told them she was the most popular waitress in the city at that time. In fact, she won the *prize* as the most popular waitress in the city. She won a cash prize, I think, of a hundred dollars, and a free trip with all expenses paid to Houston, Texas. They had a woman, I forgot her name but her old man had a joint on Iberville and something. He was making plenty of money then. Nowadays he's working at a bar on Conti and Galvez. He's a bartender behind the bar there. He was halfway rich at one time but this woman broke him. She was the first colored woman I ever saw that wore hundred- and hundred-fifty-dollar dresses. She used to wear high-priced dresses, mink coats, all that jive. Well, she was the kind of woman that gave these kinds of contests. She wanted to be a big wheel and get her name in the papers in the society column, so she'd say she was going to give a popular waitress contest. She made money out of it, because people bought the votes for the "popularest" waitress. She sold the votes and, quite naturally, she made enough money to come up with the hundred dollars cash, and then enough money to send the winner to Houston, Texas, with expenses paid for a week. Eva won *that,* so I got her the job at the Plaza.

I worked there for a long time. I had the band there. I had a three-piece band in the back and they had dancing in the back. I had traded the ukelele and I had got me a tenor guitar. A four-string guitar. I played the tenor guitar just like I played the ukelele. I tuned it just like a ukelele. It's just that it was bigger and the frets were wider. I had a piano player and Cagnieletti, the trumpet player, his brother was playing drums with me. He stayed drunk all the time. Liquor's what killed him, but what *actually* killed him is, he tried to work night and day. He'd work at night with me, get off around four o'clock in the morning, and go home. He'd just have time enough to drink some coffee and change into his working clothes and go work all day. Then he'd come back that night. That's why as soon as he'd get a few drinks he'd get so sleepy he'd be playing all out of time and everything. Sleeping! I had to wake him up half the time but he played with me for a long time while I played there.

While we were at the Plaza I went up to the Grand Terrace on Seventh and Howard. I was off that night. They had some cats up there that had heard about me so I sang some blues. Of course, I had brought my tenor guitar with me up there. We had a ball, so the man *hired* me. The man told me, "I'll give you ten dollars a week." I wasn't getting but seven down there at the Plaza, so I told Eva I was going to take the job and I went to work up at the Grand Terrace.

That's when the trouble started between me and Eva. I'd come down to the Plaza when I'd get off in the mornings; I used to get off at two o'clock. She'd still be working when I got off so I'd come down there and wait for her and take her home. This is where the humbug was: the place was packed at first and the evening was very busy. After things slowed down the man that was spending the *money* in the place was still there. *He* started dancing with Eva and I got mad. Oh, I was terrible. I was really jealous of that woman. I walked up to her and I separated her from him. I made one grab, like *that*, and her whole uniform came off in my hand! She broke and ran into the toilet and one of her friends went in there and gave her a coat to put on. I left there and I went home and got the gun and came back, but her friend took her down to Claiborne Street where *she* lived at. She took her to *her* house till the next day.

By the next day I had cooled off. I was in the back, sleeping, and the kids were sitting on the porch. When she came back she asked them, "Is Joe inside?"

They said, "Yeah, Mama. He's asleep." So she came in there. I was sleeping and she woke me up and she talked to me the way she'd talk to one of her kids. She said, "Now, listen. Lemme tell you somethin. You don't have to worry about no man with me. You the only man I love, and you the only man that I ever *will* love, long as I *live*." In fact, that's the truth. She did. Till she died. But she told me, "Now, that's part of our living. This man was the biggest spender in the place," and she showed me how much money in tips she'd made.

"Well, honey, I'm sorry," I said. "You know, I love you so much I just can't stand to see nobody holdin you so close like that."

"Well," she said, "you never have to worry about that."

So I said, "Okay," and I didn't give her any trouble after that.

Eva was the inspiration for the tune of "Little Eva" that I wrote in New York. She was still my old lady at the time. We weren't married, but we were common law. I was thinking about a tune to complete a recording date; you needed at least four tunes. That's the main reason why I wrote the tune. I had three tunes and I thought about her and I just wrote the tune. I actually wrote it about her.

I had to think of the ideas to try to put the tune together to make it materialize the way I wanted it to. Like, if I'm calling her and she doesn't want to come, well, I said, "you three times seven and you should know what you want to do." She's over twenty-one, understand? She's her own woman. She wasn't married to me and so she could do what she wanted to do. But I also told her to be careful, too, because while I was gone I didn't want her "giving away none of my jelly roll." If I found it out, she'd have to "ask the Lord to have mercy on her soul." I was going to fix her up if I found it out, or if I would catch her when I came home. When I came home she wouldn't *know* I was coming home. I always had a key to the house. Everywhere I'd go I'd bring my key so I don't have to knock on the front door and somebody be goin out the back! I'd just open my door and come in. And suppose it's during the night when both of them are sleeping in the bed. They wouldn't hear me when I came in. That's trouble right *there.* So that's why I told her that I was "gonna ring up" Geddes and Moss. That's the undertaker on Jackson. I was going to ask them "how much her funeral cost," because I was gonna kill her!

All that was in the tune. What made me put it in the tune was I had all that in my mind—what I was going to do if I would catch her in that kind of situation. That's what gave me the inspiration to write it.

Little Eva, Little Eva, baby, don't you hear me callin you?
Little Eva, Little Eva, don't you hear me callin you?
I know you three times seven, you should know what you
*   want to do.*

But don't ever let me catch you giving away my jelly roll.
Don't ever let me catch you, baby, giving away my jelly roll.
If you do, just ask the good Lord to have mercy on your soul.

Gonna ring up Mr. Geddes, wire Mr. Moss,
Ask the undertaker how much your funeral cost.
Yeah, Little Eva, baby, don't you hear me callin you?
I'm also three times seven and I know what I want to do.

10

It takes two to tango,
It don't take but one to mess around . . .

THE GRAND TERRACE used to be called the Black Gold. That was the first name of it. They changed the name after a young fellow, about my size, killed the cook. They had a little short-order place in the front, and they had a big black guy, about six feet four, weighed about two hundred forty pounds. He was the cook. Every time this kid would come in the place, the cook would say, "I told you to stay out of here." The kid wasn't doing anything. The cook just was a bully, and he didn't like the kid for some reason or other. But the kid waited till he turned his back on him and he reached on the counter and got the ham knife and . . . Like to cut him in *half!* Just one whack! By the time they got him across the street to the Flint-Goodridge Hospital he was dead. Blood all over the place.

They cleaned the place up and they changed the name—from the Black Gold to the Grand Terrace. I had a job up there. I had a band there. I got a man who could read! A piano player named Louis Givens. He could see music around the corner! Louis Givens played piano, and I had John Handy playing clarinet. Albert De-longe was on alto sax with us. He used to live down in Buras and he was a good saxophone player. We had a drummer, too, but I forgot the drummer's name. I had this band and I was the front man with the guitar.

While I was up there, at the Grand Terrace, I traded the tenor guitar and I bought me a six-string guitar at Peterson's Music Store on Claiborne and St. Peter. I paid seven dollars and fifty cents for it. I didn't even know how to tune it, but Battle Ax taught me. He was a guitar player who was taught by Johnny St. Cyr, and he knew how to read music. Johnny St. Cyr played guitar with Louis Armstrong when he had his Hot Five. Johnny St. Cyr taught Battle Ax and Battle Ax taught me. He told me, "I'm gonna tune this guitar for you, and if you like, until you learn how to play the whole six strings, you can play it just like you played the ukelele.

The last four strings on the guitar is just like that on a ukelele and you can make the same positions. You just got two more strings. And I'm gonna show you where you can make your C chord and your F chord and your B-flat chords in more than one position." He taught me all that. That was about nineteen thirty-four or five.

The Grand Terrace was at Seventh and Howard. In the Garden District. There were supposed to be some bad cats up in the Garden District. A policeman owned the place. Him and his brother. His brother was a racketeer and he was a policeman. He was from the Twelfth Precinct—the baddest precinct in the city on Negroes. They used to beat them up when they'd get them in the cell.

They had a cat named Riley around there, who used to rent rooms—twenty-five cents for an hour. Every time I'd pick up on a chick—oh, I don't know, I must've been oversexed or something—every time I'd get hold of a fine broad I'd tell Handy, "Take over till I get back." I'd go around to Riley's and knock off a piece and come on back. Then, before the night was over, I'd pick up on another one.

Riley told me, before I took the job there, "I wouldn't take this job if I was you. You look like a nice fellow." Then, after I took the job he said, "Now, you took this job, but you got to be careful, man, cause they got some bad cats around here."

I said, "Ain't no man too bad that he can't be talked to."

So this bad cat came there. The owner had told me he didn't want nobody in there without a coat, collar, and tie. I was standing right where they come in. Everybody had a tie on but him. He came in and I said, "Wait a minute. Sorry, man, but you can't come in like that. You have to get you a tie."

He said, "Nigger, do you *know* who you *talkin* to?"

I said, "Nooo. I don't know who I'm *talkin* to, but, I'm still *tellin* you, you can't come *in* here."

He looked at me and said, "What makes you think you could get away with talkin to me like that?"

I said, "Now, listen. Lemme tell you something. They told me you was *bad*. I don't care how bad you are, cause all bad mens is *dead* right now. I don't care how *bad* you are, my friend, but you could be *talked* to. Now, you wouldn't want that police from the Twelfth Precinct to come and drag you outa here and bring you to the precinct and whip your ass with them old rubber hoses, would you?"

He told me, "You know somethin? These chicken niggers . . . There ain't no nigger ever talked to me like that *before!*"

While I was up there, at the Grand Terrace, I traded the tenor guitar and I bought me a six-string guitar. . . . Johnny St. Cyr played guitar with Louis Armstrong. . . . Johnny St. Cyr taught Battle Ax and Battle Ax taught me. (p. 62)

I said, "Because they didn't have *sense* enough, man. Trouble is so easy to get in, man, but it's very hard to get out."

He looked at me and he said, "You know somethin? You got somethin."

Me and him got to be best of friends. He went back home and got a tie and came back. And I didn't have any more trouble with him. There were no fisticuffs or anything like that. All I had to mention was the police from the Twelfth Precinct and he didn't want to come in contact with *them!* The Twelfth Precinct—oh, they'd beat you up so bad it'd be pitiful.

I worked there a long time. I was still staying with Eva, but I met a girl from Chicago. She was a nice-looking brownskin woman, but she was kind of heavy set. She had *money.* Her husband worked for Paramount Pictures. He used to make the designs and things to go on the front of theatres. He had a whole lot of money. She had a pocketbook chockablock with money, and she fell in love with me, too. I don't know, I must have had magic or something. Women would just look at me and they were ready to go. Her mother liked me, too. Anyway, me and her got together and when I got off, she wanted to take me home. So she took me home. That was on Monday. On Tuesday I told her I had to go home and she said, "Why you have to go home?"

I said "Cause I gotta go change my shirt and things, and take a bath."

She said, "Look, what size shirt you wear?" She went downtown and bought me some shirts and I stayed a whole *week* there. Eva was waiting for me to come *home*, and I stayed there a whole week!

So, Eva came up there to the Grand Terrace. She had the thirty-eight in her pocket book. This girl from Chicago had a table with all her friends and her mother's friends and all, with fifths of liquor all on down, and she paid all the expenses and everything. Handy knew Eva was my old lady and he used to have a habit of saying, "My God, be careful!" to let me know Eva was coming *in*, so I got away from the table and I went back to the bandstand.

The owner of the place knew Eva was my old lady, too. She told him, "I come to get my old man. He's comin home with me tonight or I'm gonna kill him. Now, you the police and I'm tellin you in front," and she went in her pocketbook and *showed* him. That was a concealed weapon but the boss, he liked *me* so much, he wouldn't arrest her for that. He told me, "Now, you goin *home* tonight cause I'm gonna put you in that squad car and I'm gonna *take* you there.

I don't wanna lose you and that woman gonna *kill* you. I'm gonna be truthful with you. I seen the gun, but I ain't gonna say nothin."

So I had to tell this girl from Chicago, "Well, I'll see you later," and I went home that night. The owner of the place brought me home. Eva, she didn't say anything. She didn't ask me where I'd stayed all the week or anything. I was terrible, man. I'm telling you. Then this other girl went back to Chicago and that broke *that* up.

Then I met another girl around the corner from there. She was black but she was nice looking. I met her and I went around the corner by her house and laid out with *her*. Her uncle was a member of the FBI. Black! I didn't know they had any black men in the FBI but he showed me his credentials. She was crazy about me. Bought me anything I wanted. I was lucky like that. Bought me anything I wanted, took me over to meet her people and everything. She was staying with her mother, and me and her, we'd lay out through the whole night. When I left the Grand Terrace and went to play with Billie and DeDe Pierce at the Kingfish, that broke that romance up.

The Kingfish was actually named for Governor Huey P. Long. It was on Ursulines and Decatur, right across from the French Market in the French Quarter—the Vieux Carré. All that was Vieux Carré then. That was the French Quarter because it was around the French Market. Billie and DeDe are the first ones who caused me to be in the Vieux Carré.

I'd met Billie and DeDe when I first went up to the Grand Terrace. They had the show at the Kingfish. The owners had got Billie and DeDe to come play out there, but they wanted a guitar player with them, and a singer and a drummer. I was the most popular thing in the city then, at that time, so they come got me and they brought me to the Kingfish. They thought about me because I could sing, too. Billie sang, DeDe sang, and I sang, and they hired a boy on drums named McGhee. McGhee was so black! In the sun he looked blue. He was the blackest man I'd ever seen in my life. And he used to wear a derby and have a cigar in his mouth all the time. Go to sleep, too. He'd be sleeping, but he never missed a *beat*. Sleeping just as sound . . . And dreaming! He'd sit next to me and when I'd touch him he'd jump! That's the truth. That's the truth.

That's the only place I ever worked at that I was scared to go to work. That's where the seamen used to come in and bring their stuff to the French Market. Every Saturday night the sailors used to come off the riverboats and they used to come in the joint. They used to drink their beer in those glass mugs with a handle on them. Glass! When they'd get full of that beer, when they'd start a fight, you talk about the biggest free-for-all you ever seen in your life! Mugs would be flying all over the place. They'd be busting them and blood would be jumping from people's heads. Me, I'd be under the piano, myself. Hiding. I was so scared I didn't know what to do.

Those white boys were bad out there. They were bad on blacks. They were as bad as an ape with a walking stick. Once they got to like you it was alright. Once they got to liking the way we played we didn't have anything to worry about because they were the baddest cats that ever walked the streets, out there by Ursulines and Decatur. If you could sing, dance, do anything, those white people wouldn't bother you. They wouldn't let anybody else bother you either.

I remember one white fellow walked up to the bandstand and he just deliberately struck a match and popped all the strings on my guitar. Well, I'm scared to say anything, but one of those fellows, short, dark, like Mister Five-by-Five—five feet across, five feet wide—he was strong as a bull. He walked over there and told this white fellow, "I saw just what you did. Now, you get in your pocket and pay that boy for them strings." Then he said, "Joe, how much do strings cost? Five dollars? Six dollars?"

I was scared. I didn't want to say anything. So he said, "Get it out your pocket or they'll have to carry you out here head first. Get it up now!" and he gave me the five dollars. I had a new set of strings in my guitar case and I put them back on. You talk about scared . . . !

Well, this white fellow kept on harassing us and pestering us. He stayed there till we got off and then *he* got up to leave. We had just hit the nickel slot machine in the front. McGhee, the drummer, took that black derby he used to wear and was collecting all those nickels. This white fellow asked him, "Nigger, what you gonna do with all that money?" So another one of those white boys came and said, "Say, buddy, come here. Now, them fellows are not bothering you, but I know that you've been harassing them all night."

Then, *he* called *him* a nigger-lover, and boy, he hauled off and hit that son-of-a-bitch and knocked him down and picked him up and knocked him down again, and the rest of the cab drivers stomped all over him. When he got up, he left his hat. We didn't have any more trouble after that.

All the cab drivers and everyone liked us. The cab drivers used to park around there, picking up fares. After the cab drivers took a liking to us they wouldn't let anybody bother us.

Then Milton Shots wanted a show in there, so we got in contact with the Fairfield Sisters and they got in contact with Matty Johnson and with "Muts" a little girl we called "Muts." I've forgotten her name; she died of TB, I believe. Then we had another girl; she was a contortionist. She could wrap herself up—her legs and arms—in such a way that she looked ill-formed. But, could she *dance*. She was the *best*. I mean, like you see them make those flips and then walk like a crab upside down on their arms and feet—she'd walk like that. Then she'd flip over and then flip *back* over backwards, and then she could jump and make a double flip and land on her feet. Oh, she was marvelous! I don't know where she learned it from. She died, too. Her name? I'll be damned if it wasn't Irene. That was her name. Irene.

We used to have crowds down there because Milton Shots used to go to the airport and meet all the tourists that came to town and tell them that he had a colored show with some of the finest black colored gals you had ever seen. We were the first ever in the city with black shake dancers. The place used to be packed all the time. All the time. And we were making money! We had a big old coffee can—a Luzianne coffee can—and McGhee, the drummer, used to take it and pass it around. When he'd come back that can'd be full of quarters and halves and dollars and things. Billie had a big old pocketbook—a *big* old bag—and we'd pour it all down in there. Every time we played a number or two, or the place'd get crowded, or the people would leave that had seen the show and the place would get crowded again, we'd pass that coffee can round *again*. We used to make so much money, it was pitiful. We weren't getting paid but a dollar a night, but we were making that money. Making that money.

After Billie and DeDe left, *I* had to play for the shows. I had Theodore Mazell on trumpet, I had Walter Daniels on piano, I had Alvin Woods on the drum, and Joe Harris on the saxophone. I was playing the guitar and leading the chorus, and I was tap-dancing, too. I had to do a few singles by myself. The chorus—the chorus girls—would do their routine, then they would go in the corner and sit down, and then I'd come out and do my tap-dancing act. Then we would pass around the can and pick up a whole can full of money.

That place was named after Governor Huey P. Long and we

3 Cousin Joe dancing at the Kingfish in the 1930s. (Pleasant Joseph and Alvin Woods)

I was playing the guitar and leading the chorus, and I was tap-dancing, too.   (p. 68)

4 The Kid Rena Band and the dancers at the Gypsy Tea Room; Joe is in the middle of the top row; Eva is fourth from the right in the front row. (William Ransom Hogan Jazz Archives)

I had the shows in the Gypsy Tea Room; they were sort of like vaudeville plays. . . . I was dancing, too. (p. 71)

were working there when Governor Huey P. Long was assassinated. Milton Shots had sold the place. Sold his share to Milton Sirio. After Huey Long was assassinated the place closed. We worked there until they closed it and then we left.

I don't know where Billie and DeDe went, but I went to work in the Gypsy Tea Room on St. Anne and Villere. Eva was the one that caused me to get the job there. She told them her husband was a musician. Eva and I had been living together for a good long time then and she had been working there ever since they had first opened. She talked for me to get the job at the Gypsy Tea Room just so she could be near me, where she could watch me.

Johnny Tessitori was the owner. He opened it up, and when he hired me he paid me ten dollars a week. I had Eva and the three kids and he *gave* me the four-room apartment upstairs, too. I didn't have to pay any rent. Nothing. He had a grocery store on the corner, too, where I could get all the groceries I wanted for nothing. In other words, we had the ten dollars a week and the money Eva made. Sometimes Eva would make ten, fifteen, twenty dollars a night. She was working with me. She was a waitress and I was playing the guitar and producing the shows.

Kid Rena had the band. The trumpet player. His brother, Joe Rena, was the drummer and they had a banjo player but I can't remember his name. Joe Harris was playing saxophone. When the band would stop playing, during intermission, I'd take my guitar and go around the tables. I never made so much money off of colored people! We used to have doctors and lawyers and accountants—all colored people. Doctor Gautier and some other doctors and their wives all used to come. The Gypsy Tea Room was the most popular colored club in the city at the time. It used to stay packed night after night after night. On the sidewalk they used to have big barrels full of half-pints and fifths and pint bottles where they sold all the whiskey during the night. They had barrels full of beer bottles and stuff on the outside, too. Every night.

I had the shows in the Gypsy Tea Room; they were sort of like vaudeville plays. Thelma and Anita Fairfield were in the chorus and they had their chorus girls with them. We had Benny Williams; we used to call him "rubber legs." He could *dance*, man! I was dancing, too. Everybody thought I was the best dancer in the city. Benny Williams and me. I worked there a long time.

I left out of there for a while and I went to work with Paul Barbarin and his band. Paul Barbarin had left Luis Russell. He had been playing with Luis Russell and he came back and formed his own band. He needed a guitar player, but mostly he needed one who could sing, and he hired me. We used to work out of a little town called New Iberia. The manager in New Iberia was a big fat man—Japanese—who used to drive a T-model or an A-model Ford. He booked us in all of those little country towns, like New Iberia, Lake Charles, St. Martinsville, St. Francisville, Franklinton—all those little one-horse towns. He used to book us in there, and we'd play.

Sometimes we'd get on a truck in the daytime and they'd have a sign on the truck for where we were playing at. We'd play on this truck and I'd sing through a megaphone. We'd drive down the street and stop at every corner and every barroom at the town where we were playing.

The only trouble we had was when we played at a place called Morgan City. We went into Morgan City and we were playing for a colored fellow that used to give dances at this dance hall all the time and used to hire bands. We were playing for him. But we got there during the night the night before; we were supposed to play the *next* night.

What happened was, we went in the restaurant. They had the sign up there on the front that said, "White Only," and, around the side, "Colored Only." We all went in the back there and we had something to eat and had a beer or so, and before we came out I went to call up Eva. I went to call her up but the telephone was in the white section. So I walked in the front door and acted like a typical "nigger," you might as well say. You had to take off your hat first, and then make a bow and say, "Excuse me, sir. If you don't mind, can I use your telephone to call my wife in New Orleans and let her know where I am?"

He said, "Sure."

So I went over there and I used the telephone and when I got through I hung up. I thought I had put enough money in it so I hung up and I walked on out. We all walked down to the bus and we took off.

We were supposed to be going to the place where we were to sleep that night, but here come the police. From where, I don't know. They pulled in front of us and we stopped.

They got out and one of them said, "Which one of you niggers made that phone call?"

Well, I had to tell them who it was because they would've put all of us in jail, so I said, "Me."

He said, "Now, you get on back there to that goddamn telephone and pay the rest of that goddamn money. And when you do that, we want y'all to get out of town."

So I went back and paid the money and we got in the bus and we drove out of town on the highway. We pulled on the side of the highway and that's where we slept. In the bus. We had to keep the windows up because the mosquitoes would've picked us up and taken us out of the bus.

First thing the next morning, this cat that was driving the bus was going into town to tell the man that we were playing for. So I said, "Wait, man, I'm coming with you."

Paul said, "Man, you go back in that town and you gonna go to jail!"

I said, "Man, are you crazy? To white folks all niggers look alike, man. They don't know the difference between me, you, or nobody else. If you're black, what the hell, they don't know the difference." Our driver was a Creole boy. You couldn't tell him from white to save your life. He was light. Light complected and had curly hair. But he was "black." He was a Negro. Creole from the Seventh Ward. So I went back to town with him.

We told this colored fellow that we were working for what the policeman did. He must've had a little influence, or maybe he was just a good, honorable, citizen, but when we told him, he went and told the Chief of Police. The Chief knew which policemen were on that beat that night but he called all of them in his office and he said, "I want to know which one of you policemen put these boys out of my town."

The two of them got up red-handed and said, "Well, we told them to get out of town."

"Who the hell do you think you are? Who gave you the authority to put anybody out of my town? Now, all these young men are well-raised citizens. Instead of harassing these men, you ought to be looking out for them damn crooks that's robbing and stealing and holding up people. Now, what I want y'all to do, I want y'all to go up there tonight where they're playing at and I want you to call that little colored fellow and apologize to him, or else you ain't gonna have no more job. You can look for yourself another job."

That night, when we were playing, the way the band was situated, I was on the *front* of the stage playing the guitar and the band was circled around me. I was in front but I was close enough in for the rhythm section to hear me. I saw these two cops walk in, and I said to myself, "Oh, my God. There they is again." When we had intermission, they called me. I got scared. I said to myself, "I wonder what they want with me. They must've recognized who I was and that I came back into town." So I went over there and I said, "What is it, Officer, sir?"

And they said, "Well, young man, we got some good reports about you all and we're sorry that we did what we did to you—ordered you and the band out of town."

We shook hands, and that was a load off *my* shoulders. That was the only trouble we had.

Somehow or another, Paul's band broke up and I went back to work at the Gypsy Tea Room.

Then I left *again* for a four-week tour to Cuba and Florida with Joe Robichaux's band. We had a show with us—chorus girls—because we were going to play theatres. Chorus girls and single singers. I was a pretty fair country tap dancer, myself, at that time, and I had a spot in the show doing a dance number, with about a chorus of ten girls in back of me, and leading the chorus in a tap-dance session. Earl Palmer's mother and his aunt—Thelma Fairfield and Anita Fairfield—were the choreographers for the all-girl chorus and they were great, they were really great. Thelma Fairfield was Earl Palmer's mother and Anita Fairfield was his aunt. They were the top terpsichoreans—dancing teachers—in the city at that time. They were the chorus girls in every show that came to the Lyric Theatre or came to the Lincoln Theatre. They used to teach dancing to almost all the kids. Girls that were ambitious to be show girls and chorus dancers used to go to the Fairfield Sisters. That's what they did, and they were with us on the trip.

We had another boy—I can't think of his name but he was a baritone singer and he had a great voice. He sang something like Paul Robeson. Like, "A-ME-RI-CA" and things like that. He was great. He had a wonderful voice, and he was with us.

We got on the bus from the club where Joe Robichaux was playing at—the Rhythm Club at Jackson and Derbigny. We left from there, in the bus. The bus was so crowded with the musicians and entertainers and everybody else like that, I was sitting right behind the driver with my legs all cramped up. Well, I was young then. I could take it.

So, we were traveling. When we went to gas up, we were in Pensacola, Florida. I never will forget that as long as I live. We stopped at a station to get gas and Joe Robichaux told the man, "Fill it up!" I wanted to get a drink of water, so I walked over. I knew where I was, see? I *knew* where I *was*. I knew I was in Gumboland and I knew what I was supposed to *do*, so, I went *in* that station and I asked the man in there, I said, "Mister, is it alright if I get a drink of water at that fountain?"

He said, "Sho, go 'head." So, I went to get me a drink of water, and, man, I'm drinkin, I'm drinkin and I look down and I see a pair of big feet. They looked like they were about size seventeen. Then I looked up. And then I looked up *again*, and there was this big, tall—looked like he was as tall as Wilt Chamberlain—big, tall cat, man. White man.

He said, "Nigger, don't you know better than to be drinkin at that fountain. You reach down there and git you a bottle and put some water in it and drink out that *bottle* and don't you drink out that fountain cause they ain't no niggers supposed to drink out that fountain."

I said, "Yes, sir." So, I reached—I had done drank all that I wanted, but to satisfy him—I reached and got the bottle and put some water in there and I drank the rest of it out of the bottle. I got back on the bus, and I told Joe Robichaux, I said, "Man, let's get the hell on out of *here*, cause you don't know what that man told *me*." So, that was *one* that I think I experienced. And we left there.

We played most all the principal cities in Florida. We played Fort Dearborn, Fort Smith, Fort Lauderdale. We played Ibo City, which is in Tampa, Florida. Ibo City—that's "Niggertown." The concert was sponsored by the Elks Club, and that's what we were playing for. The Elks Club set up the tour, but we were playing for a percentage of the *door*, there. *That's* the way that was. So, we played it, and then we played in Miami. We played Daytona Beach, Miami.

We crossed the Gulf at Miami. On the boat. Overnight. We crossed at Miami and the next morning we were in Havana. Now, I had a friend of mine, used to work with me, he had a job on the ship. He used to be a little jive dancer. I was teaching him some things, too. Anyway, he was a good friend of mine, and he *knew* that I was coming to Havana because he read the posters. When he saw my name, he had a police escort meet me on the wharf at the boat, with a special motorcade. Oh, that was a cheeky little son-of-a-bitch. He was cheeky. He was pretty well known in Cuba, and the people around there, the police and everybody, knew him. So, they came and they met me. Man! He came and told me, "You got your escort waitin for ya. Your motorcade."

I said, "Well, I'll be damned."

I'm sitting in the car—and I'm the only one they *took!* All the rest of them, they didn't pay them no rabbit-assed mind. But me, I'm the star. I didn't know what to make of that. I can't think of that boy's name to save my life, but he was a real gone cat.

So, we got all set up and everything, got ready to go to the theater. We were playing at the National Theatre. My hotel was on Obrapia Street and the National Theatre was on Central Avenue, right across from the biggest barroom in the world—Sloppy Joe's. Sloppy Joe's was a whole square block. Nothing but bar. You stand up at the bar all around the block. You ain't never seen so many bartenders in your life, all around that full square block. All the bartenders right next to each other—side by side. And all the recipes for all the thousands of different kinds of drinks, for mixed drinks and all kind of stuff like that, well, those bartenders out there *wrote the book.* That's where it come from. Sloppy Joe's.

This theatre was so big, in the lobby they had a life-sized airplane. In the lobby! On exhibition! The theatre was bigger than the Hippodrome in New York. It would hold five thousand people sitting down. It had three decks, like the Yankee Stadium. For people way up there, you'd look like a dwarf down on that stage. And that stage was so big, man. Hooo, my gracious, that stage was so big, it'd make you look like a dwarf if you were six, seven feet! That's how big that place was.

That first gig we played at this theatre, I went out there, doing my number, with my guitar, singing my blues and singing my tunes, and it seemed like I couldn't *move* them, because they couldn't understand what I was saying. But, they had a *black* Cuban—he went to school over here, but he was from Cuba—and he came backstage. —

"I'm goin to teach you some songs in Spanish," he said, "Then you gonna move em."

So I said, "Okay, man," and I told him where my hotel was.

So when he came over there that next day, he taught me *La Cucaracha:*

La cucaracha, la cucaracha. Ya no puede caminar.

Porque le falta, porque no tiene, marijuana por fumar.

and he taught me this other one:

Kay, yay yay yay. Canta y no llores.

Porque cantando se allegran cielito lindo los corazones.

and man, when I started *that*—that broke up the whole show. Boy, everybody—all of them—standing up, and singing along with me.

Boy, that was the greatest time of my life, man. I had those people jumping and shouting in their seats, man, just with those two tunes. That's all. That's all I knew!

When the show was over, we went to a theatre there. Boy! They had one of those porno movies, and boy oh boy. They showed the stage show, first. All naked men and women on stage. Then after, they showed the movies. And boy, those girls in this thing with us, they had never seen anything like that before and they started getting sick in the stomach and everything else. I was enjoying it, myself.

At night all the whores and prostitutes, there's one street they'd be on. They weren't allowed to be all over the city. Just one street—Market Street. That's where the prostitutes used to hang out. They had prostitutes they had imported; some of them were from here. Some of them were from Cuba. Anyway, it was forty cents a whack. At that time forty cents was a lot of money in Cuba, because at that time, the American dollar was worth about five dollars in Cuba. Maybe ten. But, anyway, you'd give them forty cents, in American money, and boy. They didn't rush you. I mean, you could take your time. So I gave one forty, eighty, and then when I went to give her another forty, she said, "Uh, uh. Mañana. Mañana." It meant come back tomorrow because she was tired. Here, I wore her out. But she was young, whew. About eighteen, and beautiful. Beautiful Cuban girls, man.

Me and High Steppin Willie, they had told us over there about that tequila. They said, "Now when you drink that tequila you gotta drink somethin with it cause it's two hundred proof. You gotta get some Seven-Up or Coca-Cola or somethin cause if you drink it like that it'll knock you down." And that Bacardi rum over there— they cut that stuff when they get it over there. They cut that stuff because you couldn't drink it. It was two hundred proof alcohol. Tequila. It came in little bottles like about a Seven-Up bottle here. Little bottles. So, me and High Steppin Willie, we bought a bottle, but we didn't get anything to drink with it.

High Steppin Willie used to dance. He was tall, he was about six feet two, and he used to pick up this table in his teeth. That was his act. One time we tricked him. Put an iron table on the stage. And boy, that was a shame, man. He did alright, but when he found out what it was, when he went to pick it up, he just took it off the stage and brought it backstage and went and got the right one. He didn't do it with his teeth—he'd've broken all his teeth.

We were in the park, right in front of the theatre. We were sitting in the park, and High Steppin Willie kept drinking that stuff. And first thing you know, when he got ready to get up, I ain't never seen a man that drunk. His two feet came from under him like Joe Louis had hit him with a left hook and a right cross. Whop! Flat down. Now, I had to drag him to the hotel. I could't carry him, he was too big, so I put his arm round my neck and I just dragged him. And then, here come the Cuban police. The Cuban police stopped us in the block of the hotel. I told them I was bringing him in because he had drank that stuff too strong. Well, they couldn't understand what I was saying, so they took our cigarettes out and they busted the packs open and they went to smelling them, because other acts had been there from New York and places like that, smoking those reefers, and they were watching out for that. Finally, when they found we didn't have anything on us like that, they finally let us go upstairs. So, I dragged him upstairs in the hotel. Boy, that was something.

Then we left there and we went to Guanaguacoa. Man, the theatre was *packed.* Theatre was packed. And I looked outside, and saw, "Admission, five and ten cents." Ten cents for the adults and five cents for the children! That night our take was forty cents apiece! But where I got *my* money, we started shooting dice on the ship when we were *going.* We'd throw the dice under the bench and then pick them up and then put them on a seven, or eleven, put them on a winning point, things like that, and I beat the cats out of all the money. When we got to Cuba I had to lend *them* money to buy something to *eat.* But I had all the rest of the money.

Coming back we played Saint Augustine, Florida, which is the oldest city in the United States. Played Saint Augustine. That was when we were coming back. Then we stopped over—jumped over—from Saint Augustine to Waycross, *Georgia.* Hee, hee! Coming back. Boy, that was something. They had policemen all over the front, and the back, and all around the place. And they didn't have uniforms. They just had on blue denim shirts and ordinary pants, a big old forty-five on their side, and a badge. A badge on their shirt. And they told us, they said, "Now, lemme tell you niggers something. When y'all git through with this dance, this concert, hyar, I want you niggers to git back cross that railroad track. Don't let me catch y'all on this side the track. After you git through this concert you git yo' black ass back on the other side that track." Nothing *we* could say. Because we knew where we were. Couldn't say nothing. That's what inspired me to write Railroad Avenue, because anytime you want to see the black people you got to go on the other side of the track.

We wound up playing the last night in Mobile, Alabama, and we came back from Mobile. When the bus pulled up on Claiborne and St. Ann I said, "Hold that bus right there." I got out of the bus, and I got on my knees in front of the bus and said, "Now, look, Joe," Robichaux, I said, "Look, man. Don't you ne-e-ever send for me to go nowhere no mo', cause I have been gone three weeks—four weeks—and I got home with exactly twenty-five *cents.*" Eva said, "Well, you had a good vacation."

So, I went back to the Gypsy Tea Room again. But when I came back to the Gypsy Tea Room, Harold Dejan had a band, and he had a job on a ship—the Steamship Dixie—and he wanted a guitar player. He wanted somebody who could sing, and he wanted *me* because I was singing everything—blues and everything else.

So, Harold Dejan asked me, did I want to go to New York. First time I'd ever been to New York in my life!

I told him, "Yeah!"

"Of course, we're gonna have music," he told me. "You gotta know how to read." Well, Harold could *read.* "But that's alright," he said, "I'll show you what to do. If you could read you couldn't make no more changes than you make anyway." I had a good ear.

We got to rehearsing, and we had music stands and everything. But Harold was the only one could read in the whole bunch! Burnell Santiago, he couldn't read. Clio, the bass player we had, he couldn't read. One of the best bass players ever jumped out of this town, Clio, he couldn't read a note. Clio played with Celestin, he played with Sidney Desvigne on the Steamer Capitol. The Streckfus brothers owned the boat. It used to run from New Orleans to St. Paul, Minnesota, up the Mississippi River. They'd make a stop and play in Baton Rouge and they'd play oh, about a week, up to St. Paul. People used to come from all around and come on that boat and play on that boat. Clio played with all those bands, and everybody in the band could read but him. But he had a wonderful ear for music. He could play anything they *had* in the book. He couldn't read, but he could *hear,* and he knew just what notes to put with the chord changes they were making.

We went on this boat and I had to go get a passport. At that time, you didn't have to be going out of the country. You had to have a passport even to be on the *ship.* You had to have your picture taken and everything. Fingerprints and passport and all that. that's the time when they first started taking out Social Security, too. Then, I had to join the Maritime Union. They'd take so much out of your money and they'd give you a card—a Maritime Union card—till you were finished paying.

We worked on this ship for seven months. What made me get off the ship was when, well, Harold's light complected and he was a nice-looking boy and all the white women in those staterooms, they'd invite him in their room for a drink and all that stuff, and the captain caught him coming out with one of those women, so that made it bad for him. Then the captain wanted me to take over the band when we got back to New Orleans, back to port.

So I told him, "Well, first thing, Captain," I said, "would you mind taking off your cap so I can talk to you like a man? Like you're a man like me?"

"Sure, Joe," and he took off his cap.

"Now, lemme tell you something, straight. Lemme put it to you straight. When you leave Harold off the job," I said, "you leave me off, too. Because if it weren't for Harold, I wouldn't have been here at all. I would've never, probably ever, been to New York. He's the cause, and I wouldn't do him that. And," I said, "I wanna ask you frankly, Captain, tween you and I. If Harold was a friend of yours and you was in my position, what would you do?"

"I'd do the same thing you're doing. I can understand that."

"That's why I wanted to talk to you like a man, you understand? With that cap on you got me covered, because you the captain of the ship. The big wheel. But now your cap's off, you're just a man like me and I can talk to you."

"That's what I like about you, Joe," he said. "You're pretty straight."

"Well, might as well. There's no other way. They ain't but two ways to be. Either be straight or be a rat, and I don't intend to be no rat. How would I feel taking the job away from this man, and this man done caused me to be *on* the job."

That's how I left the ship. I quit rather than take Harold's place on the boat. He's the one who made it possible for me to be on there in the first place.

11   Make Me Strong as Sampson

Make me strong as Samson,
And I'll serve my God above . . .

WHILE I was in New York with Harold, the Gypsy Tea Room burned down. Eva wrote to me in New York and told me, "Send money. Everything we've got is gone."

So when I came off the boat I stayed with Harold's band. Harold got a job in a little place called Bucktown. That was where they had those women-impersonators. Later it became the My-O-My Club. We were playing for the show—for the women-impersonators—we played there a good while.

Then we got a job with A. J. Piron at the Oriental. Piron was *supposed* to go on the boat with his band, but what happened was, Piron couldn't leave the Oriental for a good while. Most of his band left him and went on the boat anyway. Manuel Sayles—guitar player—left Piron, and he was short of a saxophone player, too. Eva, at that time, was working at a restaurant on Orleans and Claiborne, and the man that owned the Oriental used to come in there. She told him about me, so he hired me to work for him. I got Harold and them and we went on to work in the Oriental with Piron. Harold wasn't much of a get-off man, but Harold could see music around the *corner*. Harold could read anything in the book—anything Piron had. He could read and play it, and I played the guitar and sang with Piron at the Oriental.

The Oriental was on Bourbon Street, between Conti and St. Louis. After that it was the Silver Slipper Club and after that it was the Bally Club. Then, when Walter Noto bought it they made a striptease joint out of it. They called it Guys and Dolls. After *that* Sam Enselmo opened it up as a nightclub called the Dream Room, and that's when he started hiring big outfits from Las Vegas and all, like Al Hirt does now. He had Sam Butera and the Witnesses. Louis Prima used to fly down when Sam Butera and them were playing there and make a one-nighter. He'd work along with Sam Butera and them, just to help out..

We worked with Piron at the Oriental and we *broadcast* from the club. Every night we'd broadcast from WWL. Then Piron left. He had a humbug with some woman, and she threw a glass of whiskey in his face. That messed up everything. Like to caused a riot in the joint. So Piron left and went back on the boat with his band, anyway. Then Harold had the band. We had a four-piece orchestra, and I was playing guitar.

While I was there, the Jazz Jesters came to town. They were an act out of Cincinnati. They came off a show and they played a week at the Lyric Theatre and they were real great. There were four of them. Four Jazz Jesters. They had a bass player and three guitars—a six-string and two four-string: one fellow played the tipple and the other played an unorthodox mandolin thing with a flat back. Then, they had a little fellow named Jackie Brown from Denver, Colorado. He played piano. They had hired him because his girlfriend had been dancing on the show. When the show closed down at the Lyric Theatre, they were stranded in New Orleans.

A white fellow had opened up the club on Bourbon Street which became the Famous Door—on Conti and Bourbon, in the next block from the Oriental. This fellow had heard the Jazz Jesters at the Lyric Theatre, but when he went back to try to find them he couldn't find them. In any case, he didn't make enough money to pay the next month's rent on the place—that was five hundred dollars—so Mr. Hyppolite Guinle told him *he* would take it over. *He* went and borrowed five hundred dollars from the fellow that used to have the club across the street, and he paid the rent and he took over the place. Then *he* went and got those boys from Cincinnati. He heard they were still around town, playing to keep in practice. When he finally found them he gave them a job when he opened this place and they started playing there.

They were packing the place. And I was playing at the Oriental in the next block. Well, it happened that the bass player died while they were working at the Famous Door. He got sick—caught a cold, got pneumonia, or something—and he died. After the bass player died, then Spike, the boy that played the six-string guitar and sang the lead, he got scared and went back home to Cincinnati. So, Billy Sherman and them came and got *me* to take his place. They had heard me singing and Billy Sherman had told me, "Man, you great. I'm gonna keep you in mind. If we happen to add another man to our outfit I'm gonna come and get you." Now, Sherman was the brains of the outfit, so he came down to the Oriental and asked me how would I like to join the act? I told him, "Sure." He

told me what time they were going to have rehearsal and everything—made a date—and I started working with the Jazz Jesters at
the Famous Door.

They cued me in on their style of singing and playing, and I got
the hang of things. I was playing six-string—rhythm. Jake was
playing the tipple—a little thing. It wasn't much bigger than a
ukelele, but they called it a tipple. A cute little instrument, but he
could play it! Sherman was out of sight! He had a mandolin. It was
made like a mandolin but not with that pumpkin-shaped body. It
was *flat* and it had *four* strings on it. It was made like a steel guitar—all metal. He had such an unorthodox way of tuning this
thing that nobody could play it but him, and man! He couldn't play
single-string—not then—but, man, oh, man, he could play those
chord changes! He'd play all the lead-chord changes, and he'd play
some of the most *lost* chords that anybody could find on that thing.
He was a *master!*

He had a tune I used to like to hear him play. It was that old
song, "Why Do I Love You?" Oh, that man was good. That man
was a genius. The way he used to arrange the music for us, at rehearsal, he used to give us all our notes. He'd give each one of us a
note and we'd practice humming just that one note—each one of
us. He'd make a chord and he'd give me my note, he'd give Jake his
note, he'd give Jackie Brown his note, and he'd take his note. Then
he'd tell us, "Now when I count 'one, two, three,' then I want y'all
to hum y'all's correct note." Then, when he said, "One, two, three,
hummmm!" you could hear that chord just as clear as a bell. That's
the way we sang, and that's the way he would arrange the music for
us to sing.

When I took Spike's place—when I joined the act—Billy Sherman had to build the arrangements and build the act around me.
Then the outfit got greater, because I taught them all the old tunes
that the people like. All the traditional tunes that the people like in
New Orleans. Billy Sherman, when I'd teach him the tunes, he'd
arrange them and give us each one our notes so we could harmonize. So that made us get greater.

Later, Spike got lonesome for the act and wanted to come back,
but when he wrote to Billy Sherman that he wanted to come
back, Billy Sherman told him, "Well, it's gonna be five Jazz Jesters
because I'm not getting rid of Joe. If you want to come you can
come, but I'm not getting rid of Joe. Joe done got to be the back-
bone of this act right now." So Spike came back. We sent for him.
We put up the money out of the tips and sent for him and he came

back. When he came back, all the money had to be split *five* ways, then.

When he came back, that made it *greater* because Billy Sherman could put all those high notes on the top, like the way Glen Miller used to have his arrangements—had the clarinets on top of the saxophones. Spike could hit those high notes because he had that kind of a voice—a high tenor voice—and he could hit those high notes. He could outsing Kenny with the Inkspots anytime. *I* couldn't hit them, but I could do everything *within* the staff that he wanted me to do. The only way I could hit them was I had to get me one of those benzedrine sulphate tablets. Then I could sing like Jeanette MacDonald. That's the truth! At that time you could buy bennies over the counter. They were legal. You could buy them in a drug-store or anywhere.

So we were playing at the Famous Door. We played there a long time. Till about 1939. We had a sign on the back wall—an electric sign—of an old man and an old lady. The old white-haired colored fellow had a pipe in his mouth. He was sitting in a rocking chair and rocking. Just a-rocking. The colored lady had a rag around her head and a big old basket like women used to carry on their heads when they worked. When they worked picking cotton they'd put the cotton in the basket and they'd carry it on the top of their head. This sign was like that. We used to have to wear overalls and a blue shirt and a red bandana handkerchief around our neck, and a farmer's straw hat, that you'd wear on the farm out in the summer to keep the sun off. We'd sit on this bale of cotton and we'd play. After we'd play a couple of tunes, then we'd get off the bale and we'd go around to the tables. That was the "Southern" exposure.

We packed that place. We made so much money for that man, it was a shame. We weren't getting but one dollar a night—each one of us. Sherman might've been getting two, but we were getting one dollar a night. If I tell you how much money we made when we'd go around the tables! We would average—apiece—fifty to seventy-five dollars a night! I made so much money I redecorated my house inside. Put crystal door knobs on the doors. Bought a brand new General Electric refrigerator-freezer and a new living room set. That's the kind of money we were making on a salary of one dollar a night. And there weren't any unions at that time.

You wouldn't believe the people we entertained in that place— the type of people who used to come in that club. The greatest people, the greatest entertainers and performers and politicians and everything like that came in those doors. That's why they call them

The greatest people, the greatest entertainers and performers and politicians and everything like that came in those doors. That's why they call them the "famous" doors.   (pp. 84–86)

the "famous" doors. I mean people like Russ Morgan, Guy Lombardo, Glenn Gray and his Casa Loma. All the bands that came to the Roosevelt Hotel heard about us at the Famous Door, and when the show was over at the Roosevelt Hotel they *all* would come in, in the Famous Door, and listen to us. They thought that was the most amazing thing, to hear five people singing five-part harmony so perfect. All the movie actors came. Wallace Beery, the Andrews Sisters, the Modernaires. They all came to get ideas. I can name you two *blacks* that I know that came in and *sat down* in there—because there never were any blacks could sit down in that club—that was Joe Louis and Billy Eckstine. The people Billy Eckstine was playing for brought him there, and they sat down and drank and talked and Billy was signing autographs. And Joe Louis—well Joe Louis was the greatest thing that ever happened at that time. He was heavyweight champion of the world and was the greatest fighter that ever lived at that time—so *he* was in there. We sang for people like Miss Dupont and like Harry Payne Whitney of the Whitney fortunes and some fellow from South America. He was a multi-millionaire. He said he had six thousand people working for him. We played for that kind of people. Mostly all the rich, rich, rich people and all the elite came in that club and we played for them.

What we didn't know was, there were a couple of fellows in there from Texas—from Dallas—and they were getting up musicians and entertainers to play for the Dallas Centennial. When they heard us, they hired us to play and they gave us a *deposit* to come there. So, we went to Rampart Street and we had some tails—some suits—made that were iridescent. When you put the light on them they shined, even in the sun. They shined and they'd shine different colors. And white shoes, and white ties and white shirt. All five of us—we were so sharp we were bleeding. Then, we didn't go there by train. We bought two cars with the advance money and we *drove* there—to Dallas.

When we got there, oh, boy, it was something else! The head man's name was Mr. Pool. He was a big man, about as tall as Wilt Chamberlain. He had this big ten-gallon hat and his boots on. And he told us, "Now, first of all, I want to brief you niggers on what's happening, on what you're supposed to do. You're supposed to speak when you're spoken to and answer when you're called. When you *are* called, or when anybody asks you a question, or anybody tells you anything, don't forget to say, 'Yes, *sir*,' and 'No, *sir*,' and 'Yes, *ma'am,'* and 'No, *ma'am.'* And when you *say,* 'Yes, sir,' you put an *accent* on that '*sir.'* Y'all understand me?

I said, "Yes, *sir.*"

But Billy Sherman and them, they weren't used to that kind of stuff. They were from Cincinnati and they didn't like that. But I got them together in the corner and I told them, "Now, look. What I want y'all to do is, don't say *nothing.* Just let me do the talking, because I was *born* and raised in Gumboland and I know what's happening. I know how to handle these people. I know *what* to say and *when* to say it and *how* to say it. So y'all just do like I tell you. If anybody speaks to you, you just say, "Yes, sir," like the man said, but let *me* do the talking—*all* the talking."

They agreed. They said, "Okay, Joe."

That night, when we had to come to work, we sharpened up and we went there and Mr. Pool brought us in the kitchen for the cook to feed us. He told him, "I want y'all to give these boys the biggest steak in the house. Give them anything they want." And in there, I met a fellow. He used to be a great prizefighter at the Coliseum and he had been whipping *everybody.* His name was Wesley Varrow and, man, he had a joint in Bucktown and he had a tailor-made white flannel overcoat and he was really sharp. During that time he passed me like a freight train passes a hobo. So who do you think was pearl diving in the kitchen? That means washing dishes. When he raised up, he looked at me and said, "Don't I know you?"

I said, "You know me *now,* but I remember the time when you *didn't.* When you were fighting at the Coliseum. You didn't know me *then,* but you know me *now.* You didn't know me when you were on your way *up,* but now you know me, since you done went *down!* You see, you never pass up anybody on the way up because they'll meet you on your way down. You see, now, *you* can't come in here where *I'm* playing. All you can do is peek through a crack, cause you can't come in there. Now, that shows you the difference. But, when I get off, I want you to meet me round by the *back* door. You can't meet me at the *front* door because you can't *go* through the front door."

This was the Dallas Athletic Club and you had to be a millionaire to even belong to that club. The club consisted of all millionaires. All oil men. After we got straight and everything, this man up on the twelfth floor called up Mr. Pool and said, "Send them niggers up here. I want them to play for me." Mr. Pool told us and we took our instruments and got on the elevator and we went up there. Twelfth floor. The elevator stopped right at his front door, twelve stories up, and he was standing in the door, waiting. When we started rushing to get off the elevator, he said, "Hold it. Wait a minute. I want to tell you niggers something. I wanna let y'all know that you the first niggers ever to cross the sill of my door! *Now* you can come in."

I said, "Yes, *sir!*"

Then he said, "Now, I'm gonna give you niggers thirty dollars to play me one tune and then I want you niggers to get out of my house."

And, oh, man, Billy Sherman was mad, then. We had made so much money at the Famous Door that Billy Sherman had got his teeth fixed—all gold inlays and everything—and he had his hair straightened and it was black and curly. He was as black as a brand new Ford with no whitewall tires on it. Me, I had left my hair bad like it was.

He told Billy, "Nigger, you look like you don't like what I say. I'll take that banjo and wrap it around your goddamn neck."

I said to myself, "Lord, I hope Billy Sherman don't say nothing." But he didn't say anything.

So, we came in. That room was so beautiful. It was ivory and green. He had a piano imported from Australia and he had that piano painted the same way. The same color as the room. And when Jackie Brown went to sit down at the piano, he told Jackie, "Wait a minute. You know you are the first nigger ever to sit at my piano? Don't put your hands on that piano. I just want to let you know that."

He was getting juiced all the time and I knew that. He asked what we wanted to drink and we told him. Scotch and soda. His wife served up the drinks, but before she served them, he said— now here was the same thing again—he said, "I want you to know you're the first niggers my wife ever served a drink."

That woman was so beautiful. That woman was pretty as a speckled pup on a July day hitched to a red wagon with the tongue painted blue. Boy! She looked like a movie actress. I don't know if she was an actress or not, but she was the beautifulest woman that I'd ever seen in my life. Her skin was as smooth as a spanked baby's ass. That woman looked like a doll. When he went in the bathroom, she came to us and she told us, "I don't like the way he act, neither, but he got *so* much *money!*" Well, I could understand that.

So, when he came out of the bathroom, I said, "Look here,

Senator." Then I put my arms around him, and we sat down on the sofa and talked.

He said, "You know somethin, you look like a good nigger."

And I said, "Who the hell said I wasn't a good nigger? Sure. I'm one of the best niggers you ever met! But let me tell you something. Just because we're niggers, you don't have to keep callin us that all the time. We *know* we're niggers, but you don't have to keep remindin us." And I had my arms around him all at the same time. I mean, my arms were on his *shoulders!* Goes to show you.

So he said, "Nigger, get off from there and go play me some music!" And he put thirty dollars in my pocket. Three ten-dollar bills. I'll never forget that.

We started playing again and we played and I sang and we sang in harmony and everything. He had told us he was going to give us thirty dollars, but when we left there he must have given us about three hundred, because he kept stuffing that money in my pockets. He had stuffed money in *all* of my coat pockets.

When we got out of there we went downstairs. That was a great big place. They had acts from all over the *country* there. They had some of the greatest guitar players I ever heard in my *life*. Especially this act they had from the Grand Old Opry. They played so much guitar, man! Those cats could play us clean out of the place. I just knew Billy Sherman and Jake could not play guitars with those fellows—neither me and neither Jackie.

We started playing—tuning up and everything—but we weren't drawing any attention at first. We weren't hitting on anything so I told them, "Wait a minute, man. Look, Sherman, if y'all think y'all can play as much guitar as them fellows, you gotta shake yourself, boy. We gotta do something different if we want to draw the people in *our* corner. Tell you what we do. We're gonna put on our *act*. Let's do 'Swing Out, Mister Wilson' and let me and Jackie do our dance routine." We had a dance routine—me and Jackie Brown. Jackie Brown would put down the bass and then Jake would play the bass.

They started playing and we were all singing in five-part harmony and swinging out Mister Wilson. Then they stopped the music and they played one of those tunes where you play in stop-time—where we could do our routine. Me and Jackie Brown could lay down some iron. We could *dance*. And that's when we started drawing the crowd all around us.

But that isn't what altogether got them. They had a fellow—he had *so much* money, and so much authority! You know, when you've got money—hah! When money talks, everybody listens. You can believe me when I tell you—or you can believe a fool from Liverpool. When people have money. I'm talking about millions. You had to be a millionaire to belong to that club. The Dallas Athletic Club. That's who gave that thing. He came from the gambling tables—the roulette tables—in a tuxedo. They had dice games and a roulette table and blackjack and all that kind of stuff. They had so much money they could get away with anything, and this was a private club anyway. He heard us and he cashed his chips and he came over to us and he said, "Where you boys from?"

I said, "Sir, we from way down yonder in New Orleans."

"Yeah? What's your names?"

"My name is Joe, that's Jake, and that's Jackie and that's Sherman—Billy."

"Which one of y'all knows how to sing any spirituals—any gospel tunes?"

"Me, sir!" and we struck up on "When the Saints Go Marching In."

I had my own version of "When the Saints Go Marching In." I had a sermon I'd preach, and that came direct out of the Bible. My father had taught it to me and I had put it in with "When the Saints Go Marching In." They were harmonizing behind me and here came the people *again!* From everywhere! All the people around were singing and I sang and preached my *sermon.* They thought that was amazing.

Man, when I started preaching my sermon, that got him. He told Mr. Pool, "Look, Pool. I wanna take these boys with *me.*"

"Sure, Jack."

That's when I knew he had a name. I didn't know what his name was in the first place. Everybody called him Jack but he was one of the most powerful men in the club.

He took us all. We had got paid already; we had bought two cars with the money. So we went with him. When we got ready to leave, he put Billy Sherman, Jake, and Jackie Brown—he put them in a taxi cab and told the cab driver where we were going. To the Adolphus Hotel. That was the highest-class hotel in Dallas at that *time.* At that time the Adolphus Hotel was the *thing.* All the movie stars and millionaires—they'd visit that hotel. They didn't stay there, but they'd go there for private meetings and things like that. They would have it in a special room in this hotel. Anyway, he put them in a taxi cab and he put *me* in his Cadillac convertible with *him*. He told me to sit on the front seat with him, so I sat there with him with my guitar in my hand.

When we got the corner of the Adolphus Hotel he pulled up to a cop and told him, "Listen, I don't want no cars comin in this block at *all*. No traffic. You stop the traffic *right here.*"

He said, "Sure, Mr. ———." He called him by his last name but I can't think of it. He didn't say, "Jack," because he was just a policeman, and this man could buy him and sell him a million times.

Then he drove down to the *next* corner and told *that* cop, "Don't let no traffic come this-a-way. I want this whole block sealed off clean—nothin come this way." We had the whole block blocked off. The hotel was in the middle of the block and he made us play right in that block. He said, "Now I want you all to stretch out and do your singin and dancin right here." And he told me, "Here, Joe. Here's forty dollars on the first installment."

I said, "Thank you, sir," and we started.

When we finished playing the street, we went in the hotel. He was in front of us and we were following behind him and he told the doorman, "Tell Mr. Summers." You see, we were the first Negroes ever been *in* that hotel. The only ones in there were the ones with a white coat on and *working* in there. Porters and waiters and ones working in the kitchen.

When we walked in the lobby, he told me, "See, that is Moran and Mack, the two block crows, and see, over there is Mr. Frank Capra, movie picture producer, see?" And most everybody—all the stars out of Hollywood—was there for that day. The Texas Centennial in Dallas. There was Roy Rogers and Dale Evans. Everybody. All the movie actors and all the directors and everybody was there. That was the biggest thing I'd ever seen.

He told the manager of the hotel, the man that was head of the whole kit-and-kaboodle, "Look, I want you to give me two of your waiters—black." When they came, he said, "Now, look. I'm gonna give you all a hundred dollars apiece, but I want one of you to serve them four boys and I want one of you all to serve me and Joe. Right here."

They said, "Yes, *sir!*"

We all went and got in the elevator and when we were going up in the elevator he made us play at every floor. We got to the first floor with the elevator—five dollars! He said, "You all play a number here." We played a number at *each* floor till we got to the top. He gave the elevator boy five dollars for each floor that we played at and he gave me a forty-dollar installment each time. Put it in my pocket. He had that cash from when he had won that money in the roulette tables; rich people usually don't carry that much cash in their pockets. He was on the night, anyway. It was cash money he had won, so he was giving it to me.

We came back down and he hired a taxi for them again. The taxi was right there at the front of the hotel. He put them in the taxi, put me and the two black waiters in his Cadillac, and we went to *another* place—*another* hotel. It was a popular hotel, too, but it wasn't as great as the Adolphus. It was the second greatest, and we went there. We got there and we went upstairs and a party was going on. There was nothing but movie actors—big-time stuff. Jean Parker and Joan Davis were the only ones I recognized; I had seen them in the movies. He had *made* the party, so we started playing, and, man, we had the house rocking. We were doing the Big Apple and I was in the middle and Joan Davis and Jean Parker were on each side—doing the Big Apple.

One of my guitar strings broke and he said, "Wait a minute." He went to the telephone and called up. He knew the man that owned a music store and he called him up at his house and told him, "This is Jack! Get up and get your ass out that bed and go open up that store and send me *all* the guitar strings you got in the house. *All* of them." And I said, "This is something else! That's sure to show you, when money talks, everybody listens." Now here came the cat. His two arms were raised up with boxes. There were boxes and boxes of guitar strings and all of them were for me! He said that. "They're yours." He paid for them and gave him twenty dollars for bringing them. We started playing again, and we played *all night long.* The party went on till about seven, eight o'clock that next morning.

He kept stuffing that money in my pocket. Jake and Sherman and them kept watching me and he kept stuffing money in my pocket. Forty dollars each time! I had the money. I had, oh, about nine hundred dollars that *he* gave me besides what we'd got from that fellow up on that twelfth floor. *He* had stuffed my pocket with money, too. He wasn't supposed to give us but thirty dollars but when I got through putting that "Jim Crow" jive on him, that Southern drawl, he was putting all that money in my pocket.

Those cats, they were watching me like a hawk. That's the reason why our act wasn't a success—because they didn't trust me enough. They had to trust *me*, because I was the one who made all the *money* for them. I was entertaining the people. What they were doing, they were just playing. Well, just playing wasn't going to get it. When you're *black* you've got to *act* to make any money off of those people. They knew that, but they were watching me right along.

The next morning this man called up one of his servants. He had ten servants and they were all black men. He'd built a ten-room house just for them; all independent rooms like in those big-time hotels. They didn't even need a kitchen or anything like that because they were working in his twenty-six-room house. and he didn't have a child in the world. Just him and his wife, that's all. They had a bridle path, with some bridle horses, and he had some private racehorses. They had a hangar with two private airplanes and a five-car garage—four cars and a big old station wagon. I don't know what kind of cars they were but they had to be those high-priced cars—Cadillacs and Rolls Royce and all that kind of stuff.

Anyway, he called up his servant—the one that drove the cars—and told him, "Dress me up. Bring me some clothes: shoes, socks, ties, underwear, and everything. I want you to match me up. I'm in my tuxedo and I don't want to walk around in my tuxedo in the daytime." This cat knew how he dressed. He was used to seeing him with those fine clothes on, so this cat got him a brown suit out of his closet with brown shoes and brown socks and a white shirt and brown tie. Oh, he was just immaculate and he was a handsome-looking cat, too. He was only about forty years old and he had all that money.

He put Billy Sherman and them in a cab and put me in his Cadillac. He took me to the Dallas Golf Club and we had breakfast on the veranda. That's what they call that screened room. I call it on the porch or in the gallery or something like that, but they called it a veranda. I was the only black man that had ever been in that club. Man, you've never seen so many pretty women in all your life. They were beautiful, and they all were movie actresses, walking around in see-through nightgowns and nothing else. Beautiful as a picture. Oh, man, it was something else! Well, I didn't want to look *too* hard. I just glanced when they passed by me. I knew where I *was*. I wasn't supposed to look at *any* white woman. You can be *standing* there with a white woman and they'll put you in jail and charge you for reckless looking. I wasn't ready for *that*.

We had breakfast and then the cat came in the station wagon with the clothes and he told me, "Wait here, Joe, cause I'm goin to change my clothes. I'm goin to grab a shower. Get ya a drink." He told the waiter, "Get him anything he wants." He was a big wheel in Dallas and they served me like I was white. I got me a couple of scotch and sodas and drank some of that while he took off his tuxedo and took a shower and shaved and cleaned up and everything. He wasn't too long. Then we left. He had a two-piece tux and all this other stuff and he brought it back into the station wagon. We left and we went to his *house*. We picked up Billy Sherman and them at the hotel, and we all went to his home.

When we got there we had to lay out in the sun in the grass out there on his estate. Everybody was pretty wined up. Me and him lay outside there in the sun, knocked out. I've never seen a white man could out-drink me and stand up, and I could drink whiskey by the water glass. That man could drink. Me and him, together, we'd been drinking all night and he drank me under the table until he was too tired. He couldn't drink anymore. Then we got up and we went on inside. Me and Sherman—the whole bunch of us—we went on inside. Brought our instruments to play for him. He told his wife he wanted her to hear us play.

But when we hit the front door his wife said, "Wait a minute. Wait a minute. *Wait a minute!* Let me get my rug up off of that floor." She had a beautiful baby grand piano but this piano was sitting on wall-to-wall Persian rug. Looked like it was about two inches thick. She called the servants to raise up that piano and take her rug off that floor. The floor was hardwood. Beautiful hardwood floor where we could dance and play, and that's where we did our act; danced and everything. Then we left him and went back to the hotel and he gave me a ten-gallon hat and a pair of lizard-skin boots and hundred dollar bills all down in those boots.

I split up all the money we had and we *drove* from Dallas in those two cars we had. But we had overstayed our time. Hyp had told us, "Now, don't forget to be back here Saturday night." Mr. Pool had sent for us to work in Dallas Saturday. But we worked there Saturday night, too, and we didn't leave there till *Sunday*. We were supposed to play Saturday night at the Famous Door, but when we didn't show up there wasn't a show.

We got home Sunday night. When we *did* get back, when we got there, Hyp pitched a boogie woogie. He raised sand. He fired us. He had been looking for us all over. He thought we had had an accident on the road or he thought we went to jail. He called up all the jailhouses in Dallas and asked if they had any black boys. He never did call us niggers. Never did. No. That's one thing I can say about him.

So we left. We had got fired so we didn't go back. But then Monday morning, Hyp sent a fellow in a great big old long black limousine. He picked us all up one by one. He had all our addresses and he came and got us and brought us to *his* place. He had a place right across from the old Union Station—a barroom. He sold whiskey and wine, but he sold more wine than whiskey. All those working men and all the people got off the train, they'd come in there. They'd drink wine. The wine was cheap and that man made a fortune selling wine. Wine was his biggest seller. He must've been a bigwig, too. That black limousine told me where *he* was. Well, he sat up in the booth and he said, "Now, listen. Let me tell y'all something. Hyppolite Guinle's a good man and I want you all to go on back to work for him *tonight*."

We said, "Yes, sir. We be there tonight."

That night we went back to work again. Hyp, he didn't raise too much hell. We started packing the joint again and we worked there till almost the last of 1939.

Then Billy Sherman and them decided they wanted to go back home, so they told me to give Hyp a week's notice; tell him that they would be leaving.

Hyp claimed, "Y'all are goin to be sorry. I know Joe ain't goin." But that's where he made a mistake, because when he looked for me I was in Cincinnati with those boys.

12

Bad Luck Blues

If it wasn't for bad luck,
I wouldn't have no luck at all . . .

I WENT with them because they told me they had a *job*. They decided that they were going to go back to Cincinnati because they had a job at some club uptown—the Silhouette Club. They had worked there before and they told me they had a job there.

We were *supposed* to have had a job, but when we got there they didn't *have* a job. So there I was. I said, "Man, what the hell y'all doin? Y'all take me this far away from *home*, man, and you ain't got no job? You niggers got to be crazy, man."

Now *I'm* in Cincinnati and I don't know *anybody*. So I stopped at a lady's house on Ninth and Jones in Cincinnati—I'll never forget that place—and I told the lady, "Miss," I said, "I'm a thousand miles from home and them boys brought me here, talked as if we had a job, and then we ain't got no job. Now, if you let me stay here, how much will it cost me?"

She said, "Seven dollars a week."

"Well, I'll tell you what. My guitar's worth at least a hundred and fifty. Okay, I'm gonna get some money but I can't pay you right now because I don't *have* no money."

She said, "Okay."

That night I took my guitar and I got me a taxi cab. I had a few dollars on me and I asked the cab driver to take me in the white section where the nightclubs were. He took me there. We got up there and I paid him. I got out and I walked into this joint, took my hat off—I forgot I was in Cincinnati, I thought I was "down there"—and I talked to the bartender.

"What you want?" he said.

I said, "Mister, I'm from New Orleans. I'm a performer and I'm trying to work my way back home. I came here to work with these boys that's from this town. We work together. We had an act in New Orleans, but they left there and came here and told me that they had a job. But they didn't have no job and here I am in Cincinnati and I don't know nobody here. So, I'm trying to make some money to get back home. If you don't mind lettin me play a few numbers and pass my hat it ain't gonna cost you nothin."

He said, "It's alright with *me*. Go *ahead*."

I started playing and singing and then I started passing my hat. I had a *hat* full of money: nickels, dimes, quarters, halves, dollars, five dollars, ten dollars. And I mean every night! Those people kept putting money in.

Now, Billy Sherman and them, they knew where I was staying at so they came to see me so we could rehearse. There was a restaurant at the corner and we went in the restaurant. I pulled out all this money and I paid for my food and put my money in my pocket and they were wondering, where did I get the *money?* But I told them, "Now, I'll tell you what. Y'all was gonna leave me, but I'm gonna beat y'all, livin in your own home town."

So, they started to trail me. They watched me then. They got in a cab and they followed me, and they found out what I was doing. Then they brought their instruments and they fell in there with *me* and we started picking up money from everywhere.

They had a cat in there who was from New Orleans. I told him *I* was from New Orleans, so he told me, "I tell you what. There's a club back of Central Avenue—in the alley—and the club's called the Barn. You go in there and ask for the owners. They're two brothers that own the place. Tell either one I sent you. They've got a violin player and piano player in there, that ain't doin *nothin* and they ain't *never* doin nothin like what *y'all* got here. I'm quite sure y'all can get a job."

Well, blessed be the child . . . We went over there and the first couple of tunes we played, we all got the job. He fired those two people and we started working. He had a little stage built in the front, and we started working right in the *front*. We had a bass player. Harold Jackson I think his name was. He could play *so much bass*. He was one of the only *black* boys that graduated from the University of Cincinnati. A rich lady had talked for him and sent him to this school. He learned music and he could play that music on a bass. First time I heard that.

We worked there for two years and eight months. We weren't making a salary but we were making a whole lot of tips. Plenty of money. One of us would hold the money and then we'd separate it at the end of the night.

While I was working there they had some cats used to come in there and they'd listen to us play. There was one fellow, he wanted me to come in the booth and play for him. He had four or five guys—one fellow was standing in one corner, another fellow in another corner and another guy in another corner. I felt kind of funny. When I got through playing he stuffed a bill in my pocket. When I looked in my pocket there was a thousand-dollar bill, so I went back and I told him, "Mister, you musta made a mistake. I don't think you intended to give me this bill. That's too much money. That's a thousand-dollar bill."

He said, "Well, my boy, I just wanted to test you out. I'm going to give you a *hundred*-dollar bill because I found out you were honest enough to know that I wouldn't have given you a thousand-dollar bill unless I told you what it was and wanted you to have it."

He and I got to be real good friends. I found out they were from Cleveland, Ohio, and they came there to buy a club across the river in Covington, Kentucky. His boys were with him and they used to come there all the time. They used to like to hear me play.

One time, I was standing up with him, drinking at the bar, and there was a priest in there, and would you believe? That priest, he didn't call me nigger, but he said, "That nigger can really sing." So, this cat grabbed that priest on the collar and said, "Let me tell you something. If you just open your mouth to call him that again, they're goin to have to *carry* you out of here. You understand what I'm tellin you?" And he *pushed* him on away from the bar. That's how he was with *me*.

One night they waited till I got off and they said, "We want y'all to come with us."

"Okay."

They had a motorcade. They had four sports-model convertibles in the alley. The main man was the type who liked me so he put me in the car with him, and Billy Sherman and them got in the cars with the other fellows and we went across the river to a place called the Lookout House.

Man, the greatest musicians used to come in there. Bojangles danced at the Lookout House, Cab Calloway played the Lookout House. In spite of all that, every black man that played the Lookout House could *not* drink at the *bar* in the Lookout House. Not even Cab, and Cab looked almost like white. But they knew he was black.

When we got there, they had closed. The bartender was still in there, checking up the register and everything, so, this fellow with me, he knocked on the door. The door had a glass and we could see the bartender through it, so this fellow took out a *gun* and knocked on the door with *it*. The bartender, he walked to the door and said, "We're *closed*." And *he* said, "Well, open it up, and open it up *right now*."

He unlocked the door and we all went in. Billy Sherman and them, they sat at the table and he said, "Joe, you sit at the bar with me."

The bartender said, "What you havin to drink?" He had seen me with my guitar and he thought I was just going to be playing so he got to the other fellow and he got what he wanted to drink. The other fellow said, "Joe, what *you* want to drink?"

I said, "I'll take a scotch and soda."

The bartender said, "I'm sorry, man, but we don't serve no blacks in here. Never did. Blacks that *work* here can't drink at the bar."

The other fellow said, "Well, I'll tell you, man, *this* black is gonna drink at this bar or they're gonna be minus a bartender." And he looked at me, kind of smiling.

The cat said, "Okay." So he served me the scotch and soda and we drank and played, and then we paid him off—gave him a good tip—and we left. We came on out of there and he gave us some money and we went on home.

Danny Barker was with Cab, then, and when Cab played the Lookout House Danny found out I was working in Cincinnati, in the alley, at the Barn. He came there to the club, to *see* me. And he came over to my *house*. I had made some gumbo and we ate it.

Now, while I was working at the Barn, some students came in from the University of Cincinnati. They worked in the lab and they had these rats for experiments and they brought me this little rat for a pet. He was so small he looked like he would disappear in my hand; if I closed my hand you couldn't see him. He was white with pretty tan stripes. I asked them what to feed him, and they told me he was a *vegetarian*. He didn't eat no meat. I had a cage for him with rings and things in it and he'd run all around and up and down in the cage. When he wanted to get out, I'd let him out and he'd run around in the room. Well, he was on the bed—jumping around on the bed—while Danny and I were eating gumbo!

When Danny saw him, he said, "Man, what the hell is *that?*"

I said, "That's Billy. That's my rat." Then I said, "Come here, Billy, come here." And Billy came over to me and jumped up on my shoulder, and I told Danny, "See? He's a pet, man."

Danny said, "I don't give a damn what he is. I just don't like no kind of rats. !"

Where the trouble came in—was one time I took Billy out of his cage. I put him on my shoulder. He wouldn't move unless I told him. Now, when he got on my shoulder, somehow he knew I was taking him somewhere. But he was never afraid because he knew I was his friend, see? I wouldn't do anything to harm him. So, I took him to a store on Central Avenue and when I walked in the place, and the women saw him on my shoulder, they screamed, and they cleared the store out. The manager told me, "Man, get out of here with that rat cause you ruining my business." And he wouldn't show me anything I had come in to see. He just said, "Get out of here and *stay* out. *You* can come back in, but that *rat's* gotta stay out." Now, if I'd've brought the cage with me that never would have happened. I could have taken him in and the women might have even admired him in the cage as to how pretty he looked. They could have seen he was a pet when he was in the cage, but they didn't know what he would do when he was standing on my shoulder.

Danny used to come to the Barn to hear me play. All the great musicians that used to play in the Lookout House used to come to the Barn where we were working, after they got off. One night in there, there were the Modernaires. There was a trombone player who had a band—I can't think of his name—and Bob Crosby. Candido from New Orleans—he came in there. They used to call him Candy and he got to be a great comedian in Hollywood. And Eddie Miller, who was playing saxophone with Bob Crosby, and one of the singers with Bob Crosby, and one of the singers from the Modernaires—they were all in there. They came up there and sang and we did jam sessions and everything, so it was really beautiful.

The director of the Cincinnati Symphony Orchestra came in there, too. He used to eat in the Barn because the Barn sold famous steaks; they had a famous cook upstairs. He—the director of the orchestra—he didn't like jazz, but this particular solo that Billy Sherman played on that unorthodox mandolin that he had made him put down his knife and fork and turn around and watch him make all these chord changes. He was playing the lead chord changes for "Why Do I Love You?" Not like these guitar players play single strings—he played *chord* changes. The way Sherman tuned this mandolin, nobody could play it but him. And he played it like a banjo. The only man I know could play lead chord changes like Billy—but on a banjo—is Kimball. He and his wife used to play with Celestin, but he plays at Preservation Hall right now, with Jaffe's Preservation Hall Jazz Band.

While I was working at the Barn it was during the war. They had just declared war on Japan, in 1941, after Pearl Harbor. At that time, Kate Smith had just made a tune called "God Bless America." I was singing this tune, and these two fellows were from Germany and they hollered, "Sing it, nigger, cause you're gonna need it!"

I put my guitar down and I went upstairs. This was a supper club downstairs and upstairs was the kitchen, so I went upstairs and I didn't come down. The boss, he came up there and asked me what was the matter.

I told him, "Well, look, man. I had to put up with enough of that shit down south where I come from and I don't intend to put up with it up here. So, now, if you don't like it you can pay me off right now." By that time we'd started getting a couple of dollars a night apiece.

"Come on down, Joe," he said. "I'll talk to them."

So, when I was coming down, they were at the head of the stairs and they said, "Your boy said he don't like us."

I said, "I didn't *say* that. I didn't say I didn't *like* you. I said I don't like what you *said. That's* what I don't like. I've got a lot of respect for my *race.*"

They handed me a ten-dollar bill and I said, "No, man, you can't buy me. You can't buy me. No. Not for ten *thousand* dollars you couldn't, because I couldn't stand for you to low-rate my race that way. It ain't worth all the money you got. It's worth more than any money you got. That's what I mean."

The boss was standing there. They said, "Well, go ahead and take the money. We're sorry we spoke to you that way and we're sorry we spoke in that tone of voice. Go ahead on and take the money." So I took the money and I went back and played.

Now, they had *another* bunch of fellows who were on their way to *Florida* for a vacation. They stopped in there. One fellow, he liked this number, "Sweet Sue." I never played so much "Sweet Sue" in all my life. They took me away from downstairs and told the boss, "We're gonna bring Joe upstairs to play for us." That man stuffed my pockets full of dollars: five-dollar bills, ten-dollar bills, twenty-dollar bills, and I'd sing, "Every star above knows the one that I love, Sweet Sue." That man had me playing that all night long! But when I came downstairs we had a whole lot of money. On their way back from Florida they stopped there *again*, on their way home, just to hear me sing.

Then, while I was playing there, I met a lady. Her boyfriend was a radio announcer, and she was playing piano at the Netherland Plaza Hotel in Cincinnati on Central Avenue. She came in there one night and she heard me singing, so she told her boyfriend, "We're gonna wait till they get off." They waited till I got off and put me in their car and we went across the river into Kentucky. We went to a place where they had a piano bar. This woman was beautiful. A beautiful redhead. Pretty. Boy, she was neat in the waist like a wasp and she was built round the hips like a thoroughbred racehorse. Boy, she was beautiful. And she could play more boogie woogie than anybody I had ever heard. Me and her played together till *day*, and then they drove me back home and gave me some money. Her and her boyfriend drove me back home.

Somewhere down the line I had met a girl. Her name was Belle. When I was working at the Gypsy Tea Room and I was producing the show, she was working in the chorus. Well, I met her in Cincinnati. Met her on Central Avenue. Man, she had a fancy mink coat, diamonds, and all kinds of stuff. When she looked, she said, "Joe?"

"Belle?" I said, "Well I'll be doggoned. Just go to show ya, huh? Two mules will never meet but two people will."

"I'm sure glad to see you," she said. "I want you to come up to my house."

"Okay."

"Where *you* stoppin at?"

"I'm livin on Ninth and Jones. Right next to the little restaurant there. Right in the front room."

"Okay."

So she came to me. Her old man, he had a gambling concession. They used to play poker and shoot dice and everything. He furnished a house for her and he gave her all these diamonds and things, but he had his own two-story building across the river. He'd send the gamblers over there. He was a real big-shot gambler but he wasn't running the game. Belle was cutting the game, and by the next morning Belle would have a sack full of money.

But Belle's trouble was, Belle would drink as much as the people. She'd get drunk and the cats would take all the money back. When this cat would come, the liquor'd be gone and she didn't have the money. So he took everything she had. Put her out and took all these diamonds and furs—took all that back.

So, she rented another house. She had enough money, but she needed money to put the telephone in, and she needed money to put the meter in for the electric lights and gas. I was the only one she knew from home, so she came to my house and she told me.

"You know, Smilin"—she used to call me Smilin because I used to laugh all the time—"Smilin, I'm gonna tell you, you the only one I know and the only one I can come to. I need some money."

"How much you need?"

I gave her the money to put the meter in and I gave her the money to open the house. After she had everything fixed up and everything, then I went to her house. She had about six or eight pretty girls there. They were hustling. When I got there, she called all the girls in there and told them who I was, and she said, "*Any* time he want *any* one of you, if I find out y'all charge him anything then you can't work in this house no more."

They said, "Okay, Belle."

So, I had the run of them. I could get all I wanted. It didn't cost me anything. Nothing! We were good friends because she remembered I put her in my chorus in New Orleans and I did her that favor when she couldn't get a favor from anybody else because she didn't know anybody else there but me. We stayed friends there till I left.

But this is the question: I got *sick.* I didn't know what was wrong with me. While I was on the bandstand. I was playing and everything turned black. My eyes were wide open but I couldn't see. Everything was black, like all the lights had gone out. I keeled over, and Jake caught me. He caught my guitar and everything. So, they called a cab and they sent me home and they told me, "Don't worry bout nothin." The boss told me, "Anything you want, just tell the boys and you can get it. Don't worry bout it."

Lord knows I didn't know what was wrong with me. I was sick from bad teeth, I had pyorrhea of the gums, and all my teeth were falling out. My teeth were as solid as a door knob but pyorrhea in my gums had separated them and couldn't hold them. Sometimes when I was eating one of them would fall out in the spoon. It's lucky I didn't swallow any of them. Some of them I could pull out with my hand! Just shake them and pull them right out. And, by me eating, and swallowing that poison—that pus—it ruined my stomach; it got in my system. Then, when I looked down there at my penis there was a little red spot on it. And every time I would pass my hand across my face, a whole lot of spots came on my neck, and pain, and everything. I couldn't eat anything; I lost fourteen pounds in one week.

I went to a drug store and the drug store man told me, "There's a doctor right off of Central Avenue. He's the head doctor of the general hospital but he's got visiting hours," and he gave me his address.

He was an old man in his seventies. When I walked in and he saw me he told me, "Get up on the scale." I got on the scale. I got off the scale. He took my blood pressure. Then he took some *blood*. He took this blood sample and told me to come back in two days.

In two days, when I got back, he told me, "Son, I don't know how you lived, *bad* as your *blood* is." I had the first stage of syphillis.

I had caught it somewhere in that *house*. I had gone with a beautiful woman. Indian-looking woman. Pretty, reddish-brown skin and her face was smooth as a spanked baby's ass. She had a *card* in her pocket where she was taking *treatments*. She didn't *tell* me that, but I found it out and I knocked her down a whole flight of stairs because that's where I caught it—from her.

He gave me a shot of Salvarsan—That's Dr. Ehrlich's magic bullet. He gave me a shot of that. That kind of stuff will knock you down. It had me walking like a drunken man and I hadn't had a drink. I was sick. Eva had come up there. I called her long distance and sent for her to come up there. She came up there and I told her the truth. I told her the truth that I couldn't have any sexual intercourse with her until I got through taking the treatments from the doctor. She understood that I had been away from home for so long. That night I had a high fever, and Eva told me that I was talking out of my head and everything, but the next morning Billy Sherman and them, they brought my money. We used to get paid every night and we used to separate the money. They brought my money and they brought me a big bunch of oranges and stuff. I could eat anything I wanted just after that one shot. Every Monday I had to take a shot and they brought me my money every day as long as I was sick and couldn't work. I think it was about ten weeks. I took about ten shots of that Salvarsan.

Now, the doctor had told me to go get my teeth pulled out. All of them. Well, I had a toothache so bad till my jaw was swollen up big, so I went to the boss at the Barn. There was a millionaire dentist on Central Avenue. He had dental offices in that whole block and he had not worked on any Negroes. But these two brothers that were my boss, they were big wheels and this doctor had so many thousands of dollars on the tab that he hadn't paid, so the boss took me in and said, "Now, you're going to wait on him because we need him. He works for us and he's gotta sing." But the boss didn't want him to take all my teeth out at one time, because he said, "He's got to sing."

I'm just as scared of dentists and doctors and hospitals as the devil's scared of holy water, so Eva came with me. I thought she could come in the dental office. He told her, "I won't hurt him, cause he's scared."

They gave me gas. I'm in this big room, all covered in white and everything. Got all these tubes and everything. It's bad enough to scare the shit out of you. I'm sitting up there, and the nurse brought this big tank in back of me and after she hooked it up, she tested it. I could hear, "ssssss," and that was gas coming out. She hooked me up to it, and she put a rubber clamp in my mouth to hold my mouth open. She said, "Once you go to sleep, if you close your mouth they couldn't get it open to take your teeth out." Then she said, "We ready, doctor?" and the doctor said, "Yeah, we're ready." And she started. I could hear that gas coming out—that "ssssss"—and I had my eyes open. She said, "Close your eyes. How you expect to go to sleep?" So I closed my eyes. "Breathe normal." I was breathing, man, way after a while it looked like my stomach was going to bust. After a while, all I can remember was "Uh!" and I was gone. I was dreaming I was playing in the club.

This gas smelled like perfume and when I woke up I said, "Say, Doc, when y'all gonna pull my teeth?"

They said, "Look on the floor."

I looked on the floor and there was all of them. They took them *all* out.

I went and told the boss, "Well, Mr. ———, I'm gonna tell you the truth. It's no sense in me just keep takin your money like that and not workin for you. You could do me a great favor if you would buy me a train ticket home. If anything gonna happen to me I would like for it to happen at home, amongst my people. I don't have nobody up here. I'd hate for my people to hear if anything happened to me up here and they're down there."

So he did. He bought me a ticket and gave me some *more* money. I never will forget those two people in all my days. They were real good to me.

13   **Lonesome Man**

Like the prodigal son,
I believe I'll go back home . . .

IN NEW ORLEANS, I went back to work at the Gypsy Tea Room. It wasn't owned by the same man; it was owned by a man that used to have the Japanese Tea Garden on St. Claude and St. Philip. Louis Messina. That was his name. He bought the Gypsy Tea Room, too, so he had two clubs, and then he went into the prizefight management business, which he's still in today. He's a local prizefight promoter. He used to go to New York and different places, and he was in New York for some reason or other when he heard that the Ink Spots had busted up.

The Ink Spots were playing at the Zanzibar and they got in a fight on the stage and they broke up. When they broke up, Joe Glaser was looking for somebody to take Deek Watson's place. Joe Glaser was the biggest agency in New York at that time for black audiences. So, this man, Mr. Louis Messina, told Joe Glaser, "I got just the man for you—down in New Orleans." And Joe Glaser told him, "Well, send him on up here."

That's when I went to New York. Lou gave me a round-trip ticket and gave me about eighty-five dollars and told me who to go see. They didn't have commercial planes then, but I caught the fastest train leaving out of New Orleans. It was called the Silver Streak. It made about four stops before we got to New York. It was considered as a fast express train. The train station was right between Rampart and Basin Street. It was the Southern Railway Station. The train was to leave out of there. I caught the train and I went on to New York.

I had my guitar with me. I had a big old white Epiphone Emperor. I'd bought it when I played with the Jazz Jesters in Cincinnati. It was all white. The tail piece was gold-filled and the keys were ivory and, oh, it was something else! I bought it in Cincinnati in 1941 for four hundred and seventy-five dollars. Cash! And for the electric pickup, I bought one of the first amplifiers designed by Les Paul. Les Paul was a pretty fair country guitar player, himself. The amplifier was called a "Les Paul Forty." I played on Indian Hill, in Cincinnati, for some rich people, and I didn't know that they only had DC current. I plugged into the DC current with my old amplifier and that just burnt it up. All I could see was the tubes in the back turning *blue*. That's what got me to buy this Les Paul amplifier.

So, I had my guitar in New York—my Epiphone Emperor guitar—and I went to see Joe Glaser. I think he was on the twenty-fifth floor up in the Brill Building—1619 Broadway, somewhere up there. He had his office up there. I went up there and I gave him an audition. Him and Ben Bart were together then, and I gave them both an audition. So here come all the people: the scrubwoman and everybody, coming in from all the offices and everything, coming in this office and hear me play.

Ben Bart told me, "Okay, now, I want you to come down to the Apollo Theatre and sit in the audience and see how the Ink Spots work."

That's when I told *him*. I knew how the Ink Spots worked because I knew the Ink Spots before they were the Ink Spots. I knew the Ink Spots when they were King Jack and Jesters. Deek Watson was the one who wrote the talking part—from a radio play. Every Sunday morning they had a radio show, called The Little White Church on the Hill, in Cincinnati. Deek went to this church and he heard this preacher talking, so, he thought he'd put that talk in the act. They made it in one of the biggest selling records: "If I Didn't Care," by the Ink Spots.

And Deek did all the swing singing, like,
I love coffee and I love tea,
I love the Java Jive and it love me.
Coffee to tea and it's jivin me,
A cup, a cup, a cup, a cup, a cup. Bop!
I was supposed to take Deek Watson's place when they split up. We had a little Ink Spot act that we were doing. We were imitating the Ink Spots, and I used to do the talking like Hoppy, one of the original Ink Spots. I told him, but I went down to the Apollo Theatre anyway and I watched how they worked.

I went backstage after they came off, during an intermission, and I talked to Kenny, the lead singer. Kenny was the leader of the

6 With Danny Barker. (New Orleans Jazz Museum)

Danny Barker and Freddie Green are the greatest six-string rhythm guitar players in the world. . . . He brought me on Fifty-second street to meet all the cats. (pp. 109, 110)

outfit, then, after Deek left. I gave an audition to Kenny and Kenny told me, "You got a lot of talent. I like your work. But you wouldn't fit in our act, man, cause you got your own style. But I tell you what I can do," he said. "I can get you in with my agency." He was with Universal then.

I said, "Joe Glaser told me to come talk to *you*."

"Well, you wouldn't fit the act."

So there I was. In New York. All by myself. Had eighty-five dollars in my pocket, and my guitar. They had got me a room at the Braddock Hotel, where they didn't have any more chinches because the roaches ate em all up! But they hadn't paid for it. I had to pay my own money for it, out of the money I had. Twenty-three dollars a week, and in the forties that was a whole lot of money.

And I didn't know anybody.

But Danny Barker found me. Danny and I were practically raised up together. I remember him when he first met Louise, and I remember when they first got married.

Danny Barker and Freddie Green are the greatest six-string rhythm guitar players in the world. Danny was with Cab Calloway. Freddie Green was with Count Basie. Danny stayed in New York about thirty or forty years; something like that. He went to New York and played with some of the greatest musicians in the world and he became one of the greatest musicians in the world, too.

Danny heard I was in town, and he found me and took me to his house. He lived in the Bronx. I went to his house and I explained him the situation. I showed him my round-trip ticket and said, "Man, I'm goin home."

He said, "Man, you ain't going nowhere, except downtown. I'm going to take you downtown and introduce you to some people."

My daddy had a barber shop in Brooklyn, so I told him I was going to see my daddy and he said, "Well, I'll pick you up and we'll go over there together."

We went over there to see my daddy and Danny told my daddy, "Between you and me, we're going to keep him here. We ain't going to let him go back, because he's got too much talent to go back. He can make it here."

My father said, "Okay."

Danny got Cab Calloway's road agent to get me a room on 126th Street. I got that room for five dollars a week. It was small. It was so small I had to walk sideways to get inside. But it saved me a lot of money.

After that, Danny would take me to his house. A couple of times I *slept* at his house and the next morning, under my plate, Blue Lu Barker had a ten-dollar bill. Under my plate. Now, *that* was my friend, and we still are the greatest of friends, right now.

Danny practically took care of me. He introduced me to John Hammond of Columbia Records. He introduced me to Teddy Rieg. He introduced me to Bill Simon. He introduced me to Mark Davis, who had something to do with Imperial Record Company. He introduced me to all the greatest musicians. He brought me on Fifty-second Street to meet all the cats. *All* the cats: Dizzy Gillespie, Charlie Parker, Thelonius Monk, Red Allen—well, I already knew Allen. He's from across the river. Red Allen was playing on Seventh Avenue at the Metropole. I knew Red Allen and Red Allen knew me. And Earl Bostic. I'd been knowing Earl Bostic, because Earl Bostic started down *here* on the boat. I met Tiny Grimes and Sid Catlett, Al Casey and Earl Hines, Harry Carney, Al Sears, Art Tatum, Hot Lips Page, Billie Holiday, Ella Fitzgerald . . . All of them. All those kind of people.

Danny told me to always stay down on Fifty-second Street— where something's happening—just like out on Bourbon Street. If you're looking for a job you can't expect a job to come to *you*. You go out *there*, cause a lot of times an opportunity presents itself and you have to be right there to grasp it, and if you *don't*, well, then, ain't nobody going to bother looking for you. Unless somebody recommends you. And you have to be real good for somebody to recommend you.

All this time Eva was under the impression I was *working*, but I was *not* working. She hadn't heard from me so she came up to New York. I didn't have a job. I didn't have any money. I had pawned my guitar for fifty dollars. A five-hundred-dollar guitar! I pawned it for fifty dollars. Then, I'd had about ten suits when I went there, and I'd pawned about eight of them by the time I made some connections. That's the kind of predicament I was in.

I had this little room, and I came to my room that night—that *morning*—and I opened my door and I smelled perfume. I smelled perfume! I didn't put the light on, but I said, "Now, some woman is in my room, because I don't use *that* kind of perfume and I ain't never had a woman round my room before. Somebody's in here!" She didn't say anything. She's just lying there, under the covers. I put the light on and I looked . . . And I said to myself, "Now, who the hell could this be?"

7 Louise "Blue Lu" and Danny Barker; photo taken around 1980. (Holly Miller)

Danny and I were practically raised up together. I remember him when he first met Louise, and I remember when they first got married.   (p. 109)

She surprised me! I didn't know she was coming, because I'd've met her at the station if I knew she was coming. But, anyway, I found Eva in there, in the bed. Now, the bed was so small that one half of the night she was sleeping on top of me, the other half of the night I slept on top of her. That's how small it was—one little bitty bunk. Little bitty room. You could hardly turn around in that rascal. But it was five dollars a week, so what the hell. It was the cheapest.

I don't know if she was trying to catch me at something or if she just wanted to surprise me to find out what was happening because I hadn't written her. But as long as I wasn't working I didn't want to write her a letter to know how conditions were because she'd've wanted me to come back home. She'd've sent me *money* to come back home. She'd have given me anything I *wanted*, but the thing about it is, I didn't *want* to let her know. My pride stopped me from letting her know anything. I said, "I'm a man. I'm supposed to be able to take it." So what I did was, I took it. Until I did get a break. With Sam Price.

Danny had told Sam Price about me. He had me make a record and he was going to introduce the record to different agents and things.

First I started singing the blues like Cleanhead Vinson, but they told me "You'll never make it singing the blues like Cleanhead Vinson. If we want Cleanhead Vinson to record, we'll get him. We want you to sing the blues like yourself." Well, that inspired me to start writing my own blues tunes. I hadn't written any blues tunes before that, but I was forced to do it if I wanted to make a recording date. I had to write something original in order to get the date because it was my first time recording. During the session you make four sides: you make two records, one tune on one side and another tune on the other side, and the same thing with the other record. In three hours that was considered as a session. Now, if any one of those tunes would have made a hit, then I could've put the whole four tunes on an album and it would have sold, too. After that, they probably would have had writers to write for me, because I would have made it famous as a blues singer, and they'd write a lot of tunes for me.

Then I made four sides with Sidney Bechet, Hot Lips Page, Sammy Price, and Mezz Mezzrow, but they weren't released until later on. Mezz Mezzrow was a white boy. Clarinet player. He wrote a book called *Really the Blues*. Anyway, he was the one who owned King Jazz Records. He had an angel that bought the company for him.

But, the person who actually got me a *real* record date was Leonard Feather. He was at the Spotlight when Danny introduced me to Clark Monroe.

Clark Monroe was the only black man that had a club on Fifty-second Street. Called the Spotlight. Danny introduced me to Clark Monroe. He said, "Clark, I want you to meet the greatest blues singer in the world. I want you to say hello to Joe. Joe, this is Clark Monroe."

I put my hand out and Clark said, "How you doin, Cuz?" That's how I got the name, "Cousin Joe." From Clark Monroe.

I said, "Fine, man, how you doin?"

"Great, Cuz! Would you like a drink?"

"I don't mind." I was drinking then. Drank Scotch. And he kept on pouring.

Then Danny said, "Let Joe sing some blues for you."

The main attraction in there was Billy Daniels. He was singing in there, and Billy Daniels was a pretty fair country singer, himself. Ernie Washington was playing piano for him and Buster Bailey was playing clarinet.

Earl Hines was standing up at the bar, *and* Leonard Feather—one of the greatest music critics in the world. Leonard Feather asked Earl Hines would he play the piano for me.

Earl Hines said, "Sure."

So, they announced me and Earl Hines asked me what key I'm in.

I told him "B flat," and he made me a *hell* of an introduction in B flat. I patted my foot on the *time* I wanted him to do it, and he just played. And I said, "Make it as low down as you can make it."

Danny had told me, "Whenever you do anything down there, do your best. Don't let anybody be able to follow you." And I was away from home, wanting me a job, and I put *everything* I had into it.

Leonard Feather liked the way I sang the blues. After I got through singing these blues, he asked me would I like to record! I told him yes.

He told me he was going to call me and I told him, "I ain't got no telephone." I said, "I barely got a room. Got a little bitty place."

He said, "Well, I'll write you a letter. Give me your address." I gave him my address and he wrote me a letter and told me he had a record date set up for me. Did I have any material?

I told him, "Yeah."

He set the date, got the studio, and *he* selected the musicians. We had a big band. *He* played the piano, and he got Harry Carney, a baritone player from Duke Ellington's band. He got Al Sears, the tenor player from Duke Ellington's band. He got Dick Vance on trumpet, and a little drummer called J. C. Heard, who was playing with Cab Calloway.

We had a guitar player—he was amazing. Danny Barker was supposed to play, but Danny had to go on tour with Cab Calloway, so Danny sent me this guitar player called Jimmy Shirley. Boy, could he play! He used to play all that pretty stuff behind Ella Fitzgerald. Oh, he was a master. He could play anything. He could read fly shit on paper!

Danny took me to the Y where Jimmy Shirley was staying at and he told me, "I want you to hear one of the greatest guitar players in the world." You know what he could play, from the book? On guitar? "Nocturne," by Chopin. Jimmy Shirley took out a guitar *score*—no chord changes and all that—with *notes,* and up and down strokes. And he sat there and played that whole score. "Nocturne," by Chopin! I didn't know *what* he was playing, but I saw on the top of the sheet, "Nocturne," by Chopin. I could see how fast his fingers were playing. They've got some fast passages in there. And they've got some lost chords in there that I could *never* find. Now, he could play *that,* and then he was one of the funkiest blues players you'd want to hear.

Jimmy Shirley played so much guitar he made me put my guitar in the pawn shop. I got a hundred dollars from the pawn shop on it and when I got ready I went back and got it out. He was on guitar, and I think we had a bass player out of Boston. His name was Lloyd Trotman and he could *play.* He used to play with the bow, and hum like Slam Stewart. He also played a week at the Zanzibar with Duke Ellington after Braud left Duke Ellington's band. Braud was such a great foundation man—had such a great tone on the bass—that Duke had to hire *two* bass players.

So, we did the session, and it was great. I did one of Danny Barker's tunes and one that was written by Leonard Feather. The rest of the tunes were written by me. And that was my first recording. The label was a company out of Los Angeles, called "Philo," but after we made the record they had to change the name, because it was too close to the name of the Philco people. So they changed the name to "Aladdin."

Clark Monroe used to have sessions every Monday, and after I made the record with Leonard Feather, he put my name on the front of his place: "Cousin Joe from New Orleans." Then the sides I had made with Mezz Mezzrow and Sidney Bechet were released. And *then*, here came *all* the record people! Here came Teddy Reig. At my house! He heard about me and he came to record me for Savoy Records, in New Jersey. And here came Bill Simon. Bill Simon was with Gotham records, then.

Then I picked my *own* musicians, and I tried my best to pick out most of the musicians from New Orleans. Like Pops Foster. I had Danny Barker on guitar a couple of times, and when Danny was out of town with Cab I used Jimmy Shirley. I used Dick Vance and Shad Collins and I used a tenor player out of Houston named John Hardy. He was real great. I had Ernie Washington on piano— he was from New Orleans, too, but he had been living in New York for a long time—and I had J. C. Heard again on drums. I had piano players like Billy Kyle, and I had an alto saxophone player named Pete Brown. I had Earl Bostic and Dickie Wells. Dickie Wells was a great trombone player. I had the famous guitarist named Al Casey. So you see, I recorded with the best! Well, at that time I was recording independently; I wasn't under contract with *anybody*.

Then, I made a *tour* with Sidney Bechet. I played the guitar in his *band*, and started getting writeups and everything. In magazines! My picture in the magazine with the guitar! I worked nine months with Bechet's band, playing guitar, from New York to Washington, D.C., for two weeks and from Washington, D.C., back to New York, then from New York to Boston for two months at the Savoy on Columbus Avenue. We excited those people in Boston and upset them in Washington. When we came back to New York from Washington we upset them in Ryan's. When we came back from Boston I went to work at the Downbeat, with Billie Holiday and Tiny Grimes and Ella Fitzgerald, and knocked them out. After that, Eva—my old lady—went back to New Orleans.

I had got Eva a job when she came to New York. I got her a job on Fiftieth and Broadway—at a hot dog stand. I went over there and talked to the man on the corner. The man knew me, because from Fifty-second Street we all used to have to pass right there, to get hamburgers and stuff. Me and Sonny Greer and Duke

Ellington—we used to pass by there all the time, going to a place
called Beefsteak Charlie's.

I ain't seen a beefsteak in there *yet* but that was the name of it.
Beefsteak Charlie's. They sold liquor in there. Duke was playing at
the Zanzibar, then, on Forty-ninth and Broadway, and, *all* the musicians, when they'd get off in the morning from the Zanzibar,
that's where they'd go. Sonny Greer and Johnny Hodges and Milt
Hinton—all of them. When I'd get off, I'd come over there and eat.
I knew just where they were—at Beefsteak Charlie's—in the mornings. Drinking. They weren't too much for those high prices where
they worked at. That liquor was high-priced where they worked at,
but they had liquor at Beefsteak Charlie's for forty cents a drink!
Hah! You can drink a whole lot at forty cents a drink. And we'd be
in there, just having a ball.

Sonny Greer was *my boy.* He was my closest buddy in Duke's
band. He'd say, "Where y'at, Cuz?" and I'd say, "Whatcha say,
Greer?" When I went to Boston with Sidney. We're going to Boston
for two months."

He said, "Yeah? Great, man!"

I said, "Well, now. Look. I want you to keep an eye on my old
lady for me."

He said, "Don't worry about her. We'll take care of her. She'll be
in good shape because she gets off round the time we get off. We'll
see that she gets home safe."

I said, "That's all I want to know, man."

See, they were all going uptown to Harlem on the subway, so he
would see that she got home. And they did.

She stayed there, and when I came back from Boston, well, you
know how it is, she wanted to see her kids. She hadn't come to stay
long. She was only working to help out until I got this job with
Bechet. I didn't mean for her to work there all the time. When I got
the job with Sidney, everything was okay. I was making ninety dollars a week and that was a whole lot of money. So, when I came
back from Boston I sent her home. I bought her a ticket and I gave
her some money and I sent her back home to watch out for the
kids. The kids were still down there, and she couldn't stay that long
away from the kids. So, I told her, "I'll see you. You know how it is
up here. You've got to grasp your opportunity when it presents itself. Well, now, the way things are with me right now, if I leave
here now and go back home, it's just the same as if I had never come

here." So, she left. I sent her back home, and I went to work back in the Downbeat.

While I was in Boston, with Bechet, I got a telegram from Bill Simon. *He* told me when I got back to New York he had a recording date for me with Gotham Records, which was owned by Sam Goody.

Well, when they found out I could sing *spirituals*, I did a spiritual album.

I did the tunes, and I got Earl Bostic to write the introductions and the endings. Earl Bostic was writing and arranging for different bands. He had records by the Golden Gates Quartet. They were the greatest at that time, but they weren't doing it the way *I* was going to do it. So I had to go to his house. He'd pick up his guitar and I'd sing it the way *I* was gong to sing it. I gave Earl the privilege of being the leader of the session, and I got the man to pay him a hundred dollars extra for writing the introductions and the endings.

Earl Bostic had a job working down at the Rendezvous, down in the basement on Seventh Avenue, when I went and got him. He played so much horn, he was making nine thousand notes a second. When the record company heard Earl Bostic playing such great alto, they spent ten thousand dollars to build him up in advertisements and write-ups and all that kind of stuff. Earl Bostic won the Pittsburgh Courier's poll as the number one alto player of the year. Then he formed his own band and he hit the road. Then he got *big*. And I'm the cause of him being the superstar that he was because if *I* didn't go get him out of that *basement* in the Rendezvous and didn't get him to record with me, they probably wouldn't have known he was there. It was through me that he got the right connections.

I don't care how great you think you are, if you don't have the right connections with the right people, you just ain't gonna get nowhere! Not on your own. You need the right people with the right kind of money to back you. That's what it takes to make a star. You could be the greatest singer in the world, but if nobody knows about you, then what? You're just there.

After that, Sammy Price talked to Decca. He took me to MCA— the Music Corporation of America, and he got me a five-year contract with Decca. That's the first time I had a contract with a record company. With Decca. They also gave me a contract for moving pictures and radio artists and television and all that kind of stuff.

They had contracts on that, too. Decca had Louis Jordan, who was a superstar in his time. They had Billie Holiday. All her life she was a superstar. And I was one of the only blues singers, outside of Louis Jordan and Billie, on Decca Records. At that time they used to call them race records.

I made a couple of hit tunes like, "Beggin Woman," and "Baby, You Don't Know It All," and "Death House Blues," and "You Ain't So Such a Much." Then, too, I wrote this tune, "Lonesome Man." I actually was a lonesome man at that time. I mean, when I *first* got to New York, I didn't know anybody, and I was in this room all by myself except for this fellow, Slim, that was sick. I got acquainted with him. I helped him out while he was sick. Pawned a couple of my suits to pay his rent when I didn't even know him. So, I thought about it, and I said, "Now, I'm really a *lonesome* man." I started thinking about it, and then I started elaborating on it. I had been *so* lonesome, I wanted to come back home. So I started off like this,

Like the Prodigal Son, I believe I'll go back home.
Like in the Bible, this man had three sons went in three different directions. Well, two of them went in the *right* direction and the other one went in the *wrong* direction. When he went in the *wrong* direction, when he *realized* he was in the wrong direction, then he wanted to go back *home*. Things didn't work out alright for him. So I said,

Like the Prodigal Son, I believe I'll go back home;
I'm gonna tell my baby that I'm sorry that I done wrong.
Something like that. I'm sort of apologizing for what I did so she can accept me back home. Then I said,

If you ever been lonesome, then you know just how I feel.
And I said,

I can't even wake up in the morning and buy myself a decent
meal.
I didn't have a job at the time and I didn't have *any* money. So I wrote something according to the lonesome life I led. And I said,

If I could catch a freight train I'm goin back home.
Even if I don't get my fare—if I've got to *hobo* back home,

I'm going back home because I'm tired of sleepin all alone.
Leonard Feather wrote something in a magazine about the type of blues I sing. He was a critic for Metronome Magazine and he wrote up my tunes in the magazine. Most of my blues tunes—the womenfolks imagined I was prejudiced against women. Like "Beg-

gin Woman." Well, that actually happened to me in life, you see. In certain times in my life. Like when I was considered to be making more money on Bourbon Street than any other entertainer. Quite naturally, when I'd get in some of these "joogie boogie" joints, the waitresses and everybody would flock around me because they know that my heart's big as a washtub. I was drinking then, too, and I spent a lot of money. I gave away a lot of money just out of the clear blue sky. One time, when I came down to New Orleans from New York I heard this record—"Beggin Woman"—on St. Louis and Burgundy in a place called the Golden Pumpkin, right across from Baby Green's where we played pool. Right across the street. I had just got back from New York and I'm standing in there, in the barroom, and somebody put a nickel on "Beggin Woman." The record was playing and a woman said, "Whoever made that record, I wish I had him here right now. I'd put one of these beer bottles on his head, cause I don't beg nobody for nothin." She got real mad. Yeah! And she didn't know I was standing right there. That was the funny part about it. Well, that's what the women thought. Probably that's why I didn't sell too many records to women.

Don't get me wrong. I love women and I love everything about them, and I'm an old man. I just thought if I did something different from the average blues singers I could probably sell more records. So I talked about the women. I'd say,

I've been givin you money,
Since you was my girl;
Now I'm through with you,
As a dead man is with the world.

and all that kind of stuff. That's in "You Ain't So Such a Much." You very seldom hear me use it. Then the first part is,

I treated that woman nice,
I did everything I could;
Now, she's tellin me,
That I was no good.

I was no good because I didn't give her anything; I always wanted something free. No matter how long I'd been with her I wouldn't give her anything, and that's what made me say,

I wouldn't give a blind sow an acorn;
I wouldn't give a crippled crab a crutch;
Because the woman I was lovin,
I found out—she ain't so such a much.

So, from her, that put other women in the same category.

I didn't have any particular woman in mind. It was just women, period. And I wouldn't say I felt that way about women, but at the time I was in New York I had to think about something different. In New York, at that time, you had to write something nobody ever heard before. You had to write something that wasn't even close to the idea of anybody else. That's why I wrote it that way. Everybody was singing about how beautiful a woman was and how much they loved her and what they would do for her and everything. So I just wrote the opposite: what I *wouldn't* do. Just to be different. That's all.

I tell the ladies in the clubs sometimes—I say, "I don't want y'all ladies to get mad with me, now. It's just in the tune." Like when I say,

I picked up on her conversation,
Heard every word she said.
She had on a fifty-five-dollar hat,
Sittin on a nickel head.

I make an excuse to the ladies. I say, "Don't y'all get mad at me now. It's only in the song." In other words, I don't want them to think *all* the women ain't got no sense. It's not that I was antisocial with women, because at that time I had a *lot* of women. At *that* time. I was able to take care of myself and take care of them, too.

By that time I was earning a hundred dollars a side. I was coming up in the world a little bit. At that time, they were paying off in uppercuts. Now they pay off in money. At that time, when you first started recording, the company paid you by the *side*, and you started off at twenty-five dollars a side. If you made *two* sides, you got fifty dollars. Well, I did pretty good for myself. I used to go down and get an advance against the royalties on my tunes. If I wrote four tunes I got four hundred dollars—one hundred-dollar advance off of each tune—against the royalties. I went down to Sam Goody and collected this money, "against the royalties," because when he made out the check, he'd write beside it, "against royalties."

I didn't get too much in royalties, but a little while later, I talked to Leonard Feather. "I tell you what," he said. "I aint' going to get you no lawyers that's going to cost you a fortune. I'll get you one of those lawyers that's just starting out. They're the ones gonna work for you." So, he got two of them and they went to Gotham Record Company, and they checked up on those books and they found out that I had nine hundred dollars coming to me that I didn't get. They took the case on a percentage basis so I came out with five hundred and they came out with four. That was five hundred dollars more than I had, so I thanked Leonard Feather for doing that for me.

I played in the band at the Downbeat, with Skippy Williams and his brother. Skippy and his brother both played with Duke Ellington. Well, they needed a band for when the regular band was off—for two nights—so Skip went down to the union and talked for me. They said I couldn't play on a *regular* job till I was there a year. But Skip said, "Look, I done lost twenty thousand dollars with bands and I've been in this union long enough. I need this man. This man is a triple threat man. This man can play, he can sing, he can dance, he's a comedian, he's a triple threat man. And there's nobody in New York doing what this man's doing. He's a writer. He's a creator." So, they let me play with him. But I told him, "Now, look, Skip. Let me tell you something. When you write the arrangements that y'all do there, now, I don't know nothing bout them minor sevenths and minor ninths and augmented ninths and all that kind of stuff. When you write out my line, simplify it for me. Please!" And he said "Okay."

You see, when you act *that* way, then the musicians *respect* you for not knowing and *know* you don't know. Because if they knew you came from somewhere and you could play, they'd send you the best—and boy, they could put you in Nelly's room. They could play more with one finger than you could play if you were an octopus. And that goes for piano players, too. Don't sit on a piano stool in New York if you don't know what you're doing. Don't pick up any kind of instrument, because all those pros up there, they've been to conservatory in New York and they know what they're doing. So, you don't go there telling them you know this and you know that, because they're going to make you know that you don't know *nothing*. The best thing for you to do is be humble and they will take sides with you. Don't be ashamed to ask somebody nor be ashamed to tell somebody that you don't know. They respect you for it.

I played with them, and they wrote the chord changes on the top, like: B flat, B flat 7th, A flat, A flat minor, E flat, and all kind of stuff like that. I could *make* those kinds of changes, but when it came to those thirteenths and those ninths and those augmented ninths and diminished sixths with a flat fifth and all that kind of stuff, I didn't know anything about that.

So, I got along great with them. I got along great with all the musicians on Fifty-second Street. They all were in on that "kicks"—

smoking those cigarettes—but I would tell them, "Well, man, I tell ya. I don't dig what you do." They would say, "Come on, Cuz, take a drag." I'd say, "No, man. I would, but I been juicin so much, you know, and juice and that stuff don't mix." They'd say, "Well, okay, man." and I got along. For five years. I got along great with all the musicians.

I was at the Downbeat when here came Joe Glaser's representative, Ben Bart. When I saw Ben Bart, on Broadway, Ben Bart said, "Hey, Joe!"

I said, "How ya doin, Ben?"

"Alright. You ain't goin back home yet?"

"Who told you I was goin home? Man, I done sold the other end of my *ticket*. I ain't goin nowhere. Who told you I was goin anywhere? If it was left to you and Joe Glaser, I'd've *been* goin back, but you see, it didn't turn out like that. See, y'all didn't take the time to find out what I could *do*. Now, you *know*."

"Well, Joe Glaser say come over and see him."

"You can tell Joe Glaser for *me* that when I first come here and gave a audition for him he didn't offer me a *pork* chop. Now I ain't givin away *nothin*. You tell him, just like I'm tellin you, cause I don't *need* him, *now*. He didn't need me at first, now I don't need *him*."

That's the way those agencies are. They're interested in you as soon as you get popular with the public. Other than that they didn't know me from Adam. Those little things that I did, they didn't know whether it was going to take with the public or not. So, they don't take any chances. But as soon as you make a hit tune all the agencies in the United States are looking for *you*, and then, if you *wrote* the tunes, all the publishing companies are looking for you. Danny told me the same words. Danny said, "You don't have to worry. They're going to be knocking at *your* door. They're going to be coming and looking for *you*." And sure enough, they *were*.

So, that's the story. From the beginning, when I first got to New York up until I got a break to work with *anybody*. When I first started out, I started at twenty-five dollars a side to make a record. I'd get a hundred dollars for the session. The next session, I went *up*: fifty dollars a side. Then the next session I made, I went up to a hundred dollars a side. Then I'd say I wanted a hundred dollars advance on each one of my tunes and they gave it to me. That made me get eight hundred dollars for a session of three hours. So you know I was not worried about them at *all*. I went to the pawn shop and got my guitar out. Got all my clothes out of pawn. Got my diamonds out. Got everything out. And then I wasn't worried about *nobody*. Then, after I met Mary, that's all! I didn't have to worry about *anything!*

14   **Come Down Baby**

Baby, baby, you're traveling through space,
I can tell by your eyes and the look on your face . . .

MARY WAS little. Nice looking little brownskin girl. She was in my corner, though. I mean, she'd make that money, and just like she'd get that check, she'd just bring it to *me* and *ask* me can she take and buy something for herself. That's how she was. Innocent.

Mary had never been downtown in her life. She was nineteen years old, and she was working in a factory that made eyeglass frames. She was going with a fellow in the block but something happened to him. He had an operation on his jaw. He must have had cancer or something. They had to take his whole jawbone out on one side and that made him look like Frankenstein. He went down to his people, and she took a liking to me.

I met Mary in a little club, across the street from where I stayed at, called the Silver Rail. I used to go there just for kicks. That's where I first met Brownie McGhee. In there. They used to have a little show. Three acts. With a master of ceremonies.

There was a bright lady in there. She was kind of stout and I thought she had money. She had her own apartment building down on 114th Street. So, instead of me taking Mary home, I took *her* home. She didn't have a husband or anything so we laid out. I used to go there practically every day, and she'd fix me something to eat and we'd lay out.

But I kept going to the Silver Rail, and Mary happened to come over and talk to me. So I finally got to talk to her, and she came on up to my apartment. It was about five walk-ups—stairs. Her old man had had this operation and had gone down to his people. He was gone for a couple of weeks, and she stayed with me all that time.

I was living on 131st Street and Lenox Avenue. I used to get off the subway right at 130th and Lenox and *walk* to 131st. That was Hell's Kitchen. The young cats had their gangs and everything—

they would mug you and hold you up. But I got in with them. I walked in the Silver Rail and a *bunch* of those cats were up in there. I told the bartender, "Give everybody a drink." A drink was forty cents, and I spent eighty-five dollars on that bar, buying drinks for all of them.

They had one of those portable record players and one day they hollered, "Hey, Cuz!" I was in a five-flight walk-up, up on the top floor. I looked out the window, and they said, "Come on down, man. Bring your guitar." I said, "Okay. I'll be down there." I got down there and they had my records on the thing, playing, and they had some of my records on the juke box inside the place, playing, and they said, "Man, we want us some wine." They had a liquor store right across the street, next door to this barroom, and I said, "You want some wine?" I gave them a ten-dollar bill and said, "Look man. Go over there and get y'all a whole gallon of wine. Get any kind you want."

They got the wine, and all of them passed the jug around. No glass. Just drinking out of the jug. Glug glug glug glug glug. I didn't drink wine—I wasn't drinking anything but scotch—but I drank it *then*. When it got to me, I said, "Give me that jug, man," and I drank wine along with them. I didn't want them to think that I thought I was more than them.

The cat that was head of the gang was running a newsstand. He was a little short cat, but he was built like Atlas. He was the boss. Anything he said, they did. Those cats had to walk like they were walking on eggs, afraid to break them. He was as bad as an ape with a walking stick. He used to carry a *machete*. In New York, they didn't allow you to carry any guns, but he had one of those machetes.

He got them all together and said, "Now let me tell y'all one thing. You see this man, Cousin Joe? I don't care what time of night he come home, and I don't care how drunk he is, if I find out any one of y'all messed with him, I'm gonna cut your throat. And I mean that, cause he's a real man. Now, you ain't never been treated like that by nobody. Not in New York. But he's a real man and I want ya'll to see that nobody bothers him." That was always my object, all the time. When I was in Cincinnati and everyplace, I'd look for the baddest cats in town. When you get in with the baddest cats in town, ain't nobody going to mess with you. So, that's the way I got along in New York with no trouble.

Now, when Mary's old man came back, she thought she was

going to have trouble with him. She peeked out my window, peeked downstairs, and saw him standing down there. There was no back way out of this building, so she couldn't get back to where she'd been staying with him. But the little fellow that ran the newsstand downstairs—that bad cat that carried a machete—*he* told him, "Now, don't you mess with Cousin Joe. If it's anything, you take care of it with your old lady, cause he ain't forced her to go upstairs. She went on her own free will. You wasn't here, so she had to find *somebody* to entertain her." So, he finally realized that she was in love with *me*. After that, when I'd come downstairs, me and him'd shake hands and have a drink. But, she left him and stayed with *me*.

One night, she went out and didn't come back till about four o'clock in the morning. I was home. It was my night off. I was working at the Downbeat Club downtown, then. Anyway, when she came in, she looked at me and said, "You ain't gonna beat me?"

"Beat you for *what?*"

"For stayin out so late."

I said, "Look, girl, lemme tell you something. You got the wrong man, honey. I'm no fighting man. And then again, I don't have no business to beat you. You're already grown!"

She just had that complex that if she had a man, and she did something wrong, he's supposed to beat her up. I guess that's what that other cat was doing. Beating her up. Taking her money. But I got her money more easily than *that*—by being nice to her. She'd cash her check and give me all the money and then ask *me* to give *her* anything I wanted. Or, she'd say, "Honey, when I get paid can I buy me a pair of stockings?" and I'd say, "Sure! Buy what you want!"

I took her down on Fifty-second Street. She had never been downtown in her life! I met Teddy Reig and he had two royalty checks for me. One for four hundred and something and one for three hundred and something. I took them and just signed the back of the three-hundred-something one and cashed it in. Then I took her down to the Twenty One Club. Billie Holiday was singing in there. I knew the man because the man knew me from when I was singing in Hot Lips Page's place at the Onyx Club. Hot Lips Page had had a week's engagement somewhere and he had told the man, "The only man you put in my place is Cousin Joe." Me and Hot Lips Page were the only two blues singers on Fifty-second Street. All the rest were playing that modern jazz and that Dixieland jazz.

Stuff Smith was at the Onyx Club with Hot Lips Page. Dizzy Gillespie and Charlie Parker were at the Three Deuces. Bud Powell was at the Spotlight with Sid Catlett. Bud Powell was the greatest modern jazz piano player the world has ever known. I took Mary down on Broadway and I took her over to Beefsteak Charlie's to meet the musicians, and then we went back home.

Then I met a cousin of mine who had an apartment somewhere around New York. I took her to see him and he took us to the Yankee Stadium to a baseball game. She had never seen *that* in her life. She had just stayed in Harlem, where she was raised. She had never been on Broadway all the years she stayed there. It was very expensive down there. Most of those cats stayed in Harlem because they couldn't afford to be downtown. Just like a lot of people can't afford to go to Bourbon Street, now.

I stayed in New York till 1948. Billie Holiday's the one that made it possible for me to stay as long as I did. She's the cause that I had the job at the Downbeat, because I did a favor for Billie, and for Joe Guy, who was her husband at that time. They say Billie was a prostitute, but I didn't believe it, and that she was a junker. Well I knew *that*, because she came to my room when she didn't have any place to stay. She used to have a big boxer dog, and they wouldn't let her go in the hotels with that dog. Then, they wouldn't give her a work-permit in New York. She had to work in Philadelphia on account of that junk. They barred her from working in New York altogether.

But before that, she came to my room about nine o'clock in the morning.

"Hey, Cuz! Hey, Cuz! I was on a third-floor walk-up, then. I had moved from the back of the building to a bigger room in the front and I could look out my window—look down and see her standing down there. She's calling, "Hey, Cuz!" I was asleep and it was like, in my sleep, I heard somebody calling me.

So, I got up and I looked out the window, and I said, "Woman, where you going this time of morning? We just got off work at four o'clock in the *morning!*"

She said, "Cuz, throw your key down."

So I threw my key down for her to open the door to get up the steps. When she got up the steps she had that boxer with her and had that big ranch mink coat all the way down to the ground. And she walked in.

I said, "What's the matter? What happened?"

"I ain't got no place to stay." Can you imagine—woman making seventeen hundred and fifty dollars a *week* and doesn't have any place to *stay*! Can you imagine *that*?

She had all this *stuff* in her pocketbook. And I tell you the truth, that's the saddest thing in the world to see a person in that position when they need a fix. Oh, Lord! Boy, it's a crime! I swear. I could've cried when I saw that woman doing what she did.

I said, "Look, Billie, lemme tell you something. I'm gonna let you do it *this* time, but don't come back no more. You ain't got no place to stay, but I don't fool with that stuff, and if they catch you in here with me they're goin to take me, too, and I'll have to go through a whole lot of blood tests and examinations and all that, to prove that I don't fool with that stuff. You're gonna fix it for *me* not to have a place to stay."

She said, "Alright, Cuz." And she took off her ranch mink and she made her old boxer sit down and she sat down. Then she got out of her gloves; she had those gloves on with no hands on them, to keep people from seeing those needle marks. She couldn't find any more places on her arms, so she looked for the veins in between her fingers. Then, she struck a match and cooked that stuff in a Coca-Cola top and put it in a syringe, and when she found the vein, I saw the blood coming back up into the needle and I said, "Oh, my God!" There she was, shaking . . . and she put all that stuff in there. Then she pulled the needle out, took a piece of cotton, wiped it off, and in about ten minutes she was just as straight as an arrow.

After she got straight she said, "Cuz?"

"What?"

"You got any pajamas?"

"Yeah! I got pajamas. But the pants ain't gonna fit you, cause your ass is too wide."

"Well, I'll take the shirt." And she took off *everything*—her drawers and slip and everything—and put the shirt on.

Then, she said she was hungry, so I went down to the restaurant. I bought a Porterhouse steak for the dog and I bought two chicken dinners for me and her. And we sat down and ate. She ate just like she was—in that pajama shirt and everything. I had a little table and I had one of those little apartment electric stoves.

Then I said, "Well, Billie, I'm gonna be frank with you. If you want to sleep here, you're gonna have to get in this bed with me, cause I ain't sleeping on the floor."

She said, "Well, that's alright. I'll get in the bed with you."

"All right," I said, "but you ain't got nothing to worry about, honey, cause I don't like you like *that* in the first place. You're alright with me. You're my friend, babe." I'm not a man to take advantage—and I could have. Since I did her that favor, she would've let me, I know. But I didn't want to force myself up on her. Billie was a beautiful woman, but when you see all those needle marks on her body, you get disgusted. I took the Sunday paper and I put it across *there* on her and turned my back and went to sleep. She slept all day, and she slept like a log.

That night, I put on one of my suits—I had a wardrobe trunk full of suits, about ten or twelve suits. Danny said I was the sharpest cat around New York at that time. I put on a suit and said, "Now, look, Billie. You're the star. You come when you get ready, but I've got to be at the Downbeat for ten o'clock. One thing I want to tell you: please lock my door when you leave. Lock my door and bring my key with you to the club."

"Okay, Cuz," she said, "and thank you. You hear? I never will forget you for that."

So, when she got down there she called me over and she told Tony, the owner of the joint, at the cash register, "Tony, you see this man? Anything you can do for him, you do it, cause he's a real man. He might be little, but he's all man cause he proved it. Do you know, I slept in this man's bed, naked as I come in the world, with just his pajama shirt on, and he never even put his hands on me! He's a real man. He could've took advantage of me, but he's the kind of man you don't see every day." He said, "Well, sure, Billie, I'll do anything I can." And I could go *anywhere* and come right back in there and go to work. That's right.

She never forgot me because she wrote in her book, *Lady Sings the Blues*, "There's a little blues singer living down in New Orleans named Cousin Joe. He's the only man that treated me like a lady."

That's why I say that Billie made it possible for me to stay in New York as long as I did. I could always be working because of her.

After that, here came Joe Guy, Billie's husband. He wanted to borrow some money from me. He needed a favor, he said, till his old lady came to the club. I told him, "Man, I ain't got no money." I had money but I wouldn't give him any. You trust a junker with money and you ain't never going to get it back, so I said, "No, man. I ain't got no money," and I stayed close to the door of my room, where I had my knives, because sometimes when junkers want money for that stuff, they'll try to take it from you. He was sweating big drops of sweat, but I said, "No, man. I'm fixing to go out anyway and I ain't got no money." So he left. I don't know where he went.

I was downtown one morning with a pocket full of money. I had just made a recording date. I was making a hundred dollars a side, then, and I was getting a hundred-dollar advance against the royalties on the four tunes, and I had about nine hundred dollars in my pocket. That's when one of the musicians—I won't call his name—was looking for somebody to buy some coke and he had no money. The boss, Tony wouldn't let him have any money. He was playing with Tiny Grimes anad Tiny Grimes wouldn't let him have any money. Nobody would let him have any money.

So, when I walked in, he said, "Say, Cuz."

"What?"

"Man, you got any money?"

"Like what?"

"Man, I need fifteen cents. The man gonna be round here, and I've got to get me some stuff, but I ain't got no money, you understand?"

I said, "Come on with me," and we went downstairs in the men's room. You're not going to pull out any money in a club like that, because you wouldn't have a *head* when you got outside. So, we got downstairs and I went in my pocket. I had to take two of my hands to get that money out of my pocket.

He said, "Why, you blues-singing son-of-a-bitch! Where'd you get all that money?"

I said, "Well, my boy, every man must have a girl, and I got one! Now, what d'you need?"

"I just need fifteen cents."

So I gave him three fives and I put my money back in my pocket and went upstairs.

He never forgot me for that. The first time he got a gig in Philadelphia, he told the man, "I got one of the greatest blues singers in the world." The man said, "Bring him." So, he called me up.

I didn't have a phone at my place but the landlady—she didn't own the building but she was the maintenance woman and collected the rent—she called me to the phone. So, I went to the phone and he said, "Hey, Cuz. This is T——."

"What's up?"

"Look, man. Come by my house." He was living in Central Park. "Come by my house."

"Where you live, man?"

"Hotel So-and-So at Central Park"

"Okay. What time you want me to be there?"

Meet me after six o'clock, because we've got to go to Philadelphia."

"What!"

"Well, I want you to sing two blues with me and I'm gonna give you a hundred dollars."

"Great!"

I went to Philadelphia with him and just did two blues. He gave me a hundred dollars, *cash*, in my *hand*. That's because I did that favor for him.

Tyree Glenn borrowed some money from me, too. The musicians got paid through the union when they'd record, but I got paid the same *day*. All I'd do was go up to Sam Goody's office and one cashier was writing out a check. The other one would cash it right there, and I'd have cash money in my pocket. Tyree Glenn died and didn't pay me my money.

Bob Dorsey owed me money, too. He was playing tenor with Cab Calloway. When he was playing with Cab he was living on Lexington Avenue. Down there on the East Side where all the high-class people live. But when Cab fired him, he wound up on Amsterdam Avenue. The last time I saw Bob Dorsey he was sitting in the gutter with a pint bottle of wine. I swear it was a shame to see the condition that man was in, as high on the hog as he was when he was with Cab. But you never get bigger than the man who pays you. Some people think that because they're stars and superstars and can play, that it's alright. But you still have to play by the rules of the man that pays you.

I *gave* Danny Barker money, because Danny took care of *me* when I first went there. Danny could get anything I *had*. Danny told me he was sending Sylvie, his daughter, up in the mountains on a vacation. I said, "How much you need?"

"Well, lend me twenty-five dollars."

Lend you! What! Man, you must be losing your mind. Here, you need fifty or a hundred?"

"No, all I need is twenty-five dollars."

"Well, you *take* that. Don't tell me about lending me anything.

As nice as you've been to me, man. You must be kidding."

I got to be pretty good. Shucks! I used to go out and have three or four hundred dollars in my pocket. I'd take Mary to the Turf Club. That's where the waiter with the frocktail tuxedo's waiting to meet you at the door, take your hat and coat and hang it up, and then escort you to a table. And there are four waiters come to the table at one time. One comes with the bread, one comes with the water, one comes with the menu, and the other one comes with the cocktails. Big time! That Turf Club was something else!

That's where I first met Erroll Garner. Great piano player. Supposed not to know how to read, but he was the greatest piano player in the world. And a writer. He wrote one of the greatest songs of the day and they'll be playing it a hundred years from today— "Misty." He first came from Dillard University—in New Orleans—and he went up to New York and sat down at the piano and played for Billie Holiday and that *got* it. I mean, he's so great, it's something else! I don't know if he's *from* New Orleans, but I know he went to school at Dillard. It's a funny thing. He went to school at Dillard and didn't know how to *read*. Look like they should have taught music there. But what happened was, he just went up to New York and that style of playing he had—it upset those people. Nobody was playing like *that*! With those block chords like that. Crossing the hands and all that kind of jive. Hoo! He was something else. Then, when he played with the New York Philharmonic Orchestra, those fellows were dumbfounded. How could he play that music they had there by *ear* and *perfect*? Never made a mistake. They say they thought it was phenomenal.

I met Mantan Moreland there, too. Mantan Moreland was a comedian in Hollywood. A little, short, dark fellow. Used to play with a little white fellow. He used to make big eyes and everything. He'd see those little fellows with white sheets over their heads, like ghosts and things like that—he would see them and break off and run. He had just bought a brand new car for his wife. His wife was coming from California and he said, "Well, I wanna surprise her when she come here." He had the keys in his hand. She was supposed to meet him. He was working at the Zanzibar. Upstairs. The Zanzibar was owned by the Turf Club. Well, he was working upstairs at the Zanzibar with Cab or Duke—either one of them. Cab and Duke had a contract with the Zanzibar that each one of them played a certain time every year in that place for so many years—

ten or twenty. They had a signed contract and wherever else they were, they had to be there at the Zanzibar for that certain time.

Mantan Moreland took me and Mary for a ride up to the Apollo Theatre to see Rochester. Rochester was at the Apollo. And Rochester—the saddest thing you want to hear—Rochester had a partner with *him* and they were at the Sebastian Cotton Club in California together. Rochester was the comedian and this fellow, Wilson, I think his name was, was the straight man, and the man that Jack Benny came to look for was Wilson. But Wilson was full of wine somewhere and couldn't be found. Rochester was on, so he got Rochester and asked him could he read those lines. Rochester said, "Yassir, Mr. Benny," and that's *just* what he wanted. Boy! He got rich. Wilson was in the audience, at the Apollo, and Rochester called him up on the stage and announced him and said, "This is the man that's the cause of where I'm at today. If he'd've been home at the time, I wouldn't have *been* here. He'd've been here. I wouldn't've been with Jack Benny. He'd've been with Jack Benny."

So that's the people I met around there. I met Milt Hinton. Oh, boy! One of the greatest bass players I ever heard in *my life*. Me and Milt Hinton were tight. I saw him up at the Copper Rail. They had a place across the street from the Metropole, on Forty-seventh, called the Copper Rail. That's where they'd sell *all* New Orleans Creole food. Yeah! Corn bread and cabbage, and pig tails and turnip greens, and red beans and rice and ham hocks, and all that stuff. It was a southern woman that was the cook in that place. She'd cook all that kind of jive, and that's where me and Danny used to go eat at when we'd be downtown. Or we'd be at Jack Dempsey's. I'd get off, and we'd go in Jack Dempsey's and eat in the mornings.

I met Pearl Bailey. Sister Rosetta Tharpe was supposed to work that night with Cab, and Sister Rosetta Tharpe had a *virus* so Cab didn't have anybody in that spot. So, Bill Bailey, one of the best dancers since Bojangles, Pearl's brother—he was on that junk but he could *dance*. Oh, my God! Bill Robinson says he's the only man in the world could take his place. He introduced Bill Bailey to Cab while he went to California to make a picture with Shirley Temple and Bill Bailey stayed with Cab. So Bill Bailey told Cab, "Why don't you go down in the Cafe Society and get my *sister*, Pearl? You ain't got nobody in the spot." So Cab sent Bill down there, and Bill went down there and got his sister and she brought her arrangements with her for the couple of tunes she was doing. They weren't that much. Cab's band ran over the things, boogity boog boo boo boog, and by showtime they had it down pat. And then, when she started to working those *hands*, and talking with Cab, saying, "Well, Honey," and "so-and-so." Oh! She upset those people. I'm telling you! First night. She upset them, so Cab *kept* her. See, Sister Rosetta Tharpe would've been where Pearl Bailey is *now*, if she'd've *been* there at the *time*.

I probably would've been with Cab, *too*, but the night when Cab was looking for *me* to take Rosetta's place, he sent Danny all over Harlem looking for me. Rosetta couldn't show up, so Cab said, "Well, Danny. How about your boy, Cousin Joe?"

Danny said, "Well, man, I don't know where to find him. He *should* be on Fifty-second Street. I told him to stay on that street."

"Well, we'll play till you come back. Go till you find him."

Where do you think I was? Over in Brooklyn. Playing for those women. My daddy taking me by all those women's houses that had a piano. I'm sitting there playing and I could have been *on* the *stage* at the *Zanzibar* on *Broadway*. Boy! I'd like to kick my own self. Boy!

Danny was *so mad* with me! He didn't want to *speak* to me for two days. He said, "Man! Now, *that* was your break, my boy. But you have to *be* there when it comes."

But I was tired. I hadn't seen my mother and sister in five years. So I decided to go back to New Orleans. When I got ready to leave, I told Mary, "Well, honey, I'm goin home. But I tell you what I'm gonna do. You dress yourself and come with me." I took her down on Fifth Avenue and I dressed her up. Bought her everything, from shoes on up. Because she was so nice to me. She never did take any money from me. Just *gave* me all the money. So I said, it's time for me to spend something for her and I spent a hundred and fifty dollars on her. I bought her a coat like she'd never seen before—a coat with a hood that came over. Beautiful. Pure cashmere. Well, I had a pocket full of money. I had bought my ticket already but I told her, "I'm gonna send for you." And I did.

15

You Ain't So
Such a Much

I wouldn't give a blind sow an acorn,
I wouldn't give a crippled crab a crutch,
Since I found out, baby,
You ain't so such-a-much . . .

LEFT New York in 1948, but I didn't go directly to New Orleans. First I went to Chicago to work with Adam Lambert at the Silhouette Club. That job fell through, so I got a job with Phamous Lambert at Club 21 on the West Side of Chicago. I played there for nine weeks and *then* I left for New Orleans.

I came back home to Eva. Now, how Eva found out about Mary was when Eva started unpacking my trunk. She found a pair of Mary's drawers in my luggage and she told me, "I know you don't wear these kind of drawers!" We didn't get in any argument or anything like that. She didn't fuss because she understood that I had to have a woman, being five years in New York. I just thought about Mary, and how good she was to me. I had promised her I would send for her so I looked for a room for Mary to live in and then I sent for her so she could be my mistress and I could keep Eva, too. But Eva and I broke up anyway.

I found a room on Roman Street between St. Philip and Ursulines with a friend of mine. His name was Lawrence Sigue but we all called him Double. He was a waiter at Pat O'Brien's, but I knew him from years ago, during the red light district days. He used to be one of the oustanding pimps in the district in those days, and he saved the money that he got from the whores. He bought a couple of houses, and he's the first black man I'd seen in the district that drove a Cadillac. He used to wear hundred-dollar suits and English derbies; he was an immaculate dresser, with diamonds galore. I rented a room at his house on Roman street for ten dollars a week.

Then I went to work, back at the Famous Door. Hyp had a Mexican band there, and he told me, "Well, I don't know how it's gonna work, Joe, but I tell you what. How many pieces you got?"

"Three."

"Well, you bring em."

So, I brought Alton Purnell on piano and his brother, Theodore Purnell, on sax, and I was playing guitar. This Mexican band was playing and singing in their language and people couldn't understand what they were singing. When *I'd* come on, we would rock the house, then when I'd come *off, they'd* come back on and everybody'd leave. So, Hyp hired Sharkey Bonano and his Dixieland Band and he kept *me* to play—half hour on and half hour off—with Sharkey. That's how I became the first *black* man to play opposite a *white* band on the same bandstand on Bourbon Street. Hyp Guinle's the one who started that.

After that, when Sharkey left, here came the Dukes of Dixieland. They were kids. Their mother and father used to have to chaperone them. They'd come there when they'd start and take them home that night. The Dukes of Dixieland. Frankie and Freddie Assunto were their names. When they came, they found me there.

When Hyp went to remodel the place we had a month off, so I went to work at the Robin Hood. A colored place. Me and my band. They had a drummer there named Alonzo Stewart. He still works at Preservation Hall, right now. I'm the first one to bring him onto Bourbon Street, because when Hyp got everything fixed up at the Famous Door he came to the Robin Hood to get me. When he heard Alonzo playing and singing with me he said, "Bring that drummer with you when you come."

I said, "Okay," and I brought Alonzo with me. We worked there for thirteen years—for Hyp Guinle at the Famous Door.

During that time, while I was in New Orleans, I got a card from New York with some musicians' names on it. It was for a concert in Town Hall and my name was on it! They were looking for me *there*, but I was home!

Eventually, I got a car. This man gave me a Studebaker—paid the down payment on it and gave it to me—because I was the cause of him marrying a girl. He owned an automobile place on Canal Street and he met this girl from Nebraska. She came to New Orleans on a vacation. She liked *me*, so he used to bring her to the Famous Door every night. A lot of musicians get the wrong conception. They think a woman likes them for sexual reasons when she pays them and they take it the wrong way. She liked my *entertaining*. She liked me, but in her *way*.

He told me, "Joe, I wanna marry her. She likes you, and she

begs me to bring her here to listen to you every night. If you talk to her and I can marry her, I'll give you an automobile."

"What am I gonna do with it? I can't drive a *wagon*. I ain't never drove a car in my *life*."

"That's alright. You can learn."

They got married and they had the reception at the Famous Door. Champagne was flowing like buttermilk. The next morning he called me up and asked if I had twenty-five dollars.

"Yeah! For what?"

"Come get your car!"

You know, when fellows have been drinking you don't pay attention to what a lot of them *say* they're going to do, so I said, "Well, I'll be damned. He did what he said he was going to do."

So, I told Double. I said, "Double."

"What?"

"Come with me and get my car."

"Why I gotta come with you to get your car?"

"Cause I don't know how to drive."

"You mean to tell me you buy a car and don't know how to drive?"

"I didn't buy it. Man gave it to me."

So he came with me and he drove it home for me. A brand new 1950 Studebaker Champion. Shaped like a bullet. Like an airplane in the front.

After a while, I sent for Mary. I bought a railroad ticket and I sent it to Mary for her to come to New Orleans. She came, and I met her at the railroad station and took her to the room I rented for her. Then we started living together, but you know, it wasn't very long that she turned out *bad*.

I took her around to meet different people. I took her to a certain lady—I won't call her name—who had a house of ill repute; I wouldn't call it a house of prostitution. I brought Mary over there and introduced her.

By her being so young and inexperienced, I explained before I took her anywhere, "Now, listen, let me tell you something, they've got cats in this town that's slick as goose grease and they'll move in on you before you know it. The best thing for you to do is to watch out for yourself because while I'm working at night, that's when they will try to talk holes in your clothes and they will try to get you to go to bed with them."

But in spite of me explaining all that she turned right around and did the thing I told her *not* to do. And the worst part about it, a friend of mine—I'm not going to call his name either, but he was a very well known cat around there—*he* told me. He called me on the side and said, "Smilin, I ain't got nothing to do with this here, but I'm gonna tell you one thing. You watch that woman you got because every night, when you're gone to work, there's some cat sleeping there with her and he leaves out, just before time for you to get off."

I didn't pay any attention to him, until one time, I got home before she did. When I found out she wasn't in the room, I sat on the step to wait. I *knew* she had to come *home*. The mistake she made was that she didn't get back before I got off. Whoever had her out kept her out overtime. When she got home—when she turned the corner and saw me—she started trembling. That was just too much for me to take. Now, I *had* to believe what the man told me.

That's the time I lost my temper. I knocked her down in the oyster shells out there in front of the house. I just beat her up. I'm not in the habit of doing that. I wouldn't do it in New York City because I figured I was in New York and she was green. She didn't know, then. She had just thought that if she did something wrong she had to get chastized for it. But this time, I couldn't take it any more. I figured I had to do *something* so I took it out on her *that* time.

So, she left. And the next time I saw her, she was at the Savoy Restaurant, on Conti and Burgundy. Milton Jones owned the Savoy. That's where most all of the black entertainers and waiters and waitresses used to hang out when they'd get off in the mornings. Milton Jones made so much money off us!

Mary was sitting at the bar. I don't know if she was waiting for me or what, but this young fellow walked in and knocked her off the stool. He was the same one that had been coming to see her all the time that I was working. I don't know if she expected me to help her, but I said I had nothing to do with that because she brought that on herself. Anyway, he took her out of there.

Then, while I was sitting there, I met another girl. She was sitting at the bar. Her name was Elsie. She was big, like an Amazon. She wasn't fat. She was just big. Had big bones and everything. Tall. I don't know, I must have had some magic somewhere, because she just came over and started to introduce herself and talk to me. I'm sitting on a stool, like a damn fool. Drinking. She came and sat by me and we started talking and everything and she fell for me like a ton of bricks. She was eighteen or nineteen or something like that. Could have had all those *young* boys. But she moved in on *me*.

I had my car outside, and when I said I was leaving, she said, "I'm coming with *you*."

I said, "I'm going to my *house!*"

"That's alright. I'm coming with you at your *house.*"

So, I brought her to my pad, and we laid out. And she wouldn't move *out!* She went uptown by her mother's and got her clothes and came and brought them back there to my room and moved on in.

We stayed together for quite a while. She was tough. She used to be a prostitute for another fellow that used to be a pimp on Rampart Street but she started hustling for me. She and I happened to see him, one time, at the Savoy, but we didn't have any words. He must've figured I was just another man she picked up. But when he found out she was staying with me, then anywhere he'd see her he would threaten her.

We stayed together for a good while. She'd give me money and everything. I used to drive her down to Buras—to the fishermen down there—about sixty-eight miles from New Orleans, down around Empire and Grand Isle. Down that way. She used to hustle the fishermen.

I'd go in the pool room and play pool. I'd give the man five dollars just to play around on the pool table—waiting till she'd get through the work she was doing and get back with the money. She'd come back with a whole *stack* of money. She even told the man that I was her cousin and she made him pay her extra money to give me for my gasoline for driving her down there and back. She'd be carrying the money down in her bosom and she must've worn about a size forty-hour. She had titties looked like two eggplants, but they were shaped like navel oranges. She was big!

When we'd get back at night we'd go to Milton Jones's and that's when she'd come out of her bosom with all that money and give it to *me*. For Easter she bought me a whole new outfit—suit, shoes, socks, shirt, tie—all new stuff.

Then, we had a humbug on Orleans Street. She and I got in an argument. All of my friends were standing out there in front of the barroom and me and her were arguing. She hit me and knocked me down in front of all my friends. I fell on one knee and that knee I fell on, it put a hole in my pants. Of course, good, expensive, clothes, when they snag, they snag in an "L" shape. When you damage them in any kind of way, they strip down one way and across the other.

They started laughing, and she told them, "What the hell you all laughin about? *I* bought it for him and I'll buy him some *more*." Then she got in the car—*knew* she didn't know how to drive—and she tried to back up between two other cars and she didn't make it.

She was going with some white fellow that owned an automobile repair shop on Ursulines and Claiborne. I know that because when he used to call up at the house and she'd answer the phone, she'd let me listen to what he was saying. I'd be in the bed with her at the time and he'd be making a date with her. Anyway, by her going with him, she got the car fixed for nothing, so that turned out all right.

But what made me mad with *her*—our first major humbug we had—was when I was driving up Claiborne at twelve o'clock in the daytime, when the traffic was heavy. We were going to the pad on Ursulines Street. She was fussing with me and she grabbed the steering wheel.

I said, "What's the matter with you, woman? You losing your mind? You trying to wreck us? Trying to get us killed?"

It was near Ursulines so I just turned left on Ursulines and I stopped the car and I hit her one punch—boom—in the eye. She jumped out of the car and she outran a spotted-assed ape. She ran into the house.

When I got to the house I went to open the screen door, and it's a good thing I wasn't close to the screen because she had a butcher knife and she shoved that butcher knife halfway through that screen trying to get to me. She thought she was going to get me when I was coming in but the door swung to the outside and she missed me. I didn't say anything. She pulled it out and then I opened the door and went inside—my liquor told me to go inside. Then she and I started arguing, and I started squaring off like a prizefighter. I knew I had to treat her like a man because she was drunk and she was stronger than me. So, I threw my left hand at her and tried to block her arm and the butcher knife whacked me right across my left hand.

The blood was running but I got a turkish towel on it and I drove to Alonzo Stewart's house—my drummer—and showed Alonzo. I could wring the towel out with the blood. Alonzo drove me to the hospital and I had nine stitches put in it. The doctor asked me how did I cut my hand like that and I told him that I slipped and fell down on a broken bottle and cut my hand.

I went back home and we made up but it went on like that till I said, "Well, that's it. It's time for me to either put this woman out or leave out myself, because she might hurt me severely if I stayed with her."

16   Driving My Engine
to the Roundhouse

I'm driving my engine to the roundhouse,
I've been switching boxcars all night long.
I'm slightly inebriated,
And I'm trying to make it home . . .

WHILE I was working at the Famous Door, during intermission I used to go to the Savoy. Milton Jones's place. The Famous Door was on Conti and Bourbon and the Savoy was on Conti and Burgundy. Almost all of the black entertainers and waiters and waitresses used to go there after hours, so that's where I used to go. Every intermission. Half an hour.

That's where I met *Irene*. Irene was living across the street. There was a lady who had a rooming house across the street from the Savoy. Her name was Johnnie Mae, and Irene was renting a room from her. They had a porch upstairs and Irene and Johnnie Mae used to sit up there on the porch and look down at all of us. All of the musicians down there. Going in and out, clowning and going on, and drinking.

Irene told Johnnie Mae that she would like to meet me, so Johnnie May called down there for me to come up to her apartment. "Joe," she said, "Come up here. I want to tell you something." I said, "Okay," and I went upstairs. When I got up there, there was Irene, sitting on the porch. She was out of sight! She was a good-looking woman. Johnnie Mae introduced me to her. She said, "This lady's been wanting to meet you." So, we sat on the porch and we talked and everything, and I told her that I was glad to have met her. "But," I said, "I gotta go back now. But when I get off, if you'll be up when I get off, we can talk some more." She said, "Okay." So when I got off I went upstairs and we talked again, and I told her that I would like to come back and see her sometime. She told me, come back anytime.

I waited about a week. I was off one night and I asked her, would she like to go *out* with me? I told her that I was off Sunday and we

could go around to clubs and things Sunday night. She said "Yeah."
So we went out. I dressed and I picked her up. I took her to the
colored clubs around town. At that time they had little clubs all
over the city, with little bands and little floor shows and things like
that and I took her to these places. A lot of times, the people knew
me from Bourbon Street and would want me to *do* something, so
I'd get up there and play the piano and sing a few numbers and get a
big hand. Then we'd sit down and drink. Well, when we left that
night, instead of me going to *Irene's* house, Irene came to *my* pad.
And that's where we slept that night. We got together. We laid out,
and the next day I drove her to work. She used to work at the Hotel
De Soto, on St. Charles, as a maid. Cleaning up and fixing beds for
the next people to come in.

I kept going to see her on Conti Street. One day, Elsie passed
around there, just for kicks, and she saw my car parked out there.
She told me, "I saw your car parked out there. Now you moved!"
and I told her, "You ain't got nothing to do with me right now." She
had met another cat, anyway.

Irene wanted to move out of that neighborhood. She wanted to
leave that one room she had at Johnnie Mae's. So, the lady she was
working with, a lady named Miss Jenny, asked Irene and me if we
wanted to move in with her. Miss Jenny was like a mother to Irene.
They both used to work together, in the same restaurant. Irene
used to be a cook, somewhere in the Vieux Carre—around Char-
ters Street. Miss Jenny was a cook, too. Miss Jenny had moved
onto Liberty and St. Anne. Miss Jenny's husband, Mr. Mahoney,
was a *prince*. He really liked me. He said if *Irene* liked me, and it
was alright with her, it was alright with him. So we stayed there.
I brought my car around there, put her clothes in my car, and we
drove on by Miss Jenny's. Miss Jenny and Mr. Mahoney had the
front room and they let us stay there with them.

Then they got married and between them they bought a house
at 3229 Eagle Street. Miss Jenny asked Irene if she wanted to come
up there and stay with them *there*. There were two sides to the
house and they would have one side and she would let Irene have
the other side. Irene asked me did I want to come *with* them. I said
I would like to, so I came over there. We had to wait until the white
people that had the house found another place to live. The white
people were on the one side of the house and we were on the other.
Irene and I, we stayed on a sofa in the kitchen, in a little hallway—

a back room—by the kitchen, till the house was empty. When those people left, and the house was empty, I took Irene down to Kirschman's Furniture Store and furnished the house from front to back. I bought a bedroom set, a living room set, and a kitchen set. I bought her a stove, I bought her a General Electric Frigidaire and I bought her a Whirlpool washing machine. At that time, in the early fifties, for about six or seven hundred dollars you could buy a whole *room* of furniture. That's how we got to staying together. We stayed like that from that day until today. We stayed there from 1951 until we moved to 2315 Washington Avenue, and Irene is the *last* and the *only* woman I will *ever* live with *anymore*.

While we were still up there—on Eagle Street—Irene's sister had Michael. Her sister came down to us and went to the hospital the day he was born. She had promised the baby to us, whether it was a boy or a girl. Irene had taken me up to her people in New Roads and I met her mother and father and sisters and everyone. They all liked me; until today they all like me. When we got Michael, Irene told me, "Now! You gonna have to *do* or you gonna have to go." I didn't want to lose her, so, I'll tell you the truth, I prayed to God to stop me from gambling.

Even before we lived on Eagle Street I was gambling. I used to drink and raise hell and go to the Fairgrounds—the race track—every day. I wasn't *bad*, but I was just gambling and throwing away my money. One time me and the band had ordered some matching suits for Easter. They were suits that we could wear anytime but they were also the band's uniform. Everybody had their money and had bought their suits and everything. Everybody but me. I had paid on mine but I hadn't got it out. I had gambled all my money.

That Easter Sunday, I told Irene what the case was. She was real, real, real, real good to me. She'd sit down and talk to me and say, "Honey, lemme ask you something. How can you work all the week and then lose all your money in one day?" Well, her husband that married her was still in the army and he was sending her allotment checks. When she'd get paid like that, she'd buy me shirts and socks and things like that. So, she took her money from one of those allotments, and she told me to meet her on Rampart and Canal. The name of the store was the Shobilt; it was between Rampart and University Place. I stood there about a half hour or forty-five minutes. I didn't know if I should call her, because I didn't see anyone coming, but about five minutes after two she was standing on the corner and I saw her. We went in the store and the man showed her the suit and the shoes and everything. He asked her, "How much you wanna put down?" and she said, "I wanna get it *out*." She paid for it, and that's how I had my outfit for that Easter Sunday. The cats in the band thought I didn't have it but I did. I told her, "You will never regret it. Believe me. I'm gonna pay you back somehow."

But I was just a no-good son-of-a-bitch. Later on, when I'd lose my money, I'd go to Mister Mahoney. He became my banker and he would lend me the money to give Irene for the house till I'd get paid. Then I'd pay him back. After we had Michael, Irene couldn't go to work. So, when push came to shove, Irene told Mr. Mahoney, "Don't let Joe have no more money." That broke *that* up. When I didn't have *any*, I had to do *without*. So, I said, "The best thing for me to do is to stop." And I stopped gambling. I stopped going to the race track, and I haven't been to the race track from that day till today. I'm telling you! I stopped gambling and I started bringing my money home. Started taking care of business.

Of course I'd still get drunk, and I'd come home and raise hell and everything, and then when I'd wake up in the morning, I'd raise hell again. One night, when I came home drunk, Irene raised up from under the cover with a *big* old knife and said, "Come on! I been waiting for you. I'm gonna fix you. You just put your hands on me and I'm gonna kill you." Hah!

Finally I *had* to stop drinking. I was beginning to get sick. I was losing weight. I couldn't stand the smell of food. I couldn't sleep for days. One night I fell asleep at the wheel, I was so sick. I was coming home from work in a storming rain, driving a brand new Mustang, and I fell asleep at the wheel, jumped the curb, and knocked down a little iron post. I wasn't drunk; I was *sick!* A policeman was right behind me and saw everything. He came over and helped me. He called more police and a wrecker to take my car to the Ford people. The police knew me from the club on Bourbon Street and while they were writing me a ticket they had the nerve to ask me to sing "Saturday Night Fish Fry!" I said, "I will if you'll tear up that ticket." They charged me with reckless driving and causing damage to city property. I got out of it by paying twenty-seven dollars for the replacement of the post.

The car was only one week old so the Ford people replaced it with a new one—same kind, same lemon yellow color. Irene said she was going to take me to the doctor if she had to drag me so I went and that's when the doctor told me I had cirrhosis of the liver.

I *had* to stop drinking. *Then,* when I'd make money, instead of spending that money on liquor and stuff like that, and on women, I spent that money on Michael. I gave Michael everything he thought he wanted. Up until today.

I've been with Irene, now, about thirty-five years. About nine or ten years ago, she told me, "Now, look, old man, if anything happens to you, I'm going to have to take care of you, and with you going and making those records and all that stuff, if you come into any kind of money, I don't want nobody to have nothing to do with it, so we're going to go get married."

I said, "Okay," and I went and got the certificate. We didn't need any blood tests so we went down in St. Bernard Parish and got the license and everything and we got married. I had to give my mother's name, my father's name, where they were born, and my mother's maiden name. Irene had to do the same thing. Irene Lauralene Cato. Her middle name was Lauralene, or Laurel. She's got the marriage license and all the papers. This was after we moved to Washington Avenue. We went to some preacher's house nearby and the preacher married us right in his house. Then I went to Mrs. Casey. She's a Certified Public Accountant. Mrs. Casey had a son who was a lawyer, too; Casey and Casey, on Cortland Avenue. Cortland and Ulloa, right off Tulane. We went to her. She liked me because one time, when I went to Mexico—a one-week tour, playing on a ship—I came back with a sterling silver ring for her. It had a snap on it and you could open it up. It's the kind of ring they used to have during oriental times; anytime a woman wanted to poison her husband, she'd put the poison in that ring, then she'd take out that ring and put the poison in their coffee or whatever and then, boom! He's gone. Well, I gave that to her. She gave me a paper for Irene to have the power of attorney to cash all my checks. That was in 1974. We didn't have an account together, and I had been touring overseas for about ten years. This way, I could send Irene checks from overseas and she could just go right to the bank and cash them. So, from 1974 until now, Irene has been getting all the money. From that day until today.

Later we opened up a checking account. With four hundred dollars. But I didn't like those checking accounts for the simple reason that every time you have a checking account you have a tendency to write more checks than what you've got in the bank. Me and the manager of the bank were real close, though, and he'd call me up

8 With Irene; photo taken around 1980. (Holly Miller)

I've been with Irene, now, about thirty-five years. . . . Irene is the *last* and the *only* woman I will *ever* live with *anymore*.   (pp. 146, 144)

and *tell* me when I was overdrawn. I'd go give him the money and he'd put it back in the bank and straighten out the account.

Now, sometimes, Irene gives me a hard time but I can't *say* anything because she'll say, "I put up with *you*, you hear? I went through hell with you. Now it's *my* turn." Then I'll say, "Okay, honey. Okay." Sometimes she'll say, "If you mess with me, I'll whip your ass." And I'll say, "Okay. The way I treated you, if it had been another woman I'd be dead right now." She'll say, "Yeah, but I didn't want to kill you. I just wanted to wait till you straightened up your stuff."

Before we got married it was okay, but for *her* sake it was better for us to get lawfully married. But it caused a problem one time when my sister's husband died. I was in Belgium and I called up Irene to talk to her and tell her I was sending her some money. She told me my brother-in-law had died—my sister's husband. I had my sister's phone number with me so I called her—from Belgium— and I told her that I had heard from Irene that Isaiah had died. I said, "Now, anything you need, you go to Irene and she'll give it to you." I didn't tell her to tell Irene that I had said to give it to her. I didn't say that. I said to ask for whatever she *needed*, not whatever she wants.

I know my sister owns property. Her husband left her with two double houses. She has a double house in the back where her daughter lives; she rents one side and her daughter lives on the other side. Then she and her family, they live in the front, on Urquehart between Garden and the next street. That's the same street Fats Domino's house is on, but she lives further down. I used to go down there quite a few times and give them money, but I stopped going down there after that because it seemed my sister's family was jealous. They were jealous of what I did for Irene and Michael. They were under the impression that I should deprive Irene and Michael of everything and give it to *her*, because she was my sister. But it doesn't work like that. Once you marry a woman, that woman comes even before your mother. For a woman, her husband comes before her father. As far as his people go, she comes first. Then, if there's anything left, then it gets scattered amongst them. A wife gets the biggest portion of everything, especially if her husband made it while he was married to her.

Later, when I was working at the Hyatt Regency, my niece made the mistake of coming in. I don't know if she knew I was working there or she just came in, but she was sitting there. With the lights down low it's kind of dark in there, but when I passed by her she said, "Uncle Joe! Don't you remember me?" I said, "Hell, yeah. I know you. You're my sister's daughter. You're supposed to be my niece, but the way you talk to me about my own money, it's like you didn't want to have anything to do with me anymore." I told her that in front of the man she was with there, whoever he was. Then she started crying and talking about, "Yeah, you do more for Michael than you do for us."

So I said, "Let me tell you something. Article number one: Michael is my son. I raised him from a baby and he's going to get everything he wants and my wife's going to get everything *she* wants. Don't you come telling me nothing about Michael." See, her brother isn't *her* blood brother either. They did the same thing that happened with me and Irene and Irene's sister, Mert. Mert is really Michael's mother. He knows that. We told him who his father was, too. But his mother wouldn't let him carry his father's name. He kept the family name—Cato, Michael William Cato—so his father can't come in for anything. When Michael got to be old enough, when he was going to high school, I asked him, and he said, "Daddy, that may be my father but you are my daddy."

Well, that's the whole story of me and Irene from the time we met up until today.

17

Beggin Woman

You know, she's a beggin woman,
And you can see it in her eyes;
She's got a hand full of "Gimme,"
And a mouth full of "Much obliged" . . .

LEFT the Famous Door when my piano player got loaded.
I was looking for him to play one night, and I find out he was with
a woman we both knew—a very good friend of ours named Olga
Manney. She was a big-time broad; traveled all over the country.
When she traveled, a lot of times, she'd bring five or six of her girls
with her to parties and things like that. They'd all have a ball and
she would spend the money. One time, when I was in New York, I
was coming out of Pete Robertson's Restaurant when who did I see
but *her*, walking up to me. I said, "Hello, Olga." She said, "Hey,
Smilin. How you doin, baby?" "Fine," I said, "but goddamn, every
place I go, I see you." She said, "Hell, yes!" She used to dress beau-
tifully. She used to wear those big wide hats that were in style for
women then.

Anyway, I found out that my piano player was with her! In Chicago! So, I played the piano in his place. But Hyp told me, "Now,
look! I'm paying you for *four* pieces. I ain't paying you for *three*."
So, I said, "Okay," and I told my piano player, "I'm gonna have to
let you go, man." He was just like a brother to me, but I said, "I'm
gonna have to give you two weeks' notice and let you go. I'm
gonna give it *all* up and I'm gonna start playing for *me*. I make the
money for you. You don't make no money for me. I'm the star.
I make the money. I split it up with you. And you gonna do me like
that? Well, you ain't my friend when you interfere with my living."

That's when I left them all. I gave Hyp a two weeks' notice and I
left. I went next to the Mardi Gras Lounge and played with Freddie
Kohlman and them. Joe Robichaux was playing piano and I was
playing guitar and we had an act, just me and him. One of the
greatest singers was there, too. Her name was Lizzie Miles. She
was the black Sophie Tucker, and could she sing! She could sing in

English and she could sing in French. She'd spent a long time in France and she was from a French origin, anyway. She was a big, robust woman. But fine! And she would never take a cab home; she'd walk and get the streetcar, that's how tight she was.

When I left *there*, I went across the street to the Absinthe Bar. I played the piano by myself in the Absinthe Bar for six years, till they turned it into an act called, "Nobody Likes a Smart Ass." The man that owned the place had died of a heart attack, and his son had taken over. He's the one who got this act. At that time it didn't cost him anything. The act was charging at the door. They took the door receipts, so the owner didn't have to pay them.

Then, I had to go to Oklahoma City on a job. I had a four-week contract for three hundred dollars a week, and I showed it to the boss and asked him for permission to go. He told me I could go. So I went. A fellow I knew was a great ukelele player and the new boss hired him to play in the front while I was gone. He *promised* me my job when I came back, but when I came back he told me he wasn't going to fire this man. So there I was without a job. When I went to get my unemployment checks they turned me down; that fellow had told them that I had quit the job, so I couldn't get the little money I was going to get.

So I got a job on Chartres Street. I played a couple of nights there and then I went talked to Archibald. He's a great piano player and a great singer. He was the first one to record "Stagger Lee." Archibald wasn't his right name but everybody called him that. Archie was working in a little club named Poodles Patio. They could hold about forty or fifty people in there. The piano was in the bar.

Poodles Patio was connected to a strip joint on the corner that had the same name and belonged to the same man. His name was Johnny. He told me that I could work on Sunday, Archie's off-night. On Archie's off-night I started to draw people in there like I had a magnet, so he came in there and said, "You know something? I've got an idea. I'm gonna put you and Archie to work *together*; y'all fix it the way you want it: half an hour each or an hour each. Any way you want." We said, "Okay," and we worked there like that for four or five years.

I left there when somebody else bought the place. They said they were going to keep us, but when I got there they had brought in their own people from California. It was an all-white jazz band. This man had them all over the country. He had one on Bourbon

When I left *there,* I went across the street to the Absinthe Bar. I played piano by myself in the Absinthe Bar for six years. . . .   (p. 151)

10 In the 1950s. (New Orleans Jazz Museum)

Street called the Last Straws. When they moved down the street they became Your Father's Moustache, but he had this other one at Poodles Patio. Anyway, that's when I lost my job there. Me and Archie *both* lost *that* job.

Now I had no job again. I told Irene, "Well, I'm goin back down on Bourbon Street and see what's happenin. I might be able to get me a gig or something." I went down and I went to the place where Frogman Henry was playing, on Toulouse and Bourbon. I talked to Frog and Frog said, "Well, okay, man. I'll see what I can do." Well, Frog must have talked to the owner of the place—a *big* man on Bourbon Street—because then *he* walked in to the place and said, "How ya doin, Joe?"

"Oh, man," I said, "I ain't doin so hot."

"What's the matter?"

"I ain't workin."

"You ain't workin? You want a job?"

"Sure, man!"

"Well, meet me tomorrow evenin at two o'clock. Be right here on this corner and meet me by the Court of Two Sisters. Tomorrow. And bring your contract, cause I'm not gonna *ask* him to hire you. I'm gonna *tell* him."

I said, "Okay," and I met him at two o'clock that evening. We went in the back and he found Joe Fine; went up in Joe Fine's office. He showed the contract to Joe Fine and said, "Sign that."

Joe Fine said, "What say?"

"Gonna put this man to work. Give him a job. He's a damn good entertainer. In fact he's one of the best on the street and he's worked in all the places on this street. You ain't doin no good with what you got, so there's the contract. Sign it."

Joe Fine had some white women in there, playing violin and piano, and they weren't drawing flies with flypaper, but he said, "But, I ain't never heard of him."

"I don't give a damn if you didn't. *I* heard him and *I* know he's good. Just sign it."

Joe Fine signed it and I said, "When you want me to come to work?" Well, he had to give the people in there a week's notice, so the next week I went *in* there.

· And when Joe Fine *did* hear me, he thought I was the greatest thing that ever happened, and I stayed there *eight years*. Till he closed it down.

"Meet me by the Court of Two Sisters. Tomorrow. And bring your contract." . . . I stayed there *eight years*. Till he closed it down. (p. 154)

While I was there, Henry Hawkins, the trumpet player, came in there. He used to just like to jam with anybody. He liked to play and he could *play*, too. I didn't know him, then. He just walked in with his trumpet and I introduced myself and he told me he was from Boston. I mentioned the place I'd played in Boston with Bechet, the Savoy on Columbus Avenue, and me and him got to be friends. Then he just took out his horn and started playing with me. When Joe Fine came in there, Joe Fine heard him. Joe Fine liked the way we played together, so Joe Fine told me, "Joe, hire him." I told Hawk, "Go down there, get you a contract, and come back and you'll go to work with me." He said, "Great!" and me and him worked there till they closed it down.

Then I got Germaine Bazzle. One of the greatest singers you ever want to *hear*. I got her from Mason's Americana. She was working in the VIP Lounge with June Gardner. Whew! If you heard her sing you'd swear you heard Sarah Vaughn. I got her to come down on Bourbon Street. Then I got one of Mason's *waitresses* a job in the club. She worked there a good while, until one of the bosses tried to hit on her.

I also brought Snookum Russell in there. He played the piano. That's when I was working by myself and I had no help. When I'd take intermission and come back, everybody would be gone. So I got Snookum Russell and he played with me—half hour on, half hour off.

Before that, I had sent out and got Roosevelt Sykes from Gulfport, Mississippi. Roosevelt was in Gulfport and he wasn't doing anything, so he came down here to see what was going on. That's when Joe Fine had gone to San Francisco to get ideas on how to remodel the place. While they were remodeling the club, I got a job around the corner at the Chez When club, next door to the 809 Club on St. Louis. I got the job over there through some people from the Court of Two Sisters, and I worked there till they finished remodeling the Court of Two Sisters. Roosevelt came by the Chez When and talked to me and I let him play a few tunes and everything and I said, "Now, if anything turns up, I'm gonna call you."

Now, there was a cat running the Court of Two Sisters. He was a millionaire. I'm not going to call his name, but he owned ice cream parlors and he owned cleaners and everything all over town. He had a beat-up old piano in there that was all out of tune. Every time the piano tuner would tune it up, I'd play it that night and the next night it would be all out of tune again. So, I told this man, "It ain't no good, man. You just gotta get another piano." Well Joe Fine went and got another old cheap piano from some piano house and it wasn't any good either. Finally, when they remodeled the place, this man came over to see me at the Chez When and told me, "Well, we're ready for you to come back to work, Joe, and I got you a brand new baby grand Yamaha! You don't have to play on that old hunk of junk no more!" I said, "I wanna *thank* you!"

Now, when they reopened, Joe Fine hired a manager. A fellow named Mike Papin. He worked there till the club closed down. Later on he became manager for a disco place named the Horgy Porgy, in the Hyatt Regency. Then they sent and got a white group—a piano player and an accordion player. They would play when I took my break and, *boom*, they'd run all the people out of the place. They were playing all those old show tunes. They didn't play any jazz or blues or anything like what people come down here to listen to. Then I had to work like hell to get the people back in there. We had a loudspeaker outside and people would be passing by and say, "Wait a minute. Let's go in here because I know who that is. That's Smilin Joe in there. I know his voice." And the people would just pile right in. Sometimes eight, ten, twelve at a time. They'd just pile right in there. Joe Fine thought I was the best he'd ever seen.

After about two weeks I told Mike Papin, "Mike, man, I'm working just as hard as I worked before. I get the people in here and then I've got to work like the devil to get them *back* in."

He said, "Yeah. I understand that, Joe. We got to get somebody up here."

"You don't need to get nobody," I said. "Let *me* get somebody."

"Well, *you* go get somebody."

"I already *got* him."

Then I called Roosevelt Sykes and said, "Roosevelt, bring your contract and come on!"

"Boy," he said, "that's the sweetest words I ever heard. Yeah. I'll be there in a flash." and he came down there and he did remarkably well. He sold his albums for five dollars apiece and a dollar to autograph them. One fellow from overseas gave us fifty dollars apiece just for us to sign our name on Roosevelt's album. Mike Papin sold him a house on Louisa Street—two hundred dollars down and about seventy dollars a month. It's paid for, now, and he bought that house working with me. That's why he never forgot me as long as he lived.

There's a whole lot of money people spend on Bourbon Street. I had a friend of mine from Houston who used to come there. He used to give me a whole lot of money. He was a bondsman in Texas but he ran rackets and prostitution. He couldn't even go onto his estate unless he drove around till his old lady gave him a signal with the windowshades—so many times she had to raise them up and pull them down. He came and heard me at the Court of Two Sisters and gave me some money and told me, "I'm giving a party at my house and I want you to come and play." I said, "Okay."

I went and played the job and Roosevelt Sykes played that night by himself. That's what we'd do. Whenever he had to go someplace I'd play all night for him. We wouldn't hire anybody just for that one night. And we were making good money in tips—seventy-five, one hundred, two hundred.

When this fellow sent for me, he sent me a plane ticket and met me at the airport in a Cadillac convertible with the top down. I played for him that night, and who do you think I was playing for? Judges, district attorneys, police department, detectives . . . And his mother was there. He was about forty-six and this girl he had, she was nineteen. He didn't allow her ouside the house. When he had the party she couldn't look up at the men; she had to look down at the floor. I'm telling you what I know! I'm not telling what anybody told me. I was right there looking at it. When he'd bring her to the club, he'd tell her, "You sit there and don't move unless you're going to the ladies' room, and you make sure that's where you're going." Boy, he was tough. This girl loved him, but she was scared of him.

I played for him that night and I had the whole top floor for myself. He told these big wigs, "let me tell you sons-of-bitches something. I pay you sons-of-bitches a million dollars a year for me to run my goddam business and I don't want no shit out of neither one of you."

He had a colored fellow that was running his business for him in the Negro section of Houston. He paid him a hundred thousand dollars a year and built him a twenty-five-thousand-dollar home to run his business.

Lightning Hopkins played for him, too. He liked Lightning Hopkins till Lightning Hopkins got too smart for his britches. This man called me all kinds of nigger words and everything else there in front of the people, but I said to myself, "You can call me what you want, just give me the money. I don't give a damn what you

12 In New Orleans, in 1966. (Martin Ottenheimer)

I'd be playing the guitar. . . . (p. 160)

call me, just don't call me too late to get the money!" But Lighting Hopkins got smart with him and this man told me, "Man, I beat the shit out of that son-of-a-bitch and kicked him off my place." That's where I'd say Lightning Hopkins was ignorant. If he was smart, every time the man gave a party, the man would hire him and he would make that money. No less than five hundred for a night. That's what he paid me. He gave me five hundred and I never would object to him calling me anything. Me and him would get drunk and sit down and start harmonizing. I'd be playing the guitar and me and him would sing together. He used to like that song about when you're white you're right and when you're black, nigger, you got to get back! And I went right along with him to get the money. "Sticks and stones can break your bones, but names ain't gonna never harm you."

When it time was to leave I said, "Get me a cab, Bobby. I don't want to ride with you back to the airport because if people start shooting they're going to kill me too." He laughed and said, "Alright." He got a cab. It came right to the door and got me and brought me to the airport. I already had a round-trip ticket. He just gave me five hundred-dollar bills and said, "I'll see you when I come to your club." I said, "Thank you, Mr. Bobby," and he said, "Where did you get that Mr. Bobby shit? Bobby!" I said, "Okay, Bobby." He said, "You're the only nigger I'd let call me by my name like that, too. But I like you."

I'll tell you why all Southerners like me. It's because you've got to remember where you come from. From the times during slavery times, until today, white man thinks he's always been a black man's superior. I knew where I was and I had sense enough to be cool. The money is what counts, see. I don't care what he called me. Till I get away from him. Then I can call him everything I want to call him.

So, he said, "I'll see you when I get down there." I said, "Okay," and I left and went back to New Orleans.

One night he called me from Las Vegas. They called me to the phone. "You're wanted on the phone, Joe. It's long distance."

"Huh? I wonder who the hell is that?" I went to the phone and I said, "Hello."

"He said, "Hey there, Joe."

"Who is this?"

"Who the hell you think this is?"

"Oh! Bobby."

"You goddam right. I called you to reserve a place for me and my girl at the bar because I just won twenty thousand dollars on the dice game and I'm coming."

I knew that was two or three hundred for me. He came. With her. Nineteen years old. He never came by himself. He brought a woman with him all the time. He had brought one before, but this time he brought the nineteen-year-old. This particular girl was pretty as a picture. Beautiful. Pretty as a picture. Skin like a peach without any fuzz on it. When he came in, he sat down at the table. She sat down, too and he said, "Now don't you move. Me and Joe got a little business to attend to."

He'd never give me any money in front of people. He'd take me in the men's room. He made sure the men's room was empty and then he socked it to me. Three brand-new hundred-dollar bills. And it's a Very Merry Christmas, too. He gave me a gold leaf pin to give to Irene and said, "I don't know if it's diamonds or what, but it's something with stones in it. It's for Irene to put on her dress. Now, I'm gonna know if you gave it to her or not because I know where you live and I know your phone number. I'll call up Irene and find *out* if you gave her that pin. I said, "Man, what am I gonna do with that? It's for women. I can't do nothing with that." I brought it to Irene and told her, "Bobby got this thing for your Christmas present."

After that, I didn't get any more jobs anywhere else besides the Court of Two Sisters. I just stayed there. Six nights a week and one night off. From Monday to Saturday and Sunday night off. Until Mike Papin said, "Well, Joe. I don't know, but I'm gonna tell you. Joe Fine's fixing to close this place." That was in 1972 and that's when I retired. When he closed the place.

18   Chicken a la Blues

Sunday, we had fried chicken,
Monday, chicken wings,
Tuesday, chicken fricassee,
Wednesday, chicken a la king,
Thursday, chicken giblets
Friday, chicken stew,
Saturday, scrambled eggs, and you know that's chicken, too. . . .

SINCE I'VE been going overseas I've met practically all of the musicians that played on records with me and that I used to know in New York. I met Kenny Clarke; he played drums on my records. I met Cleanhead Vinson; I played on a session with him. I played a jazz festival with Clark Terry, I played the Festival by the North Sea with Dizzy Gillespie and Ella Fitzgerald and Nina Simone and Dorothy Donegan and Teddy Wilson and B. B. King and Gatemouth Brown and Wallace Davenport and Teddy Wilson—we were all on the same bill. The next year I played there, B. B. King and Dorothy Donegan and I were all on the same bill on the same night. B. B. King, to my knowledge, is the highest-priced blues singer in the world today, and I was working at Art D'Lugoff's Village Gate in New York when B. B. King made his debut. That was when he started working for Joe Glaser, and when he left there, he didn't stop!

When I first went overseas I went to England and to France. A lot of people say, "You're going to Europe"—I've seen them on talk shows; they say, "We'll pay a fare for you and whoever you want to take with you to London, England." Now, that's a lie. Why do they want to say that's Europe, when Europe and Great Britain are separated by the English Channel and the North Sea? When you go to London, you're not in Europe. You're in Great Britain. You're not in Europe until you cross the North Sea or the English Channel.

I know my geography. But I don't only know my geography, I've *been* there. I've seen it all. I've crossed the English Channel on a Hovercraft. It looks like a spaceship. I've ridden it many times. It can cross the English Channel in thirty minutes. The boat takes four hours across the North Sea, and the North Sea is the most treacherous body of water in the universe, except the Amazon River. When it gets bad, it gets *bad.*

George Wien, the head of the Newport Jazz Festival—in Newport and in New York City and all over the country—he's the first one who sent for me to go overseas. The tour was called the Blues and Gospel Train, in 1964. George Wien sent and got me. He sent me my ticket and sent me three hundred dollars in the bank.

I went to New York first and I met Muddy Waters and them in the airport—it was Idlewild Airport, then. There was me, Muddy Waters, and Otis Spann, the greatest blues player on the piano I ever heard in my life. He could outsing Muddy Waters, too, that's why Muddy didn't ever let him sing. I heard some records of his. And we had Ransom Nolan, Muddy's bass player, and a little fellow named Smith, and Sister Rosetta Tharpe, Brownie McGhee and Sonny Terry, and Blind Reverend Gary Davis.

Where we got our kicks was, when we were on the plane, we had a bottle of gin. At that time they didn't worry about you bringing your own bottle on the plane. Now, you can't bring it on the plane because they sell it on the plane. Anyway, we must have been riding in first class, because I was in the front seat with Reverend Gary Davis. Muddy and them, they were in the back. Reverend Gary Davis would say, "Muddy." Muddy would say, "That's my pastor calling me. Whatcha say, Rev.?" He'd say, "Where's the bottle, man?" He wanted some of that gin. So Muddy would bring him the bottle and he'd take a hooker, I'd take a hooker, and Muddy would take the bottle back.

When we were about two or three hours on the plane, Reverend Gary Davis said, "Cuz?"

I said, "What?"

He said, "Are we over the ocean, now?"

"Well, Rev., that's just where you are at."

"How far down is it?"

"Well, Rev., I'll tell you. The captain says we are thirty-seven thousand feet up. That's the closest you are going to get to heaven alive."

"How *deep* is it?"

"Well, Rev., it's thirty-seven thousand feet from here to the water and after you hit the water then it's thirty-seven thousand feet down again."

Of course the Atlantic Ocean isn't that deep. The Pacific is. In the Mariana Islands, where Piccard's bathyscaphe went down. But by that, those people behind me fell out laughing.

Then I said, "You ain't got to worry about nothing, Rev. You ain't got to worry about a thing. If anything happens, just stick your head between your legs and kiss your ass goodbye!"

I had those people in stitches, I had them laughing so hard. And while they were laughing, I said, "One thing is for sure. If this son-of-a-bitch goes down, we are all going to die laughing!"

When we got over there, to that first gig, man, boy I shook them up right. I was closing the first set, Muddy was closing the second. That was the first time Muddy heard me and when I got through, Muddy said, "Man, let me tell you something. I'm sure glad I ain't got to follow *you!*"

We had an hour between sets and me and Muddy used to play coon can. Muddy thought he was a hell of a coon can player, but I used to beat Muddy all the time. Muddy used to like to drink Johnny Walker Black Label whiskey so I said, "Well, I'll tell you, Muddy, to make it interesting, we won't play for money, but if you don't win, you don't drink." Muddy said, "That's a good deal. Alright." So, me and Muddy were playing cards. After I beat Muddy in so many straight games, Muddy said, "Hey, man, gimme a drink of that whiskey, man. I ain't *never* gonna win one. I want a drink." "Okay," I said, "but look, Muddy, don't fool with me, man, because I'm a *master* in that game." He said, "I see that."

Nobody would buy any whiskey but Muddy and me, but all the other cats wanted to drink. Here came Ransom Nolan and them, reaching for the bottle, and Muddy said, "Put that down, because you ain't spent ne'er a dime. Nobody bought that whiskey but me and Cousin Joe and we are the only ones gonna drink it. Now, if you act nice, and ask us for a drink, we might give you a little taste, but don't come reaching for the bottle." Boy, we had some fun.

We stayed there fourteen days. While we were there, we did a TV show for Granada. On location; not in the studio. Out on location in the *rain!* With a live audience. The television people built stands out there, one on each side, for the people, and they hired people to sit in the stands to look at the show. They had TV cameras so high up you could hardly see them. The show was given at a railroad station that they hadn't used in sixty years. They still had all those old flat carts that the porters used to use to carry suitcases and stuff on, and they had some old suitcases on them, with holes in them. They had two goats, a white one and a black one, tied to a post on one side, and when they heard me doing this number, "Chicken a la Blues," they brought a whole crate of live chickens and set them on the piano! On the baby grand. While I was playing they used invisible strings and opened up that cage and the chickens were running all across the railroad tracks. All that came out on the TV. They hired a train and as many of us as were in the act, that's how many coaches they had. They hired people to fill all those coaches and they took pictures of the train. They had a tunnel that the train went under; it went under and turned around and came back. Best thing you want to see.

Reverend Gary Davis was sitting in the bus saying, "I ain't playing in all that rain and cold. I ain't playing!" They went and got his ass and he came out there in the rain, too. Who the hell did he think he was?

For the finale, Sister Rosetta Tharpe was in the middle, I was on this end, and Muddy was on that end. We were the three stars. We started singing,

He's got the whole world in his hands,
He's got the whole world in his hands . . .

The people were clapping and clapping. In the *rain*.

We worked all that *day*. We knocked off for lunch and they took us all to a restaurant and fed us and we came *back*. We worked till six o'clock that evening. Let me tell you something. Television is a hard job. When they brought us for lunch I thought it was all over with, but they said, "Oh, no. We were just adjusting for sound. Now we're going to do the real *thing*." And we had to do the whole thing over again. From twelve to about six that evening. And we had to play that same night. That was something else.

Sister Rosetta Tharpe's old man used to be one of the Ink Spots. He called George Wien, all the way in America, because he wanted to get *paid* for that TV show or he wasn't going to let Rosetta Tharpe come on. But the TV show was included in the contract. If the TV show ever got shown in the United States, then they would have to pay us, but as long as they showed it over there, that was alright. It's different now, but that was in 1964.

Then we left and we went to France. When I got to Paris, who was in the lobby of my hotel but Hughes Panassie! Him and his wife! They had driven two hundred and fifty *miles* to see me. I had done a spiritual album in New York with a spiritual on it called, "Make Me Strong as Sampson and I'll Serve My God Above." Well, Panassie's old lady invited us to her home for dinner and when I walked in, she said, "Here comes my Sampson." They must have had about twenty-five thousand albums, all over the room, in sections. They had one section just for me, "Cousin Joe," and they played all of them all night. Yeah! Played them all. That was great.

Hughes Panassie wrote the French Dictionary of Jazz and he had me written up in there. I'm on two pages and they have a page of one of the tunes I recorded; they had it in English and they had it interpreted into French, too. They named me one of the four greatest blues singers in the United States in that book.

19 Life's a One-Way Ticket

Life's a one-way ticket, baby,
And there ain't no second time around . . .

CAME BACK after that and I went back to work in the Court of Two Sisters. Then in 1971 I went to France again on a tour with the Chicago Blues Festival. Roosevelt Sykes played in my place while I was gone. That's when I played with Jimmy Dawkins and his Chicago Blues Band. They didn't have a piano player so when we had rehearsal that evening, I sat down and played with them during the rehearsal. Now, what got me was all those guitar players in Chicago all played in E natural and A natural. I couldn't play in those keys, but I'd find a note they were playing and then I'd take it from there, so Jimmy told Jean-Marie Monastier to let me play the piano with them when they played.

There was Gatemouth Brown. He was a show-stopper. That man could play some guitar! He made a video tape where he played with Roy Clark. You know Roy Clark can *play* some but Gatemouth Brown showed him the way to go *home!* That man can play! I got to give him credit. (I ain't got no cash, I've got to give him credit!) He was a show stopper.

We were in Orange, France, playing in a stone mountain. The club must have been a winery because they didn't have any toilet facilities in it. It was cut way far back in there and all you could see was wine barrels on each side. You could go about two or three blocks back up in there and you couldn't see anything; it was pitch dark. You could do anything you wanted back up in there but you couldn't see anything. It was so cold, they had floor heaters all around the stage where I played. This mountain was made out of pure stone; I could look up over my head and see stone. When they said, "Where you want the piano at?" I said, "You see where that door is, right there? That's where I want it. So if anything starts to fall I'll be able to get out of here." He said, "Don't worry, they ain't fell in two thousand years." "But," I said, "there's a first time for everything, man. Don't tell me that." So they put it there and we played.

They had a doctor who came there that night and heard us, and he invited us to dinner at his house. They had a piano in the house and I sat down and played. The doctor's wife liked some tune I played called, "Touch Me." That's what she wanted to hear me play and I played it for her.

The next day, we played somewhere near there and they invited us out to dinner again. They had a swimming pool in the back yard—a great big long swimming pool—but it was wintertime and they weren't using it. All the leaves from the trees had fallen in it. The doctor's wife wanted her picture taken with me by the swimming pool, her daughters wanted their pictures with me by the swimming pool, and they wanted their pictures taken with Jimmy Dawkins, too. When we went to pay the bill at the hotel we were staying in, they said, "The bill has already been paid." The doctor paid our hotel bill, too! We didn't have to pay for anything. That was beautiful. After Orange we played Dijon, France, and who was in the audience? The same doctor and his wife! They had followed us to Dijon. We played Toulouse, Bayonne, Villeneuve, Bordeaux, Paris, and Orange, France. While we were in Toulouse we made a record together.

Big Joe Williams, who played the guitar, was supposed to go to Nancy to finish out his contract, but he told Monastier, "You give me my money and you drive me to the airport because I'm goin home." Monastier said, "Well, you can't go home." But Big Joe had a knife. To tell you the truth, I don't know how that man got through customs with that big knife. It had two blades on the same side and he ran Monastier all over the hotel with this knife. Monastier came up to me and I said, "Don't get behind me, man." Well, Monastier got scared, paid him his money, got somebody to drive Big Joe to the airport.

Now Monastier was in trouble. They had advertised Big Joe coming to Nancy and playing, and Big Joe was on his way home. I was *supposed* to leave that day but I had heard that some Palestinians had held up the airport. See, they have what they call a world radio station—it comes out of London—where they speak English. I heard those people talking about the Palestinians having held up the airport. They said they were going to kill everybody in the airport if they didn't get some food and medicine. They had a plane full of people. But the police dressed up like mechanics and they caught them; there's a place where they put the baggage in the belly of the plane and they came out under there, put those guns on those rascals, and got them all without even firing a shot.

So I said to Monastier, "Well, I don't have to go today, man. I can go *tomorrow.* I tell you what, *I'll* go to Nancy." Monastier said, "Oh, man, that's great! Wait a minute. Let me talk to the man in Nancy." He talked to the man and asked the man, "Well, Big Joe got sick and went home, but I can send you *Cousin* Joe."

He said, "What? You got Cousin Joe with you?"

"Yeah."

"Man, send *him.* That's *better* than what you were supposed to send me. I've got all his records here."

So I went. He met me at the train and brought me to the hotel first. Then he had an apartment he took me to. The outside was like a garage and you would never think that there was an apartment inside there, but once you opened the doors—boy, that was a beautiful place. He had a room that looked like a studio where you could record; he had all kinds of equipment in there. I met his wife and everything and had dinner with him, and while I was having dinner with him he was playing my records. He had some of my records that I forgot I had written. He had "Lightning Struck the Poor House," and all that kind of stuff. He had about ten albums of mine.

When I went to the joint they *forgot* about Big Joe. The place wasn't very wide but it was *long,* and just from the spotlights I could just look out there and see all those people, way back there. Then they had a whole lot of them sitting on the stage. Around the piano and around me. I met one colored girl who was there from America. She had come over there because she had majored in French. When I told her I was from the States it was like I was from home.

That man treated me royally. He paid me more than he was supposed to pay me—for doing a good job. He brought me to the station and I went back to Paris to meet Monastier. He was supposed to settle up the money with me but he only gave me a certain amount and told me that he would send me a check from Bordeaux to the Bank of France. We were in Paris and Bordeaux—where he had his money—was on the border of the Atlantic Ocean. It wasn't really his money; it was his mother's. She was rich and she was backing him up in the business.

I said, "Okay," because I had sent most of my money home, anyway. He only had about four hundred dollars for me. The record I made in Toulouse became the Album of the Year in all of France for 1972. I've got a plaque, signed by Panassie—the president of the Hot Club of France. Album of the Year in all of France. Can't beat that with a stick. Well, that's what happened in the tour of France.

Now, an English promoter heard about me. He had the Blues Legends of 1974, and he was associated with Big Bear Records, in England. He sent for me. He had a lot of cats. He had G. P. Jackson. He had Dr. Ross, the Harmonica Boss; he's a one-man band. He has a headpiece where the harmonica sits in his mouth and then he plays the drums with his feet and he plays the guitar and he sings. He plays right-handed, but he's got his guitar tuned for a left-handed player. The way he plays it, the little string is at the top and the big string is at the bottom. Now, I ain't never seen nobody play like that! Then he had Big John Wrencher. *He* had one arm and you know how he lost his arm? He lost his arm in a wreck. The wreck took his arm off up to his shoulder blade and he got up and picked up his arm and walked, till he found a house, and he went in there and told the lady he was in an accident and he had his arm in his *hand*. The lady put him in bed and tried to stop the bleeding and stuff. When the doctor came, his arm was on the dresser and he was sitting up there drinking cognac! He was a great big man!

When I got to the airport, there was Eddie Playboy Taylor. He's the one who played twenty years with Jimmy Reed. Played all that guitar with Jimmy Reed.

Dr. Ross missed the plane so where Dr. Ross was supposed to play, this promoter sent me there. I went and played that night and they didn't miss Dr. Ross. Dr. Ross didn't know me. He came the next night. He's supposed to have a lot of Indian in him and when he gets into that firewater, he gets mean. Well, he must have been drinking from somewhere and he got to cussing, "Goddamn. No son-of-a-bitch gonna take my job. So-and-so and so-and-so." I said, "Wait a minute, buddy. You talk to the promoter because *he* sent me on the job. *You* missed the plane and *you* didn't show up and somebody had to *be* there so the promoter sent *me* there. And," I said, "don't fool with me, man, because you don't know nothing *about* me and I don't know *you*. And I don't *give* a damn about you neither."

Big John told me, "Take it easy, Joe, please."

I said, "Take it easy for what? He come jumping on *me*. I know he's talking about me because I'm the one who went and played the job. He ain't man enough to come to me and talk to me and tell me. He does his wisecracking around y'all, talking about 'Nobody takes my job from me' and all that. Well, I know he was talking about *me*." See, the promoter had told him he had to send me on the job or he would have lost the job. Well, that all went down alright.

Now, we were traveling on the road and we got to Germany. When you cross the border into Germany and you're on the road you've got to show your passport. They have a place where you show your passport and all that so you can go across the border. Those Germans have a racket on the highway. It's a million-dollar-a-year racket. Just before you hit the motorway there's a policeman on a motorcycle with a walkie-talkie. Every time a British car goes by he probably relays the license number and everything to a group of policemen up ahead on the motorway.

Me and the promoter were in his Jensen-Healey; it's made by Austin Healey and Jensen. A little white sports car. I looked like I was sitting on the ground when I sat in that rascal. And you talk about *fly*. This man was a speed demon. We were up ahead and the rest of them were coming behind us, back in the bus. After we got a certain distance onto the motorway, a whole lot of German police cars came out across the highway and stopped the bus. We had passed that spot but I told the promoter, "Back up, man. Let's go see what's happening—what they're stopping them for."

We went back there and they were telling the bus driver, "You were speeding back there."

The driver said, "Well, why don't you take me to jail and let me pay the fine?"

"No, you pay right here." They don't want to take them to jail because they're going to put that money in their pocket. So they said, "How much money you got?" They've got a lot of Germans who speak English. "How much money you got?"

"I got pounds." Their money was German marks.

"We take that."

He had about twenty pounds and they took twenty pounds. There wasn't anything the promoter could do. Nobody could do anything. They'd have put us *all* in jail, so he paid it and we went on. They do that to every British car that goes through Germany. They don't like the British because the British stopped them during the war; stopped them from crossing the North Sea—or the English Channel. They're terrible. And that racket—they make a million dollars a year from that.

13 In Birmingham, England, in the 1970s. (Pleasant Joseph)

Now an English promoter heard about me. . . . First he sent me all over England. Then he started sending me to Belgium, Holland, France, Germany . . . (p. 170, 174)

14 In a record store in London, in the 1970s. (Pleasant Joseph)

One time we played a college. This little cat that drove the bus, he was a dope head. He wasn't on hard drugs, but he smoked reefers. We got to this college and, of all people, he met a brown-skin cat there; he was colored, but his mother was white. You know all those black soldiers had all those white women over there and some of them came out light brownskinned. He didn't know the man from Adam, but he asked him where he could buy some grass. The man said, "Come on, I'll show you," and he brought him around somewhere in the dark, stuck him up and said, "Now, give me all your money." He had all the money in his pocket to pay for our gas and all that stuff and here he came back crying, "They stole my money!" When I found out he had gone and asked that boy where he could buy some grass, I said, "You got to be kidding, man. You ain't got no better sense than *that?* That man could have been a narcotics agent. How would you know? You could have gone to jail for about twenty years, man. Are you crazy?"

After I finished the '74 tour I became the star. The promoter stopped sending for all of us and started sending for me. He brought me to Heathrow Airport and put me on the plane from London to come home. He had a contract in his hand and he said, "Now, this is your contract. I've signed it and I want you to sign it. It's for you to come back." He told me what day I was coming back and said he was going to send me my ticket. He sent me my ticket, I went on back, and he's been sending for me ever since. He used to send me a round-trip ticket, which was about seven hundred and fifty dollars. First he sent me all over England. Then he started sending me to Belgium, Holland, France, Germany . . .

At that time he used to travel *with* me. When he found out I could travel *by myself,* then he stopped traveling with me. In the last part of '74 he came with me on the boat—with his car—as far as Tilburg, Holland. He had a friend that was living in Tilburg, so he ran the European business with me out of Tilburg. He sent me from Tilburg to Berlin and then my itinerary from Berlin was to Nuremberg, Würtzburg, Freiburg, Heidelberg, Mannheim, Hanover, and Frankfurt. Then back to Mannheim. The promoter met me in Mannheim and drove me to Tilburg from there.

I'm traveling all by myself, collecting the money, and then I'm a secretary on the road: I have my book, I get a taxicab, I get the receipt and mark that down in my book, with the date. Then I catch the train and I tell them, "Now, I would like to have that ticket back, please. Can you scratch that up there, so I can have that for my company? I travel for a company on an action-packed expense account." They say, "Alright," and they cut-cut-cut on the ticket and they give it back to me. Now, I have all those receipts and all those train tickets, plane tickets, and everything. I have to have all that when I get back to the promoter.

I had a big old envelope of German marks. Full! Stacks of them. Every time I was ready to stay in a hotel I'd say, "You got a safe back there?" They'd say, "Yeah." I'd say, "Well, okay." I'd go upstairs, put up my stuff, and then I'd bring my money downstairs. They'd put it in a big envelope, put my name and room number on it, and give me a receipt. They didn't know how much was in it but they'd give me a receipt for the package. Then, they'd tell me, "Now, if you lose the receipt you can't get your money." I'd say, don't worry about it. I'm not going to lose it. I'm going to put it where I put my passport and you know I can't lose that because I can't get out of your country if I do." That's what I had to do. All the time.

We finally made an agreement. I'd get five hundred dollars a week, all expenses paid, and he would send for me any time he needed me. Now, this was a verbal agreement. There were no witnesses to hear him tell me that. Just me and him. Five hundred dollars a week, and all expenses paid. And every time he sends for me it's for three, four, sometimes even five weeks at a time.

I know he couldn't find anybody in his office that could do what I did for him. I traveled *alone* for him. Usually they have somebody representing the office to travel *with* you; that's what they're *supposed* to do. But I went to France and Germany and Holland and Belgium and Finland and Norway and Austria and Switzerland and Sweden *alone,* and I couldn't understand any of those languages. I *know* he couldn't get anybody else to take those kinds of chances. And in all the years I've been working for this man, I've never missed a train, I've never missed a plane, I never was late on the job.

In Germany he had the name of the *strasse*—the street—but he didn't have the number! When I got into Nuremberg it was as cold as a welldigger's ass in Montana. I'm struggling with my bags and everything and I'm walking up and down, asking every cab driver, "Excuse me. Do you speak English?" until I get the one that says, "I speak a little." So I show him the paper and I say, "I'm looking for this address. Do you know where this club is?" and he says, "Man, that street runs all across Germany. Where's the number?"

This man hadn't put down any number and the hotel he had me

registered in didn't exist and I was there by myself. Then, when I went to call him in the post office, the woman—the German operator—couldn't understand me and I couldn't understand her. I couldn't get any number because the woman couldn't understand what I was talking about, so I hung up. They made me deposit fifty marks before I made the call and they give me a receipt. I brought my receipt back to them and they gave me forty-seven marks back. They took three marks out and I didn't even get the number I called. That's what I had to go through for this promoter.

So I said, I'm going to find that son-of-a-bitch if it's the last thing I do. I got another cab driver—a woman. She told me she didn't know where the place was but she knew the man because the man's name was on the contract. She started driving, and she was driving and driving and the first thing you know, we were in some housing project. I said, "Wait a minute, lady, you don't know where you're going. Article number one, all this is a residential section. These are projects where people live. They haven't got a club within ten miles of this place. I tell you what you do. You cut that meter off, right there, because it isn't my fault that you don't know where you're going. I'm going to pay you, but you take me to the Army base. I know everybody speaks English there, because that's all American soldiers."

I went to the Army base and I had them call the promoter in Tilburg. The promoter had said, "If you have any problems, call me," but I couldn't get any answer.

So I got another cab and I told the next cab driver, "You take me to a hotel around here. I don't care where it is, just take me to a hotel." He took me a hotel and charged me nine marks. Okay. I paid it and I got a receipt for *it*. I got receipts for *all* those marks. Then I paid thirty-seven marks for the hotel. Paid that in advance and got a receipt.

Now it's about seven o'clock that night. Since seven o'clock in the morning I've been trying to find this place. I can't rest and I can't sleep because I can't find the place. So what I did, the lady at the reception desk could speak *good* English and I had her help me. She called up the operator and asked the operator about the name of the hotel I was supposed to be staying in. The operator told her that the number had been disconnected and that the hotel wasn't there any more. Now I didn't know *what* to do.

Then another lady relieved that lady in the lobby and she looked at a map of the city. Now, on the contract it said Wolbreckstrasse and she said, "Come here. This must be the place you're looking for. Volbreckstrasse." I said, "I'll be John Brown." Then, when I showed her the name of the club, she said she knew where it was! I said, "How far is it from here?" She said, "About two minutes' walk. Right around the corner!"

I got around there and I knew it was the place because I saw my picture up there and, "From Big Bear Records: Cousin Joe, appearing tonight." And the date was that night. Boy, did I cuss that son-of-a-bitch out. I found the manager and I put all those receipts out and said, "Now, before we start, article number one, they don't have the same name of this place as you've got on this contract. That's your handwriting, isn't it?"

"Yeah, that's my handwriting." He was a German fellow—a promoter—who owned the club, and he had changed the name of the club since he signed the contract with the promoter, about six or seven months earlier. But he hadn't let the promoter know he had changed the name.

That's what I had to go through for this man. Since 1975 that's what I've been doing. Every year I had to travel by myself. He would send me an itinerary and I would take the itinerary and just follow it for three weeks. He would keep in touch with me because he knew, from the itinerary, which hotel I'd be in. He could bet his bottom dollar I was there, too, and they'd call me downstairs and say I had a telephone call. He'd say, "How ya doin?"

"Okay. How *you* doin?"

"I'm doin great. How was the gig last night?"

"Great, man. Had a nice crowd."

"Yeah?"

"Yeah. Well, you'll hear about it."

If it's bad, then he's going to know about it, but if it's *good*, they're going to put it in the paper and the promoter's going to let him know, too.

I traveled like that all over Europe. I went to Stockholm, Sweden, by myself. I went to Finland by myself. In Finland I played the Hotel Hisperia. I had a suite there that was out of sight! A penthouse on the eighteenth floor. With everything. I did a television show there for a live audience, right from the stage. When I came downstairs to do the sound check I'd never seen anything like that. The seats were situated in a circle. They were red vinyl chairs but they swiveled. You could be sitting down and have to go to the ladies' room or the men's room and all you'd do is just turn yourself around, get up, go to the restroom, come back, get in your seat, turn yourself back around and watch me. All the seats were like that. Some kind of expensive red vinyl. I looked in the lobby and I saw that Ella Fitzgerald and Oscar Peterson had been there for a week, so when I came, I followed *them* in there. Later on, when I came downstairs to do the show, I didn't see anybody there. It was nine and the show was supposed to begin at nine-thirty. There were a few people sitting at the table where you pick up tickets so I said, "Hey, man, I don't see anybody *in* this place."

They said, "Don't worry about it, Joe. It's been sold out before you *got* here. This is just for standing room." Well, before I started, at nine-thirty, the place had packed up and at the bar they were standing about four deep and I told myself, "Well I'll be John Brown. I didn't know it was like that."

A lot of the places I played were the same places I'd played before. Every year I'd be booked in the same places. The promoter would tell me, "You're going to *this* place; you've been there before. You know the people. You know the promoter. His name is so-and-so-and-so," or "his name is Dave." Like this:

June the third, DeVille's Night Club, Westport Road, Stoke-on-Trent. The promoter's name is Ian McClendon. A hundred pounds up and fifteen pounds back. Cash. You leave New Street Station at 3:55, arrive in Stoke-on-Trent at 4:50 P.M. You will be met at the station and taken to George Hotel where you pay 11 pounds, 50.

I'd have to pay that out of the hundred pounds I started with and I'd have to keep tabs on that.

June the fourth, the Blue Note, 1480 Saddlegate, Derby. Dave Milton. A hundred pounds again. Seventy percent of the gross door take. Arrive at 8 P.M. Cash. Train from Stoke-on-Trent. They will meet you at the station. Stay at the Friary Hotel where you pay 11 pounds, 50.

Thursday, the fifth of June, take any train to Birmingham in New Street. Go to Gilly Lodge. Play at the Green Dragon, Stratford-on-Avon. You will be picked up by Dave Tickles around 7 P.M. and taken to the gig—about 30 miles. Ninety pounds cash and seven pounds hotel accommodations.

The sixth of June, a day off. At the Montana Hotel.

Saturday, the seventh of June, the Zodiac, Oxford Street, in Manchester. Ninety pounds plus fifty percent after 350

> pounds door take. Check the door take. Roger Eagle. The
> management provides accommodations.

I'm supposed to check the door take! That's a hell of a thing. Now,
what is that man thinking?

> *Saturday,* go to Manchester Airport. Depart at 12:30, arrive
> in New York City at 4:15. Standby ticket. (Standby ticket!)
> Ninety-seven pounds. Depart New York at 10:20 P.M., arrive
> in New Orleans 12:10 on Delta 199. Cash $1,900.

Cash, $1,900! That's what I had in that belt on me. When I was
there the pound went down to one sixty-seven, and I told him, "I
don't want to get paid in pounds. Just pay me cash in American
dollars." We've been dealing in American dollars ever since.

Usually he would get a hundred pounds for me. With the pound
at two-thirty that would be two hundred and thirty dollars a night,
but a lot of times he'd get more than that. He has gotten a thousand dollars a week just for six nights in Neuchâtel, Switzerland,
but that was *his* money. He paid me five hundred dollars a week
and all the rest was clear profit.

I played almost all the principal cities in England and Ireland and
Scotland. One time I flew from Finland to Glasgow, Scotland,
played in Glasgow, and then flew to London. From London I flew to
Belfast, Ireland. That was during the time they were killing people
on the street. In Northern Ireland. Belfast. They were fighting like
I don't know what. Talk about scared! I'm telling you. I couldn't take
anything on the plane. You can't take *anything;* you've got to check
it *all.* And then they search you from the outside in and the inside
out, to make sure you don't have anything when you go into
Belfast. Coming out of Belfast, the promoter was driving me to the
airport and it seemed like every hundred yards those people would
stop us with those machine guns and look in the car and ask to see
his driver's license. And he *lived* there. He was *from* there. We got
to the airport all right and when the pilot said, "You are thirty
thousand feet up," I said, "Well, y'all didn't get me when I was on
the *ground* and it's too bad now. I know y'all ain't got *anything* that
can reach up *this* high." When I got back to the office, I told the
promoter, "Man, don't ever book me at a place like that no more!
You know you took a chance on my life, man. I could have gotten
killed, man."

Sometimes I'd play England first and then go on to Europe. One
time, I had to catch a train from Birmingham to Euston Station in
London, play the Zanzibar, the One Hundred Club, the Pizza Express, and the London College of Fashions, and then leave that last

night and fly to Switzerland. I was in such a rush that I left my boots at the College of Fashions. In those colleges, you have to finish around 11:30 or 12:00 at the latest or those faculties in there put the lights out on you. They kept putting the lights out and the kids kept on yelling and screaming and hollering to put me back on. So they would put the lights back on, but when they put them out the last time they stayed out. I had to change my clothes in the dark. I had a pair of Pierre Cardin boots—I had paid something like ninety or a hundred dollars for them—and I forgot those boots! I put on a pair of shoes that matched my suit and I just left the boots behind. I went back to the hotel and packed up and got a cab to Victoria Station. From Victoria Station I caught the train to Gatwick Airport to get a plane to fly to Switzerland. I never did get the boots back.

Then, I was in trouble at the airport. The promoter had bought one of those charter tickets on a charter plane—they're cheaper. He had given me the ticket and told me to rent a hotel near the airport. The plane would be leaving that evening and I was getting there early. The promoter's wife had rented the hotel for me for half a day. She paid for that and they brought me to the hotel from the airport. I had to be at the airport for six o'clock and I took the hotel bus back to the airport. When I got there, they told me that the plane was full up. I said, "How in the hell is the plane gonna be full up? Why the hell did y'all sell my boss a ticket that I was guaranteed a seat on if you knew the plane was going to be full up? I've got to be in Berne, Switzerland, for tomorrow. Now, somebody is going to get me there *some* kind of way." I went to the desk and talked to a lady there and she asked me for the name of the chartered plane. I told her what the company was—it was on the ticket—and she showed me the woman that was in charge of things at the airport. *She* told me that she could put me on *another* flight that would leave at *seven* o'clock and stop in some other part of Switzerland. Then I would have to take a *bus* from there to Berne. "But," she said, "I don't know if you can get there in time."

They put me on the plane at seven o'clock and when I got there, from there I had to catch a bus that left at about 11:30 that night. I *got* there at about 10:30 but it was actually 11:30 because there was an hour difference in time. So I made it in time to catch the bus. When I got to where the bus stopped I had to get a taxi to my hotel, and when I got a taxi to the hotel, the hotel was closed up! The taxi driver knocked on the door, the man came to the door, and

I told him who I was. He said, "Oh, yeah. I was expecting you earlier."

I said, " I would have been here earlier but those planes messed up."

He registered me in, and that was *more* trouble I had, traveling by myself. But there was nothing else to do but just try and make it.

Well, I made it. I played a festival in Berne and after that I played in Neuchâtel for a week. That was six nights where they paid all expenses. I booked in all the high-class fancy hotels when they paid the expenses. But I did all that traveling by myself.

20

Cousin Joe

I'm hotter than a plate of red beans,
Cause I'm Cousin Joe from New Orleans . . .

FROM THE TIME I started going overseas I started getting international recognition from all the different countries I went to and from all the different jazz festivals I played in. Since 1974 I've probably made at least fifteen trips overseas. I've been to practically all the cities in the western world. I haven't gone to any communist countries, but I've been to Belgium and Holland, France and Germany, Denmark and Sweden, Switzerland and Finland, Norway and Austria, and of course Great Britain. I've been to London, Cardiff, Portsmouth, Leicester, Manchester, and Newcastle-on-Tyne. I went to Scotland and played Glasgow, Edinburgh, and Saint Andrews, and I went to Ireland but I'm never going back there any more. I went to the University of Bangor, in Wales. I've also played in a lot of jazz festivals, like the Festival by the North Sea.

I enjoy playing overseas more than I do here. Here you work no less than four hours in a club and you get very little intermission out of that unless you sign a contract where you very carefully specify a three-hour gig, for example, with forty minutes on and twenty minutes off. When the owner signs that he doesn't have anything to say if you take twenty minutes off out of each hour.

The audiences overseas are ten times greater than here. These audiences don't appreciate what you're doing. You've got to stand on your eyebrows before you can get their attention. That's the reason why I don't work in those little colored joints where they have local people any more. I worked in them *before,* but after I got off of Bourbon Street they couldn't hire me any more. They don't pay enough money, in the first place, the local Negroes don't believe in tipping, and there are very few black tourists that come to town. It's mostly white people who come down here to New Orleans; they take their vacation in the wintertime when it's snowing, and they come down here. People overseas take their vacations in the summertime. They're used to the cold weather and if they came here in the summertime they couldn't stand it. Over there, in May, the big hotels cut all the heat off, but to me it's still cold.

A lot of the audiences overseas are students and they go head over heels for blues. Yeah! And that's what I played the most—colleges. The younger kids today—the students—they go to the library and read up on what people wrote about the blues. Then, when they find out there's a blues singer in town, they're going to go see and hear that person. They're curious. They want to find out if what they've been reading about is factual. They come there out of curiosity, but they'll sit down there and the first thing you know, they'll find out they like it. Then they'll sit there till it's all over; till they close the doors on them.

They keep saying they wonder why the younger musicians don't try to keep up the tradition of jazz. The younger musicians want to play hard rock and modern jazz, but they don't know what they're doing. Actually, they're playing blues when they're playing rock and roll; they're just playing it a little faster. And when they're playing hard rock, they're just playing it a little faster and louder. The louder they play, the better they like it. And singing? I don't know what they're saying any more than the man in the moon, but they've got the microphone on the inside of their mouth and they're making a whole lot of motions. They've got all those fancy pants with those sparkling jackets and all that kind of jive, and they've got all kinds of different lights, blinking all over the place. A doctor told me that all those kids are going to be deaf. That music is going to bust their ear drums. The kids don't worry about the words; they just want that beat, where they can get on the floor and do their number. And of course, you never know who's dancing with who. Two cats get up and say, "Let's dance." When they hit the floor, *she* starts, then *he* starts, and the first thing you know, she's way over there and he's way over here and it's just a total mess. I don't dig it, myself.

I'm a pretty fair country entertainer and I don't see that kind of music being played much overseas. I've had a rock band play before me—I was the featured attraction—and the people would be glad when they got through and got off the stage. It was too loud in the first place, and the people couldn't hear themselves talk. It was awful.

The loudest group I ever played with was in Berlin. That's the first time I saw my name in neon lights out in front. There was a little sign for the band that was going to play before me, but my name was in big letters. "Cousin Joe from New Orleans," in neon lights. This was a pretty big place and they had put some saw-horses on the bandstand with long pieces of lumber and tablecloths on them. People sat there, right on the bandstand. I guess they figured that if they got there early enough they could get close enough to hear me and see me too.

The band that played before me took an hour to set up all their amplifiers and stuff. Everything was electrified. Then they started tuning up and all that; raising the volume up high, tuning up, tuning up. When they opened up and played that first number, here came the "*gestapo*," the German police. They burst open the door and walked in—blond hair, cut short—and one of them said, "Pack up and get out. We heard you two blocks away!" Now, they had to pack up all that stuff and get out.

Then *I* had to play with just the house pianist to spell me. They had a West Indian fellow. He was a good piano player. He couldn't sing but he could play. When they didn't have any featured attraction, he'd play there—for little or nothing. They were paying him about six or ten marks for a night; something like that. That wasn't very much because it was about two marks to the dollar. Anyway, I had to play and when I took a fifteen-minute intermission, he'd play piano. I had to do that for the rest of the three nights there.

I've played with the different jazz greats of the world and from coming in contact with all of these people, *now* I can *demand* what I want. Before, they used to tell me what they were going to pay me. Now, they're going to have to pay me what I want or they can forget it. That's what I finally told that English promoter.

This makes things more progressive for me because now I can just make two or three trips over there and then stay home until I get another notice to go back over. And then, I've been booked from the English agency by other people, like jazz people in Los Angeles, California. I worked eight days in Germany for Barry Martyn and got twelve hundred dollars. Then I flew to London to work for the English promoter and made nineteen hundred dollars in just three weeks. That's over three thousand dollars. I can't make that much in any one month here. I can't make that kind of money here at all.

The younger kids today—the students—they go to the library and read up on . . . the blues. Then, when they find out there's a blues singer in town, they're going to go and see and hear that person. They're curious.   (p. 183)

16 At Kansas State University, in 1980. (Holly Miller)

17 At Kansas State University, in 1980. (Holly Miller)

18 Lecture-demonstration at Kansas State University, in 1980. (Holly Miller)

19 At Kansas State University, in 1980. (Holly Miller)

20 At the Jazz and Heritage Festival in New Orleans, 1981. (Holly Miller)

I started getting . . . recognition from all the . . . festivals I played in.   (p. 182)

21 At the Jazz and Heritage Festival in New Orleans, 1981. (Holly Miller)

22 At the Jazz and Heritage Festival in New Orleans, 1981. (Holly Miller)

23 At home in New Orleans, in the 1980s. (Holly Miller)

It's better for me now than it ever was.   (p. 194)

Anytime I'm ten thousand miles from home I send my wife money; eight or nine hundred dollars, a thousand dollars, two thousand. When I come home she gives me an account of every dime that I send her. The average woman would go through that money like a dose of castor oil or Ex Lax. That's the truth. *She* puts it in the bank. Or she puts half of it in there and takes half of it for house expenses until I get back home. She's got her own account and my name isn't on her book.

I wouldn't be gone but about five weeks at the most—maybe five weeks and three days. I never did stay six weeks—but I'd always send her the first grand as soon as I'd get over there. I found out that the best way to send it is to wait until you get to London. There's a Bank of America in London that handles American dollars. They send it by telex and she'll get it in about four days. When I send money out of the Netherlands, though, sometimes I beat the money home! Another way, that a fellow showed me in Belgium, is to send a check directly to her at home instead of to the bank.

It's better for me now than it ever was. I make more money now than I ever made in my life. I made a lot of money on Bourbon Street in tips but I'm talking now about just actual salary. Now people are beginning to pay me what I'm worth. Before, in New Orleans, when they'd hire you, they'd think they were doing you a favor. They didn't realize that without you they couldn't make any money.

The good Lord gave me a chance to make a comeback. I had messed up my whole life from drinking: from slow horses, from fast women and bad whiskey. That's what knocked me in the bleachers. But I cut all that out. I found the kind of woman I wanted and she's the best. Of course, she can get a little contrary sometimes but I can understand that from what she put up with, with me. I just say, "Well, she's the kind who'll forgive but she won't ever forget." I've been with her now for more than thirty years and when you're with the same woman for thirty years there isn't any sense in you changing because you're going to go from bad to worse.

I guess I'm going to go on until I can't go anymore. As long as my doctor keeps telling me I'm in the shape I'm in I'm going to keep going. I want to save enough money so if anything happens to me my wife won't have to worry about anything.

24 Publicity photo, around 1980. (Porter's Photo News)

Bibliography

Anonymous
  1964 A Blues Downpour. *R&B Scene*. England.
  1972 Cousin Joe, Bad Luck Blues. *Bulletin du Hot Club de France* 219 (July-Aug): 24–25.
  1972 Cousin Joe, Bad Luck Blues. *Blues Unlimited* 94 (September): 25. England.
  1979 Feeling e veccia America. *La Repubblica*, December 21. Italy.
  1980 Alright for a Poor Boy. *Dundee Standard,* May 30, p. 13. Scotland.
  1982 Cousin Joe. *Nancy Jazz Pulsations,* October. Nancy, France.
Balliett, Whitney
  1966 Sweet Tedium and Crippled Crabs. In *Such Sweet Thunder: Forty-nine Pieces on Jazz*. Indianapolis: Bobbs-Merrill. (First printed in *The New Yorker,* May 30, 1964, pp. 133–35.)
Borchet, Ulrich
  1974 Blues Stars im Neuerofneten Kolbeh in Berlin. *Jazz Podium* 23 (August): 27. Stuttgart, Germany.
Broven, John
  1978 *Rhythm and Blues in New Orleans*. Gretna, LA: Pelican. (First published as *Walking to New Orleans: The Story of New Orleans Rhythm and Blues*. Bexhill-on-Sea, Sussex, England: Blues Unlimited, 1974.)
Cummings, Tony
  1974 Cousin Joe. *Black Music* 58 (September). England.
Feather, Leonard
  1960 Pleasant Joseph. In *The New Encyclopedia of Jazz*, p. 295. New York: Bonanza Books.
Gillespie, Dizzy, with Al Fraser
  1979 *To Be, or Not . . . To Bop*. Garden City, NY: Doubleday.
Harris, Sheldon
  1979 Pleasant Joseph. In *Blues Who's Who: A Biographical Dictionary of Blues Singers*, pp. 299–301; see also pp. 202, 490. New Rochelle, NY: Arlington House.
Jepsen, Jorgan Grunnet
  1965 *Jazz Records, 1942-1968: A Discography in Eight Volumes*. Vol. 3, pp. 51–52; vol. 5, p. 164; vol. 6, p. 156. Holte, Denmark: Karl Enid Knudsen.
Joseph, Pleasant, and Harriet Ottenheimer
  1982 Barefoot Boy: Chapter One of the Life Story of Cousin Joe,

"Life's a One Way Ticket." *Louisiana Folklore Miscellany* 5 (2): 13–16.

Kinkle, Roger D.
1974 *The Complete Encyclopedia of Popular Music and Jazz, 1900–1950*, pp. 568, 1469, 1621, 1857. New Rochelle, NY: Arlington House.

Lentz, Paul
1972 Cousin Joe, Blues Humorist. *Downbeat* 39 (no. 15, September): 18, 41.

Martinello, Angelo
1979 Blues: Cousin Joe al Folkstudio: Satana d'annato. *Il Messagero*, December 2, p. 11.

May, Chris
1978 Life Begins at 70. *Black Music*. March, pp. 13–14.

Mezzrow, Milton "Mezz," and Bernard Wolfe
1946 *Really the Blues*. New York: Random House.

Miller, Holly
1980 Cousin Joe from New Orleans: Life's a One Way Ticket. *Flint Hills Journal*, March 14, pp. 4–5. Manhattan, KS.

Ottenheimer, Harriet
1973 *Emotional Release in Blues Singing: A Case Study.* Unpublished Ph.D. dissertation, Tulane University, New Orleans.
1979 Catharsis, Communication, and Evocation: Alternative Views of the Sociopsychological Functions of Blues Singing. *Ethnomusicology* 23 (1): 75–86.
1980 Cousin Joe. *Minorities Resource and Research Center Newsletter*, May, pp. 1–3. Farrell Library, Kansas State University, Manhattan, KS.
1982 The Second Time Around: Version and Variants in the Life Story of Cousin Joe, a New Orleans Blues Singer. *Louisiana Folklore Miscellany* 5 (2): 7–12.

Page, Les
1974 Crescent City Cousin. *Melody Maker* (February). England.

Panassie, Hughes
1972 Cousin Joe, "Bad Luck Blues." *Bulletin du Hot Club de France* 219, 3e série, 24–25, 39.

Panassie, Hughes, and Madeleine Gautier
1956 Pleasant Joseph. In *Guide to Jazz*, Paris: Robert Lafont.
1971 Blues. In *Dictionnaire du Jazz*, pp. 49–52. Paris: Editions Albin Michel.
1971 Pleasant Joseph. In *Dictionnaire du Jazz*, pp. 184–85. Paris: Editions Albin Michel.

Penny, Dave
1985 Cousin Joe from New Orleans. *Blues & Rhythm—The Gospel Truth* 13 (October): 18–21. England.

Ruppli, Michel, with assistance from Bob Porter
  1980 *The Savoy Label: A Discography.* Westport, CN: Greenwood Press.
Sandmel, Ben
  1980 Cousin Joe, Gospel-Wailing, Jazz-Playing, Rock 'n' Rolling, Soul-Shouting, Tap-Dancing Bluesman from New Orleans. *Living Blues* 48 (Autumn): 17.
Samuels, Shepherd
  1982 Cousin Joe. *Wavelength.* August, pp. 25–26.
Schneider, Steve
  1986 There's More to the Music of New Orleans Than Jazz. *New York Times,* January 19, p. H-26.
Scott, Hammond
  1975 New Orleans' Cousin Joe. *Living Blues* 19 (January/February): 20–23.
Shelley, Rita
  1980 Entertainer Has Fun with Hard Luck Theme. *Topeka Capital-Journal,* March 2, p. 36. Topeka, KS.
Stenbeck, Lennart
  1978 Smiling Blues. *Orkester Journalen* 46 (no. 2, February): 12. Stockholm, Sweden.
Vacher, Peter
  1980 Durable Veteran—Cousin Joe. *Jazz Journal International,* April, pp. 9–10. London.
Wilson, John S.
  1966 Pleasant Joseph Takes Pleasure in His Blues. *New York Times,* April 16.
Wisse, Rien
  1977 Niewe Grappen en Grollen van Cousin Joe. *Jazz/Press* 37 (April 29): 6. Netherlands.

Discography

I. Recording sessions

July 1945, New York City
Vocal (as Pleasant Joe), with Sam Price, piano.
    Broken Man Blues   by P. Joseph
        master no.   King Jazz KJ10
        released on: Storyville LP SLP 153
    New Jailhouse Blues   by P. Joseph
        master no.   King Jazz KJ11
        released on: Festival LP FLD 3635
Note: alternate date of March 27 suggested by Penny (1985).

30 or 31 July 1945, New York City
Vocal (as Pleasant Joe), with Mezzrow-Bechet Septet:
Oran 'Hot Lips' Page, trumpet; Milton 'Mezz' Mezzrow, clarinet; Sidney
Bechet, soprano; Sammy Price, piano; Danny Barker, guitar; George
'Pops' Foster, bass; Sidney Catlett, drums.
    Levee Blues (#1)   by S. Wilson
        master no.   King Jazz KJ17-1
        released on: King Jazz KJ144; KJ(It) KJLP 1001;
                       Storyville(D) SLP 136; JS 754
    Layin' My Rules in Blues   by P. Joseph
        master no.   King Jazz KJ18-1
        released on: Storyville(D) SLP 153
    Bad Bad Baby Blues (#1)   by P. Joseph
        master no.   King Jazz KJ19-1
        released on: Storyville(D) SLP 141
    Bad Bad Baby Blues (#2)   by P. Joseph
        (Kickin' Like a Kangaroo Blues) (?)
        master no.   King Jazz KJ19-2
        released on: Storyville(D) SLP 411
    Saw Mill Blues   by S. Wilson
        master no.   King Jazz KJ20-1
        released on: King Jazz KJ144; Storyville(D) SLP 137; JS 754

5 October 1945, New York City
Vocal (as Cousin Joe), with Leonard Feather's Hiptet:
Dick Vance, trumpet; Al Sears, tenor; Harry Carney, baritone; Leonard
Feather, Piano; Jimmy Shirley, guitar; Lloyd Trotman, bass; J. C. Heard,
drums.

My Love Comes Tumblin'   by L. Feather
 Down
 released on: Philo/Aladdin 115
Larceny Hearted Woman   by D. Barker
 released on: Philo/Aladdin 116
Just Another Woman   by L. Feather
 released on: Philo/Aladdin 117
Post War Future Blues   by P. Joseph
 released on: Philo/Aladdin 118
Record of the month, *Modern Screen Magazine.*

13 February 1946, New York City
Vocal (as Cousin Joe), with Pete Brown's Brooklyn Blue Blowers:
Leonard Hawkins, trumpet; Pete Brown, alto; Ray Abrams, tenor; Kenny
Watts, piano; Jimmy Shirley, guitar; Leonard Gaskin, bass; Arthur Herbert, drums.

 Wedding Day Blues   by P. Joseph, T. Reig
  master no. S 5882
  released on: Savoy 5527; Savoy SJL (SLP) 2224
 Desperate G.I. Blues   by P. Joseph, T. Reig
  master no. S 5883
  released on: Savoy 5526; Savoy SJL (SLP) 2224
 You Got It Comin' To You   by P. Joseph, T. Reig
  master no. S 5884
  released on: Savoy 5527; Savoy SJL (SLP) 2224
 Boogie Woogie Hannah   by P. Joseph, T. Reig
  master no. S 5885
  released on: Savoy 5526; Savoy SJL (SLP) 2224

February 1946, New York City
Vocal (as Cousin Joe), with Earl Bostic's Gotham Sextet:
Tony Scott, clarinet; Earl Bostic, alto; Ernie Washington, piano; Jimmy
Shirley, guitar; George 'Pops' Foster, bass; J. C. Heard, drums.

 You Ain't So Such a Much   by P. Joseph
  master no. Si 116
  released on: Gotham 501; King 4186; Riverboat 900.265;
       Oldie Blues OL 8008
 Fly Hen Blues   by P. Joseph
  master no. Si 117
  released on: Gotham 500; Riverboat 900.265;
       Oldie Blues OL 8008
 Lonesome Man Blues   by P. Joseph
  master no. Si 118
  released on: Gotham 500; Riverboat 900.265;
       Oldie Blues OL 8008

Little Eva   by P. Joseph
   master no.   Si 119
   released on: Gotham 501; King 4186; Riverboat 900.265;
             Oldie Blues OL 8008

June or August 1946, New York City
Vocal (as Cousin Joe), with Earl Bostic's Gotham Sextet (or Earl Bostic's
   Orchestra):
Lemon Boler (?), trumpet; Tony Scott, clarinet; Earl Bostic, alto; John
Hardee, tenor (?); George Parker or Hank Jones, piano; Jimmy Shirley,
guitar; Jimmy Jones, bass; Eddie Nicholson, drums.
   Baby, You Don't Know It All   by P. Joseph
      master no.   S 137
      released on: Gotham 135; Riverboat 900.265;
               Oldie Blues OL 8008

July or August 1946, New York City
Vocal (as Cousin Joe), with Earl Bostic's Gotham Sextet (or Earl Bostic's
   Orchestra):
Tony Scott, clarinet; Earl Bostic, alto; John Hardee, tenor; George Parker
or Hank Jones, piano; Jimmy Shirley, guitar; Jimmy Jones, bass; Eddie
Nicholson, drums.
   Barefoot Boy (#1)   by P. Joseph
      master no.   S 154
      released on: Gotham 135; Riverboat 900.265;
               Oldie Blues OL 8008

August 1946, New York City
Vocal (as Brother Joshua), with Earl Bostic's Orchestra:
Tyree Glenn, trombone; Tony Scott, clarinet; Earl Bostic, alto; John
Hardee, tenor; Hank Jones, piano; Jimmy Shirley, guitar; Jimmy Jones,
bass; Eddie Nicholson, drums.
   If I Just Keep Still   Traditional
      master no.   Si 164
      released on: Gotham 119
   When Your Mother's Gone   Traditional
      master no.   Si 165
      released on: Gotham 119
   When the Roll Be Called in   Traditional
      Heaven
      master no.   Si 166
      released on: Gotham 120; King 4246
   Make Me Strong as Sampson   Traditional
      master no.   Si 167
      released on: Gotham 120; King 4246

Discography

8 August 1946, New York City
Vocal (as Cousin Joe), with Earl Bostic's Orchestra:
Unknown trumpet; Tyree Glenn, trombone; Tony Scott, clarinet; Earl
Bostic, alto; John Hardee, tenor; Hank Jones, piano; Jimmy Shirley, gui-
tar; Jimmy Jones or George 'Pops' Foster, bass; Eddie Nicholson, drums.
   My Tight Woman   by P. Joseph
      master no.   Si 168
      released on: Gotham 121; Riverboat 900.265;
                   Oldie Blues OL 8008
   Lightning Struck The Poorhouse   by P. Joseph
      master no.   Si 169
      released on: Gotham 121; Riverboat 900.265;
                   Oldie Blues OL 8008

21 May 1947, New York City
Vocal (as Cousin Joe), with Al Casey Quartet:
Steve Henderson (Hoggie Beetle?), piano; Al Casey, guitar; Al Matthews,
bass; Arthur Herbert, drums.
   Old Man Blues   by P. Joseph
      master no.   S 3424
      released on: Savoy 5536; Riverboat 900.265
   Death House Blues   by P. Joseph, T. Reig
      master no.   S 3425
      released on: Savoy 5540; Riverboat 900.265
   Too Tight to Walk Loose   by P. Joseph
      master no.   S 3426
      released on: Savoy 5536; Riverboat 900.265
   Big Fat Mama (#1)   by P. Joseph, T. Reig
      master no.   S 3427
      released on: Savoy 5540; Riverboat 900.265

June or July 1947, New York City
Vocal (as Cousin Joe), with Dickie Wells' Blue Seven:
Shad Collins, trumpet; Dickie Wells, trombone; Pete Brown, alto; Billy
Kyle, piano; Danny Barker, guitar; Lloyd Trotman, bass; Woodie Nich-
ols, drums.
   Come Down Baby   by L. Feather
      master no.   SRC 439
      released on: Signature 1013; Riverboat 900.265
   Bachelor's Blues   by P. Joseph
      master no.   SRC 440
      released on: Signature 1012; Hi-Tone 150; Riverboat 900.265
   Don't Pay Me No Mind   by L. Feather
      master no.   SRC 441
      released on: Signature 1013; Riverboat 900.265

Stoop to Conquer   by D. Barker
> master no.   SRC 442
> released on: Signature 1012; Hi-Tone 150; Riverboat 900.265

Blues I   by P. Joseph
> master no.   SRC 443
> unissued

Blues II   by P. Joseph
> master no.   SRC 444
> unissued

16 July 1947, New York City
Vocal (as Cousin Joe), with Sam Price Trio:
Sam Price, piano; Danny Barker, guitar; George 'Pops' Foster, bass;
Kenny Clarke, drums.

Bad Luck Blues (#1)   by P. Joseph
> master no.   74008
> released on: Decca 48045; Br(F/G) 10360; Oldie Blues OL 8008

Box Car Shorty and Peter Blue   by P. Joseph
> master no.   74009
> released on: Decca 48045; Br(F/G) 10360; Decca 79230;
>   Oldie Blues OL 8008

19 October 1947, New York City
Vocal (as Cousin Joe), with Sam Price Trio:
Sam Price, piano; Billy Butler, guitar; Percy Joell, bass; Dorothea Smith,
drums.

Beggin' Woman (#1)   by P. Joseph
> master no.   74142
> released on: Decca 48091; Br(F/G) 10360; Ace of Hearts AH 72;
>   Decca DL 434; Oldie Blues OL 8008

Sadie Brown   by P. Joseph
> master no.   74143
> released on: Decca 48061; Oldie Blues OL 8008

Evolution Blues (#1)   by P. Joseph
> master no.   74144
> released on: Decca 48061; BR(F/G) 87504; Oldie Blues OL 8008

Box Car Shorty's Confession   by P. Joseph
> master no.   74145
> released on: Decca 48091; Br(F/G) 10360; Decca 79230;
>   Oldie Blues OL 8008

1947, New York City
Vocal (as Cousin Joe), with unknown accompaniment.

Looking for My Baby   by P. Joseph (and J. Thomas?)
> master no.   76149
> released on: Decca 48165

High Powered Gal   by P. Joseph
 master no. 76150
 released on: Decca 48165
Chicken a la Blues (#1)   by P. Joseph (and J. Thomas?)
 master no. 76151
 released on: Decca 48157
Poor Man Blues   by P. Joseph (and J. Thomas?)
 master no. 76152
 released on: Decca 48157
Note: Alternative date of April 1950 in Penny (1985).

February (?) 1947, New Orleans
Vocal (as Cousin Joe), with Cousin Joe and His Sextet:
Lee Allen, tenor; Paul Gayten, piano; Edgar Blanchard, guitar; Warren
Stanley, bass; Robert Green, drums.
Just As Soon As I Go Home by E. Severn and P. Joseph
 master no. 361
 released on: Deluxe 1065; Deluxe 3065 (?); Oldie Blues OL 8008
Phoney Woman Blues   by P. Joseph
 master no. 362
 released on: Deluxe 1065; Deluxe 3065 (?); Oldie Blues OL 8008
Little Woman Blues   by P. Joseph
 master no. 363
 released on: Deluxe 1067; Deluxe 3067 (?)
It's Dangerous to Be a Husband by P. Joseph
 master no. 364
 released on: Deluxe 1067; Deluxe 3067 (?)
Note: The last title of this session is listed on the cover of the Riverboat
900.265 album, but is not included on the album. Also, an alternative
recording date of April 1946 is given on Oldie Blues OL 8008. Early 1947
is the most likely date.

1951 (?), New Orleans
Vocal (as Smilin' Joe), with Alonzo Stewart, drums and additional vocals;
other personnel unknown.
Second Hand Love   by P. Joseph
 master no. 357
 released on: Imperial 5159
Dinah
 master no. 358
 released on: Imperial 5159
Misery
 released on: Imperial 5187
Won't Settle Down
 released on: Imperial 5187

14 December 1952, New Orleans
Vocal (as Cousin Joe), with Freddie Kohlman and His Band:
Thomas Jefferson, trumpet; Wendell (or Homer) Eugene, trombone; Willie Humphrey, clarinet; Dave Williams, piano; Clement Tervalon, bass; Freddie Kohlman, drums.

  I Saw Mommy Kissin' Santa
      Claus
    released on: Decca LP DL 5483

2 August 1954, New Orleans
Vocal (as Smilin' Joe), with Dave Bartholomew, piano.
  ABC I   by P. Joseph
    master no.   745
    released on: Imperial 5304
  ABC II   by P. Joseph
    master no.   746
    released on: Imperial 5304

20 December 1954, New Orleans
Vocal (as Smilin' Joe), with Dave Bartholomew, piano.
  How Long Must I Wait?
    master no.   807
    released on: Imperial 5327
  Sleep Walking Woman   by P. Joseph, D. Bartholomew
    master no.   808
    released on: Imperial 5327

10 October 1971, Toulouse France
Vocal and piano (as Cousin Joe), with Clarence 'Gatemouth' Brown, guitar; Mac Thompson, bass; Ted Harvey, drums.
  Bad Luck Blues (#2)   by P. Joseph
  That's Enough   by P. Joseph
  Take a Lesson from Your   by P. Joseph
    Teacher
  I Don't Want No Second   by P. Joseph
    Hand Love
  Levee Blues (#2)   by S. Wilson
  Box Car Shorty   by P. Joseph
  Railroad Porter's Blues   by P. Joseph
With Jimmy Dawkins, guitar; Mac Thompson, bass; Ted Harvey, drums.
  I'm Living on Borrowed Time by P. Joseph
  Goin' Down Slow   by J. Oden
  Chicken and the Hawk   by Lieber and Stoller
  Tow Down   by P. Joseph
  Life Is a One-Way Ticket   by P. Joseph
    released on: Black & Blue 33.035

rereleased on: Black & Blue 33.549/WE 341.
Note: Blues Album of the Year, 1972, France.

1973, New Orleans
Vocal and piano (as Cousin Joe), with Roosevelt Sykes, piano; Justin
Adams, guitar; George French, bass; Alonzo Stewart, drums.

Country Boy	by P. Joseph
Joe's Blues	by P. Joseph
Evolution Blues (#2)	by P. Joseph
Down It and Get from Around It	by P. Joseph
Chicken a la Blues (#2)	by P. Joseph
Beggin' Woman (#2)	by P. Joseph
Barefoot Boy (#2)	by P. Joseph
Messin' Around	by P. Joseph
Love Sick Soul	by P. Joseph
Life's a One Way Ticket	by P. Joseph
Juice on the Loose	by P. Joseph

released on: ABC Bluesway BLS 6078

February and March 1974, Chalk Farms Studio, London, England
Vocal (as Cousin Joe), with The Blueshounds:
Roger Hill, guitar; Graham Gallery, bass guitar; Peter York, drums.
Other personnel: Colin Smith, trumpet; George Chisholm, trombone;
Johnny Barnes, clarinet; Mike Burney, tenor. Backing vocals by 'Arrival':
Dyan Birch, Frank Collins, and Paddy McHugh.

When a Woman Loves a Man	by Hanighan/Jenkins/Mercer
Checkin' Out	?
Touch Me	by ? Nelson
I Got News for You	by ? Alford
Too Late to Turn Back Now	by C. Otis
Lipstick Traces	by A. Neville
Night Life	by W. Partridge
How Come My Dog Don't Bark When You Come 'Round?	by W. Partridge
Barefoot Boy (#3)	by P. Joseph
You Talk Too Much	by J. Jones and R. Hall
Railroad Avenue	by P. Joseph

released on: Big Bear 3

1975, Chalk Farms Studio, London, England
Vocal (as Cousin Joe), with Geoff Brown and The Muscles:
Geoff Brown, guitar; other personnel unknown.

You're Never Too Old to Boogie	by G. Brown
Hannah from Savannah	by P. Joseph

released on: Big Bear 14 (single)

1 and 2 October 1985, New Orleans
Vocal and piano (as Cousin Joe).

Brown Skinned Woman	by P. Joseph
Hard Work	by P. Joseph
What a Tragedy	by P. Joseph
I Had to Stoop to Conquer You	by D. Barker
In and Out of Love	by P. Joseph
Little Low Mama	by P. Joseph
Don't Let Your Head Start Nothin'	by P. Joseph
Big Fat Mama (#2)	by P. Joseph
Revenge Is So Sweet	by P. Joseph
Hard Times	by P. Joseph

With John Berthelot, piano.

That's What Love Is All About	by G. Stevenson and J. Berthelot

released on: Great Southern Records GS 11011

II. Song Titles recorded

ABC I	Imperial 5304
ABC II	Imperial 5304
Baby, You Don't Know It All	Gotham 135
	Riverboat 900.265
	Oldie Blues OL 8008
Bachelor's Blues	Signature 1012
	Hi-Tone 150
	Riverboat 900.265
Bad Bad Baby Blues (#1)	Storyville(D) SLP 141
Bad Bad Baby Blues (#2)	Storyville(D) SLP 411
Bad Luck Blues (#1)	Decca 48045
	Br(F/G) 10360
	Oldie Blues OL 8008
Bad Luck Blues (#2)	Black & Blue 33.035
	Black & Blue 33.549/WE 341
Barefoot Boy (#1)	Gotham 135
	Riverboat 900.265
	Oldie Blues OL 8008
Barefoot Boy (#2)	ABC Bluesway BLS 6078
Barefoot Boy (#3)	Big Bear 3
Beggin' Woman (#1)	Decca 48091
	Br(F/G) 10360
	Ace of Hearts AH 72
	Decca DL 434
	Oldie Blues OL 8008
Beggin' Woman (#2)	ABC Bluesway BLS 6078
Big Fat Mama (#1)	Savoy 5540
	Riverboat 900.265

Big Fat Mama (#2)	Great Southern Records GS 11011
Blues I	unissued (master no. SRC 443)
Blues II	unissued (master no. SRC 444)
Boogie Woogie Hannah	Savoy 5526
	Savoy SJL (SLP) 2224
Box Car Shorty	Black & Blue 33.035
	Black & Blue 33.549/WE 341
Box Car Shorty and Peter Blue	Decca 48045
	Br(F/G) 10360
	Decca 79230
	Oldie Blues OL 8008
Box Car Shorty's Confession	Decca 48091
	Br(F/G) 10360
	Decca 79230
	Oldie Blues OL 8008
Broken Man Blues	Storyville LP SLP 153
Brown Skinned Woman	Great Southern Records GS 11011
Checkin' Out	Big Bear 3
Chicken a la Blues (#1)	Decca 48157
Chicken a la Blues (#2)	ABC Bluesway BLS 6078
Chicken and the Hawk	Black & Blue 33.035
	Black & Blue 33.549/WE 341
Come Down Baby	Signature 1013
	Riverboat 900.265
Country Boy	ABC Bluesway BLS 6078
Death House Blues	Savoy 5540
	Riverboat 900.265
Desperate G.I. Blues	Savoy 5526
	Savoy SJL (SLP) 2224
Dinah	Imperial 5159
Don't Let Your Head Start Nothin'	Great Southern Records GS 11011
Don't Pay Me No Mind	Signature 1013
	Riverboat 900.265
Down It and Get from Around It	ABC Bluesway BLS 6078
Evolution Blues (#1)	Decca 48061
	Br(F/G) 87504
	Oldie Blues OL 8008
Evolution Blues (#2)	ABC Bluesway BLS 6078
Fly Hen Blues	Gotham 500
	Riverboat 900.265
	Oldie Blues OL 8008
Goin' Down Slow	Black & Blue 33.035
	Black & Blue 33.549/WE 341

Hannah from Savannah	Big Bear 14
Hard Times	Great Southern Records GS 11011
Hard Work	Great Southern Records GS 11011
High Powered Gal	Decca 48165
How Come My Dog Don't Bark When You Come 'Round?	Big Bear 3
How Long Must I Wait?	Imperial 5327
I Don't Want No Second Hand Love	Black & Blue 33.035
	Black & Blue 33.549/WE 341
I Got News for You	Big Bear 3
I Had to Stoop to Conquer You	Great Southern Records GS 11011
I'm Living on Borrowed Time	Black & Blue 33.035
	Black & Blue 33.549/WE 341
If I Just Keep Still	Gotham 119
In and Out of Love	Great Southern Records GS 11011
I Saw Mommy Kissin' Santa Claus	Decca LP DL 5483
It's Dangerous to Be a Husband	Deluxe 1067
	Deluxe 3067 (?)
	(Riverboat 900.265: listed on album cover, not present on disk)
Joe's Blues	ABC Bluesway BLS 6078
Juice on the Loose	ABC Bluesway BLS 6078
Just Another Woman	Philo/Aladdin 117
Just As Soon As I Go Home	Deluxe 1065
	Deluxe 3065 (?)
	Oldie Blues OL 8008
Larceny Hearted Woman	Philo/Aladdin 116
Layin' My Rules in Blues	Storyville(D) SLP 153
Levee Blues (#1)	King Jazz KJ144
	JS 754
	KJ(It) KJLP 1001
	Storyville(D) SLP 136
Levee Blues (#2)	Black & Blue 33.035
	Black & Blue 33.549/WE 341
Life Is a One-Way Ticket	Black & Blue 33.035
	Black & Blue 33.549/WE 341
Life's a One Way Ticket	ABC Bluesway BLS 6078
Lightning Struck the Poorhouse	Gotham 121
	Riverboat 900.265
	Oldie Blues OL 8008
Lipstick Traces	Big Bear 3
Little Eva	Gotham 501
	King 4186

	Riverboat 900.265
	Oldie Blues OL 8008
Little Low Mama	Great Southern Records GS 11011
Little Woman Blues	Deluxe 1067
	Deluxe 3067 (?)
Lonesome Man Blues	Gotham 500
	Riverboat 900.265
	Oldie Blues OL 8008
Looking for My Baby	Decca 48165
Love Sick Soul	ABC Bluesway BLS 6078
Make Me Strong as Sampson	Gotham 120
	King 4246
Messin' Around	ABC Bluesway BLS 6078
Misery	Imperial 5187
My Love Comes Tumblin' Down	Philo/Aladdin 115
My Tight Woman	Gotham 121
	Riverboat 900.265
	Oldie Blues OL 8008
New Jailhouse Blues	Festival LP FLD 3635
Night Life	Big Bear 3
Old Man Blues	Savoy 5536
	Riverboat 900.265
Phoney Woman Blues	Deluxe 1065
	Deluxe 3065 (?)
	Oldie Blues OL 8008
Poor Man Blues	Decca 48157
Post War Future Blues	Philo/Aladdin 118
Railroad Avenue	Big Bear 3
Railroad Porter's Blues	Black & Blue 33.035
	Black & Blue 33.549/WE 341
Revenge Is So Sweet	Great Southern Records GS 11011
Sadie Brown	Decca 48061
	Oldie Blues OL 8008
Saw Mill Blues	King Jazz KJ144
	Storyville(D) SLP 137
	JS 754
Second Hand Love	Imperial 5159
Sleep Walking Woman	Imperial 5327
Stoop to Conquer	Signature 1012
	Hi-Tone 150
	Riverboat 900.265
Take a Lesson from Your Teacher	Black & Blue 33.035
	Black & Blue 33.549/WE 341

That's Enough	Black & Blue 33.035
	Black & Blue 33.549/WE 341
That's What Love Is All About	Great Southern Records GS 11011
Too Late to Turn Back Now	Big Bear 3
Too Tight to Walk Loose	Savoy 5536
	Riverboat 900.265
	Big Bear 3
Touch Me	Big Bear 3
Tow Down	Black & Blue 33.035
	Black & Blue 33.549/WE 341
Wedding Day Blues	Savoy 5527
	Savoy SJL (SLP) 2224
What a Tragedy	Great Southern Records GS 11011
When a Woman Loves a Man	Big Bear 3
When the Roll Be Called in	Gotham 120
Heaven	King 4246
When Your Mother's Gone	Gotham 119
Won't Settle Down	Imperial 5187
You Ain't So Such a Much	Gotham 501
	King 4186
	Riverboat 900.265
	Oldie Blues OL 8008
You Got It Comin' to You	Savoy 5527
	Savoy SJL (SLP) 2224
You Talk Too Much	Big Bear 3
You're Never Too Old to Boogie	Big Bear 14

III. Albums (and singles) released, in alphabetical order by label

ABC Bluesway BLS 6078: *Cousin Joe of New Orleans* (1973)

Juice on the Loose	Country Boy
Beggin' Woman (#2)	Love Sick Soul
Chicken a la Blues	Evolution Blues (#2)
Messin' Around	Joe's Blues
Barefoot Boy (#2)	Life's a One Way Ticket
	Down It and Get from Around It

Ace of Hearts AH 72
    Beggin' Woman (#1)

Big Bear 3: *Cousin Joe: Gospel-Wailing, Jazz-Playing, Rock 'n' Rolling, Soul-Shouting, Tap-Dancing Bluesman from New Orleans* (1974)

Night Life	Lipstick Traces
How Come My Dog Don't Bark When You Come 'Round?	Too Late To Turn Back Now

Discography

Barefoot Boy (#3)
You Talk Too Much
Railroad Avenue

I Got News for You
Touch Me
Checkin' Out
When a Woman Loves a Man

Big Bear 14 (single)
Hannah from Savannah

You're Never Too Old to Boogie

Black & Blue 33.035: *Cousin Joe—Bad Luck Blues* (1972) and Black &
Blue 33.549/WE 341: *Cousin Joe—Bad Luck Blues: Vol. 10 of The Blues
Singers & Players Collection* (reissue)

Take a Lesson from Your
  Teacher
Bad Luck Blues (#2)
I'm Living on Borrowed Time
I Don't Want No Second
  Hand Love
That's Enough
Life Is a One-Way Ticket

Goin' Down Slow

Box Car Shorty
Chicken and the Hawk
Levee Blues (#2)

Railroad Porter's Blues
Tow Down

Br(F/G) 10360
Bad Luck Blues (#1)
Beggin' Woman (#1)

Box Car Shorty and Peter Blue
Box Car Shorty's Confession

Br(F/G) 87504
Evolution Blues (#1)

Decca 48045
Bad Luck Blues (#1)

Box Car Shorty and Peter Blue

Decca 48061
Sadie Brown

Evolution Blues (#1)

Decca 48091
Box Car Shorty's Confession

Beggin' Woman (#1)

Decca 48157
Chicken a la Blues

Poor Man Blues

Decca 48165
Lookin for My Baby

High Powered Gal

Decca 79230: *The Blues and All That Jazz*
Box Car Shorty and Peter Blue   Box Car Shorty's Confession

Decca DL 434: *Out Came the Blues*
  Beggin' Woman (#1)

Decca LP DL 5483
  I Saw Mommy Kissin'
    Santa Claus

Deluxe 1065 and 3065 (?)
  Just As Soon As I go Home   Phoney Woman Blues

Deluxe 1067 and 3067 (?)
  It's Dangerous to Be a Husband   Little Woman Blues

Festival LP FLD 3635
  New Jailhouse Blues

Gotham 119
  If I Just Keep Still   When Your Mother's Gone

Gotham 120
  When the Roll Be Called in   Make Me Strong as Sampson
    Heaven

Gotham 121
  My Tight Woman   Lightning Struck the Poorhouse

Gotham 135
  Baby, You Don't Know It All   Barefoot Boy (#1)

Gotham 500
  Fly Hen Blues   Lonesome Man Blues

Gotham 501
  You Ain't So Such a Much   Little Eva

Great Southern Records GS 11011: *Cousin Joe: Relaxin' in New Orleans*
(1985)
  Brown Skinned Woman   Don't Let Your Head Start Nothin'
  Hard Work   Big Fat Mama (#2)
  What a Tragedy   Revenge Is So Sweet
  I Had to Stoop to Conquer You   Hard Times
  In and Out of Love   That's What Love Is All About
  Little Low Mama

Discography

Hi-Tone 150
    Stoop to Conquer   Bachelor's Blues

Imperial 5159
    Second Hand Love   Dinah

Imperial 5187
    Misery   Won't Settle Down

Imperial 5304
    ABC I   ABC II

Imperial 5327
    Sleep Walking Woman   How Long Must I Wait?

JS 754
    Levee Blues (#1)   Saw Mill Blues

KJ(It) KJLP 1001
    Levee Blues (#1)

King 4186
    You Ain't So Such a Much   Little Eva

King 4246
    When the Roll Be Called in   Make Me Strong as Sampson
    Heaven

King Jazz KJ144
    Levee Blues (#1)   Saw Mill Blues

Liberty LP LBL 83327: *Urban Blues—New Orleans Bounce*
unknown selections

Oldie Blues OL 8008: *Cousin Joe from New Orleans: In His Prime* (1984)
    You Ain't So Such a Much   Baby You Don't Know It All
    Fly Hen Blues   Barefoot Boy (#1)
    Lonesome Man Blues   Bad Luck Blues (#1)
    Little Eva   Box Car Shorty and Peter Blue
    Just As Soon As I Go Home   Beggin' Woman (#1)
    Phoney Woman Blues   Sadie Brown
    My Tight Woman   Evolution Blues (#1)
    Lightning Struck the Poorhouse Box Car Shorty's Confession

Philo/Aladdin 115/116
    My Love Comes Tumblin' Down   Larceny Hearted Woman

Philo/Aladdin 117/118
    Just Another Woman   Post War Future Blues

Riverboat 900.265: *Cousin Joe Joseph from New Orleans*

You Ain't So Such a Much	Bachelor's Blues
Little Eva	Stoop to Conquer
Lonesome Man Blues	Don't Pay Me No Mind
Fly Hen Blues	Come Down Baby
Baby, You Don't Know It All	Death House Blues
Barefoot Boy (#1)	Big Fat Mama
My Tight Woman	Old Man Blues
Lightning Struck the Poorhouse	Too Tight to Walk Loose

Note: Two titles, *Old Man Blues* and *Too Tight to Walk Loose*, are included on this album but are not mentioned on the album cover. One title, *It's Dangerous to Be a Husband*, is listed on the album cover but is not included on the album.

Savoy SJL (SLP) 2224: *The Changing Face of Harlem—Volume Two* (1977)
    Desperate G.I. Blues   Boogie Woogie Hannah
    Wedding Day Blues   You Got It Coming to Ya

Savoy 5526
    Desperate G.I. Blues   Boogie Woogie Hannah

Savoy 5527
    You Got It Comin' to You   Wedding Day Blues

Savoy 5536
    Too Tight to Walk Loose   Old Man Blues

Savoy 5540
    Death House Blues   Big Fat Mama (#1)

Signature 1012
    Bachelor's Blues   Stoop to Conquer

Signature 1013
    Come Down Baby   Don't Pay Me No Mind

Discography

Storyville(D) SLP 411
  Bad Bad Baby Blues (#2)

Storyville(D) SLP 136/137
  Levee Blues (#1)   Saw Mill Blues

Storyville(D) SLP 141
  Bad Bad Baby Blues (#1)

Storyville(D) SLP 153
  Layin' My Rules in Blues   Broken Man Blues

IV. Recording artists

Bass:

  George French
    Barefoot Boy (#2); Beggin' Woman (#2); Chicken a la Blues (#2);
    Country Boy; Down It and Get from Around It; Evolution Blues
    (#2); Juice on the Loose; Joe's Blues; Life's a One Way Ticket; Love
    Sick Soul; Messin' Around.
  George 'Pops' Foster
    Bad Bad Baby Blues (#1); Bad Bad Baby Blues (#2); Bad Luck
    Blues (#1); Box Car Shorty and Peter Blue; Fly Hen Blues; Layin'
    My Rules in Blues; Levee Blues (#1); Lightning Struck the Poor-
    house (?); Little Eva; Lonesome Man Blues; My Tight Woman (?);
    Saw Mill Blues; You Ain't So Such a Much.
  Graham Gallery
    Barefoot Boy (#3); Checkin' Out; How Come My Dog Don't Bark
    When You Come 'Round? I Got News for You; Lipstick Traces;
    Night Life; Railroad Avenue; Too Late to Turn Back Now; Touch
    Me; When a Woman Loves a Man; You Talk Too Much.
  Leonard Gaskin
    Boogie Woogie Hannah; Desperate G.I. Blues; Wedding Day Blues;
    You Got It Comin' to You.
  Percy Joell
    Beggin' Woman (#1); Box Car Shorty's Confession; Evolution
    Blues (#1); Sadie Brown.
  Jimmy Jones
    Baby, You Don't Know It All; Barefoot Boy (#1); If I Just Keep
    Still; Lightning Struck the Poorhouse (?); Make Me Strong as
    Sampson; My Tight Woman (?); When the Roll Be Called in
    Heaven; When Your Mother's Gone.
  Al Matthews
    Big Fat Mama (#1); Death House Blues; Old Man Blues; Too
    Tight to Walk Loose.

Warren Stanley
  It's Dangerous to Be a Husband; Just As Soon As I Go Home;
  Little Woman Blues; Phoney Woman Blues.
Clement Tervalon
  I Saw Mommy Kissin' Santa Claus.
Lloyd Trotman
  Bachelor's Blues; Blues I; Blues II; Come Down Baby; Don't Pay
  Me No Mind; Just Another Woman; Larceny Hearted Woman;
  My Love Comes Tumblin' Down; Post War Future Blues; Stoop to
  Conquer.
Mac Thompson
  Bad Luck Blues (#2); Box Car Shorty; Chicken and the Hawk;
  Goin' Down Slow; I Don't Want No Second Hand Love; I'm Living
  on Borrowed Time; Levee Blues (#2); Life Is a One-Way Ticket;
  Railroad Porter's Blues; Take a Lesson from Your Teacher; That's
  Enough; Tow Down.
Clarinet:
Johnny Barnes
  Barefoot Boy (#3); Checkin' Out; How Come My Dog Don't Bark
  When You Come 'Round?; I Got News for You; Lipstick Traces;
  Night Life; Railroad Avenue; Too Late to Turn Back Now; Touch
  Me; When a Woman Loves a Man; You Talk Too Much.
Willie Humphrey
  I Saw Mommy Kissin' Santa Claus.
Milton 'Mezz' Mezzrow
  Bad Bad Baby Blues (#1); Bad Bad Baby Blues (#2); Layin' My
  Rules In Blues; Levee Blues (#1); Saw Mill Blues.
Tony Scott
  Baby, You Don't Know It All; Barefoot Boy (#1); Fly Hen Blues; If
  I Just Keep Still; Lightning Struck the Poorhouse; Little Eva;
  Lonesome Man Blues; Make Me Strong as Sampson; My Tight
  Woman; When Your Mother's Gone; When the Roll Be Called in
  Heaven; You Ain't So Such a Much.
Drums:
Sidney Catlett
  Bad Bad Baby Blues (#1); Bad Bad Baby Blues (#2); Layin' My
  Rules in Blues; Levee Blues (#1); Saw Mill Blues.
Kenny Clarke
  Bad Luck Blues (#1); Box Car Shorty and Peter Blue.
Robert Green
  It's Dangerous to Be a Husband; Just As Soon As I Go Home;
  Little Woman Blues; Phoney Woman Blues.
Ted Harvey
  Bad Luck Blues (#2); Box Car Shorty; Chicken and the Hawk;

Goin' Down Slow; I Don't Want No Second Hand Love; I'm Living on Borrowed Time; Life Is a One-Way Ticket; Levee Blues (#2); Railroad Porter's Blues; Take a Lesson from Your Teacher; That's Enough; Tow Down.

J.C. Heard

Fly Hen Blues; Just Another Woman; Larceny Hearted Woman; Little Eva; Lonesome Man Blues; My Loves Comes Tumblin' Down; Post War Future Blues; You Ain't So Such a Much.

Arthur Herbert

Big Fat Mama (#1); Boogie Woogie Hannah; Death House Blues; Desperate G.I. Blues; Old Man Blues; Too Tight to Walk Loose; Wedding Day Blues; You Got It Comin' to You.

Freddie Kohlman

I Saw Mommy Kissin' Santa Claus.

Woodie Nichols

Bachelor's Blues; Blues I; Blues II; Come Down Baby; Don't Pay Me No Mind; Stoop to Conquer.

Eddie Nicholson

Baby, You Don't Know It All; Barefoot Boy (#1); If I Just Keep Still; Lightning Struck the Poorhouse; Make Me Strong as Sampson; My Tight Woman; When the Roll Be Called in Heaven; When Your Mother's Gone.

Dorothea Smith

Beggin' Woman (#1); Box Car Shorty's Confession; Evolution Blues (#1); Sadie Brown

Alonzo Stewart

Barefoot Boy (#2); Beggin' Woman (#2); Chicken a la Blues (#2); Country Boy; Down It and Get from Around It; Evolution Blues (#2); Joe's Blues; Juice on the Loose; Life's a One Way Ticket; Love Sick Soul; Messin' Around.

Peter York

Barefoot Boy (#3); Checkin' Out; How Come My Dog Don't Bark When You Come 'Round?; I Got News for You; Lipstick Traces; Night Life, Railroad Avenue; Too Late to Turn Back Now; Touch Me; When a Woman Loves a Man, You Talk Too Much.

Guitar:

Justin Adams

Barefoot Boy (#2); Beggin' Woman (#2); Chicken a la Blues (#2); Country Boy; Down It and Get from Around It; Evolution Blues (#2); Joe's Blues; Juice on the Loose; Life's a One Way Ticket; Love Sick Soul; Messin' Around.

Danny Barker

Bachelor's Blues; Bad Bad Baby Blues (#1); Bad Bad Baby Blues (#2); Bad Luck Blues (#1); Blues I; Blues II; Box Car Shorty and Peter Blue; Come Down Baby; Don't Pay Me No Mind; Layin'

My Rules in Blues; Levee Blues (#1); Saw Mill Blues; Stoop to
Conquer.

Edgar Blanchard
It's Dangerous to Be a Husband; Just As Soon As I Go Home;
Little Woman Blues; Phoney Woman Blues.

Clarence 'Gatemouth' Brown
Bad Luck Blues (#2); Box Car Shorty; Levee Blues (#2); I Don't
Want No Second Hand Love; Railroad Porter's Blues; Take a Lesson
from Your Teacher; That's Enough.

Geoff Brown
Hannah from Savannah; You're Never Too Old to Boogie.

Billy Butler
Beggin' Woman (#1); Box Car Shorty's Confession; Evolution
Blues (#1); Sadie Brown.

Al Casey
Big Fat Mama (#1); Death House Blues; Old Man Blues; Too
Tight to Walk Loose.

Jimmy Dawkins
Chicken and the Hawk; Goin' Down Slow; I'm Living on Borrowed
Time; Life Is a One-Way Ticket; Tow Down.

Roger Hill
Barefoot Boy (#3); Checkin' Out; How Come My Dog Don't Bark
When You Come 'Round?; I Got News for You; Lipstick Traces;
Night Life; Railroad Avenue; Too Late to Turn Back Now; Touch
Me; When a Woman Loves a Man; You Talk Too Much.

Jimmy Shirley
Baby, You Don't Know It All; Barefoot Boy (#1); Boogie Woogie
Hannah; Desperate G.I. Blues; Fly Hen Blues; If I Just Keep Still;
Just Another Woman; Larceny Hearted Woman; Lightning Struck
the Poorhouse; Little Eva; Lonesome Man Blues; Make Me Strong
as Sampson; My Love Comes Tumblin' Down; My Tight Woman;
Post War Future Blues; Wedding Day Blues; When Your Mother's
Gone; When the Roll Be Called in Heaven; You Ain't So Such a
Much; You Got It Coming to You.

Piano:

Dave Bartholomew
ABC I; ABC II; How Long Must I Wait?; Sleep Walking Woman.

John Berthelot
That's What Love Is All About.

Leonard Feather
Just Another Woman; Larceny Hearted Woman; My Love Comes
Tumblin' Down; Post War Future Blues.

Paul Gayten
It's Dangerous to Be a Husband; Just As Soon As I Go Home;
Little Woman Blues; Phoney Woman Blues.

Discography

Steve Henderson (Hoggie Beetle?)
Big Fat Mama (#1); Death House Blues; Old Man Blues; Too Tight to Walk Loose.

Billy Kyle
Bachelor's Blues; Blues I; Blues II; Come Down Baby; Don't Pay Me No Mind; Stoop to Conquer.

Hank Jones
Baby, You Don't Know It All (?); Barefoot Boy (#1) (?); If I Just Keep Still; Lightning Struck the Poorhouse; Make Me Strong as Sampson; My Tight Woman; When Your Mother's Gone; When the Roll Be Called in Heaven.

Pleasant 'Cousin Joe' Joseph
Bad Luck Blues (#2); Barefoot Boy (#2); Beggin' Woman (#2); Big Fat Mama (#2); Box Car Shorty; Brown Skinned Woman; Chicken a la Blues (#2); Chicken and the Hawk; Country Boy; Don't Let Your Head Start Nothin'; Down It and Get from Around It; Evolution Blues (#2); Goin' Down Slow; Hard Work; Hard Times; I Don't Want No Second Hand Love; I Had to Stoop to Conquer You; I'm Living on Borrowed Time; In and Out of Love; Joe's Blues; Juice on the Loose; Levee Blues (#2); Life Is a One-Way Ticket; Life's a One Way Ticket; Little Low Mama; Love Sick Soul; Messin' Around; Railroad Porter's Blues; Revenge Is So Sweet; Take a Lesson from Your Teacher; That's Enough; Tow Down; What a Tragedy.

George Parker
Baby, You Don't Know It All (?); Barefoot Boy (#1) (?).

Sam Price
Layin' My Rules in Blues; Bad Bad Baby Blues (#1); Bad Bad Baby Blues (#2); Bad Luck Blues (#1); Beggin' Woman (#1); Box Car Shorty and Peter Blue; Box Car Shorty's Confession; Broken Man Blues; Evolution Blues (#1); Layin' My Rules in Blues; Levee Blues (#1); New Jailhouse Blues; Sadie Brown; Saw Mill Blues.

Roosevelt Sykes
Barefoot Boy (#2); Beggin' Woman (#2); Chicken a la Blues (#2); Country Boy; Down It and Get from Around It; Evolution Blues (#2); Joe's Blues; Juice on the Loose; Life's a One Way Ticket; Love Sick Soul; Messin' Around.

Ernie Washington
Fly Hen Blues; Little Eva; Lonesome Man Blues; You Ain't So Such a Much.

Kenny Watts
Boogie Woogie Hannah; Desperate G.I. Blues; Wedding Day Blues; You Got It Comin' to You.

Dave Williams
I Saw Mommy Kissin' Santa Claus.

Saxophone:

ALTO:

Earl Bostic

Baby, You Don't Know It All; Barefoot Boy (#1); Fly Hen Blues; If I Just Keep Still; Lightning Struck the Poorhouse; Little Eva; Lonesome Man Blues; Make Me Strong as Sampson; My Tight Woman; When the Roll Be Called in Heaven; When Your Mother's Gone; You Ain't So Such a Much.

Pete Brown

Bachelor's Blues; Blues I; Blues II; Boogie Woogie Hannah; Come Down Baby; Desperate G.I. Blues; Don't Pay Me No Mind; Stoop to Conquer; Wedding Day Blues; You Got It Comin' to You.

BARITONE:

Harry Carney

Just Another Woman: Larceny Hearted Woman; My Love Comes Tumblin' Down; Post War Future Blues.

SOPRANO:

Sidney Bechet

Bad Bad Baby Blues (#1); Bad Bad Baby Blues (#2); Layin' My Rules in Blues; Levee Blues (#1); Saw Mill Blues.

TENOR:

Ray Abrams

Boogie Woogie Hannah; Desperate G.I. Blues; Wedding Day Blues; You Got It Comin' to You.

Lee Allen

It's Dangerous to Be a Husband; Little Woman Blues; Just As Soon As I Go Home; Phoney Woman Blues.

Mike Burney

Barefoot Boy (#3); Checkin' Out; How Come My Dog Don't Bark When You Come 'Round?; I Got News for You; Lipstick Traces; Night Life; Railroad Avenue; Too Late to Turn Back Now; Touch Me; When a Woman Loves a Man; You Talk Too Much.

John Hardee

Barefoot Boy (#1); Baby, You Don't Know It All (?); If I Just Keep Still; Lightning Struck the Poorhouse; Make Me Strong as Sampson; My Tight Woman; When Your Mother's Gone; When the Roll Be Called in Heaven.

Al Sears

Just Another Woman; Larceny Hearted Woman; My Love Comes Tumblin' Down; Post War Future Blues.

Trombone:

George Chisholm

Barefoot Boy (#3); Checkin' Out; How Come My Dog Don't Bark When You Come 'Round?; I Got News for You; Lipstick Traces;

Night Life; Railroad Avenue; Too Late to Turn Back Now; Touch Me; When a Woman Loves a Man; You Talk Too Much.

Wendell or Homer Eugene

I Saw Mommy Kissin' Santa Claus.

Tyree Glenn

Baby, You Don't Know It All; Barefoot Boy (#1); If I Just Keep Still; Lightning Struck the Poorhouse; My Tight Woman; When the Roll Be Called in Heaven; When Your Mother's Gone.

Dickie Wells

Bachelor's Blues; Blues I; Blues II; Come Down Baby; Don't Pay Me No Mind; Stoop to Conquer.

Trumpet:

Lemon Boler (?)

Baby, You Don't Know It All.

Shad Collins

Bachelor's Blues; Blues I; Blues II; Come Down Baby; Don't Pay Me No Mind; Stoop to Conquer.

Leonard Hawkins

Boogie Woogie Hannah; Desperate G.I. Blues; Wedding Day Blues; You Got It Comin' to You.

Thomas Jefferson

I Saw Mommy Kissin' Santa Claus.

Oran 'Hot Lips' Page

Bad Bad Baby Blues (#1); Bad Bad Baby Blues (#2); Layin' My Rules in Blues; Levee Blues (#1); Saw Mill Blues.

Colin Smith

Barefoot Boy (#3); Checkin' Out; How Come My Dog Don't Bark When You Come 'Round?; I Got News for You; Lipstick Traces; Night Life; Railroad Avenue; Too Late to Turn Back Now; Touch Me; When a Woman Loves a Man; You Talk Too Much.

Dick Vance

Just Another Woman; Larceny Hearted Woman; My Love Comes Tumblin' Down; Post War Future Blues.

Note: While this book was in press, the following additional information was received: Big Bear 2 (single, 1975) includes *Lipstick Traces* and *I Can't Lose with the Stuff I Use.*

Appendix

A Second Time Around: The Construction of Self in Life-Story Narratives

The following is adapted from a paper read at the Joint Meeting of the American Ethnological Society, the Southern Anthropological Society, and the Association for the Anthropological Study of Play, Baton Rouge, Louisiana, 11–16 February 1983.

Life-story narratives, variously termed life histories, oral histories, life stories, personal-experience narratives, and memorates, are an important type of oral record. They usually reflect traditional attitudes and occur within established storytelling traditions. Self-conscious, unspontaneous performance pieces, life-story narratives are often repeated by their tellers almost word-for-word. It is as though a life-story narrative, told once, becomes a model or stereotype, guiding subsequent retellings. We don't expect contradictory versions of the same episode from a single narrative. But this is what I have, in fact, collected. And so, evidently, have other researchers.

Cousin Joe's telling—and my editing—of his life story took place over a twenty-year span. Many episodes were told more than once—sometimes because one episode was embedded in another or it provided the context for another, sometimes because I questioned a detail or Joe remembered a detail and the narrative needed to be narrated anew, with the detail in its proper place, sometimes because one or the other of us forgot that the narration had already been taped, and sometimes just because they were such good stories and we both enjoyed them. All of the narratives were tape-recorded and transcribed, and as a chronology developed, a copy of each episode was filed using the chronology as a framework.

Most of Joe's narratives were remarkably consistent. Some were repeated almost exactly word-for-word. Occasionally, however, there were variants which appeared to contradict one another. The sequence of night-club and touring engagements in the 1930s was especially complex, for example; sometimes the narrations implied one order, sometimes the opposite. Since a published autobiography was Joe's stated goal, I thought it necessary to develop a coherent narrative from the tape transcriptions. Consequently, I needed to confront the problem of whether—or how—to reconcile the contradictions that I perceived in differing narratives.

The existence of variant versions in life-story narratives conflicts directly with a basic cultural assumption of ours. James Clifford calls it

225

the "myth of personal coherence." Even though a person may change through time, or from one situation to another, we expect his or her life story to present a complete whole, to contain a single diachronic strand, to provide the individual with a single identity (Clifford 1978).

Yet many of us who work with life-story narratives find ourselves being forced to come to terms with a *discontinuous* self—one which is constructed through narration and which often appears to include multiple and contradictory selves. Theodore Rosengarten, working with the life-story narrations of a sharecropper comments, "he had one version for his family, one for traveling salesmen, and one for me . . . yet no version is false, once you know all the versions. Each reveals one of the hats he wore. . . . Each is a step on the way to the next, contained in, but not contradicted by his other positions" (Rosengarten 1979: 117–118).

An individual, then, can create a variety of selves, by the simple act of narration. A single narration may even be said to contain one view of one's self—perhaps just one view of many. In a life-story narrative, then, the past becomes a prism or lens through which the self is seen. Telling a life story enables one to create a self which need be "real" only to oneself and to one's listener. Different selves can be created for different listeners and even for oneself in different moods.

What are the implications of this perspective for those of us who collect, and who attempt to edit, life-story narratives? How do we edit them? *Do* we edit them? How do we present them to our various audiences?

Several possibilities exist. One is the presentation of raw, unedited narrative, complete with coughs, pauses, and the sounds of cigarettes being lit included in the text. This is what my transcriptions look like. Although it seems well-suited to archival material and should be available for linguistic and other kinds of analysis, I do not think it is appropriate for a general audience.

A second possibility is an edited presentation which includes the contradictory narrations along with some commentary by the ethnographer. Vincent Crapanzano begins his portrait of Tuhami with a fragment of narrative which, he tells us, "resists integration because it probably never took place," while it also "precludes omission because it speaks a truth that can only be called autobiographical" (Crapanzano 1980: 4). Tuhami, in all of his transformations, provides us with an exceptionally challenging narrative. Keeping track of all of Tuhami's selves is difficult, however, especially for members of a culture who assume "personal coherence."

Yet a third possibility is an edited presentation which strives for some measure of coherence and which is intended for a general reading public. This is the option which I believe Cousin Joe prefers. In his own words, he intends the story of his life to be a "best seller." To do this, some responsible editing must be done. Our audience's expectations must be taken into account.

And so, I have edited, seeking an acceptably coherent narrative. I used several tools. Historical and archival research were essential, but structural analysis of the transcribed texts seemed to be even more important. The raw transcriptions, as well as the tapes, belong in an archive—and that is where they will be when the manuscript is completed.

Cousin Joe wrote a song which expressed the entire situation in a nutshell. It's entitled "Life's a One-Way Ticket," and in it he sings, "Life's a one-way ticket, and there ain't no second time around." Life may indeed be a "One-Way Ticket," but for Cousin Joe, as for most of us, narrating a life story is, in fact, "A Second Time Around."

BIBLIOGRAPHY

Clifford, James. 1978. Hanging Up Looking Glasses in Odd Corners: Ethnobiographical Prospects. In *Studies in Biography*, Ed. Daniel Aaron. Harvard English Studies 8. Cambridge, MA: Harvard University Press.

Crapanzano, Vincent. 1980. *Tuhami: Portrait of a Moroccan*. Chicago: The University of Chicago Press.

Dorson, Richard M., ed. 1977. Stories of Personal Experience. *Journal of the Folklore Institute, Indiana University*. Special double issue, 14(1–2).

Langness, L. L. and Gelya Frank. 1981. *Lives: An Anthropological Approach to Biography*. Novato, CA: Chandler & Sharp.

Olney, James. 1972. *Metaphors of Self: The Meaning of Autobiography*. Princeton: Princeton University Press.

Rosengarten, Theodore. 1979. Stepping Over Cockleburs: Conversations with Ned Cobb. In *Telling Lives*, ed. Marc Pachter. Washington, D.C.: New Republic Books.

Titon, Jeff Todd. 1980. The Life Story. *Journal of American Folklore* 93(369):276–92.